Ibn ʿArabī and Kubrawīs: The Reception of the School of Ibn ʿArabī by Kubrawī Mystics

Ibn ʻArabī and Kubrawīs: The Reception of the School of Ibn ʻArabī by Kubrawī Mystics

Seyyed Shahabeddin Mesbahi

FONS VITAE

First published in 2019 by
Fons Vitae
49 Mockingbird Valley Drive
Louisville, KY 40207
http://www.fonsvitae.com
Email: fonsvitaeky@aol.com

Library of Congress Control Number: 2018934072
ISBN 978-1941610-077

Cover photograph: Vakīl Mosque (18th Century), Shiraz, Iran
(photo by Seyyed Shahabeddin Mesbahi)
The calligraphy (*Bismillāh*) by Seyyed Shahabeddin Mesbahi

Printed in Canada

بسم الله الرحمن الرحيم

This book is dedicated
To my wife and to the loving memory of my parents

Praise For
Ibn ʻArabī and Kubrawīs: The Reception of the School of Ibn ʻArabī by Kubrawī Mystics

"Dr. Mesbahi is to be congratulated for providing a highly scholarly and accessible work on an important subject to which not enough attention has been paid until now. The influence of Ibn ʻArabī's writings reached far and wide throughout much of the Islamic world soon after his death, but the Central Asian Sufi Order, the Kubrawiyyah, had its own distinct teachings. Yet, even this Order fell under the sway of Ibn ʻArabian theses while some of its later members developed their own interpretation of such basic doctrines as *wahdat al-wujūd*. Scholars of Sufism should be grateful to the author for elucidating in a masterly fashion the link between the teachings of the Andalusian sage and the Kubrawiyyah Order which exercised such an extensive influence in Central Asia and the Indian Subcontinent and which has survived to this day as a living Sufi order."

Seyyed Hossein Nasr, University Professor of Islamic Studies, George Washington University

"The mystical writings of Ibn ʻArabī had a profound effect on Islamic thought for centuries, but it was also complex and controversial. In this detailed study, Shahabeddin Mesbahi explores the contours of this debate, particularly among the influential Kubrawī Sufis. This is an important resource for anyone interested in the history of Sufi metaphysics."

Carl W. Ernst, William R. Kenan Distinguished Professor, the University of North Carolina at Chapel Hill

"Now largely extinct, the Kubrawiyyah was one of the principal Sufi orders between the 12th and 14th centuries, originating in Central Asia but extending as far west as Iran. All of its principal figures wrote copiously in both Persian and Arabic, leaving a rich textual legacy that until now has not been properly analyzed. Shahabeddin Mesbahi's book, examining the principal Kubrawī texts, constitutes therefore a pioneering effort, a major contribution to the knowledge of this Sufi tradition. At the same time, he traces meticulously the acceptance and transmission of Ibn ʻArabī's key concepts by the

Kubrawīs. It is therefore doubly deserving of serious attention by all scholars of Sufism."

Hamid Algar, Professor Emeritus of Persian and Islamic Studies, University of California, Berkeley

"This is the first book specifically focused on the influence of Ibn 'Arabī's worldview and his school on the well-known Kubrawiyyah Sufi masters…Taken into consideration the originality and varieties of comparative and methodological approaches in the book, this study provides a new paradigm in the study of some of the most crucial concepts in Islamic mystical tradition."

Mohammad H. Faghfoory, Professor and Director, Graduate Program in Islamic Studies, Department of Religion, George Washington University

Contents

Introduction

The School of Ibn 'Arabī and Kubrawīs

Ibn 'Arabī and His School

The twelfth and thirteenth centuries, a chaotic period for the Muslim world in which the safety and stability of Central Asia and Iran were weakened by the calamitous Mongol invasions, were, perhaps unexpectedly, a lively age for Sufism, a time when many *ṭarīqas* ("orders") of Islamic mysticism were born and flourished.[1] Although the formation of the *ṭarīqas* was already underway prior to the Mongol invasions, their significant flourishing in this period perhaps represented the culmination of this process.

Although many important places in Transoxania were invaded as the Mongols "burned,...slew, ...[and] plundered,"[2] and the 'Abbāsīd Caliphate crumbled, Sufi orders were established or revived. Amidst all these catastrophic events, many Muslims found their respite and breathing space in binding with such spiritual elements of Sufism as *dhikr* ("invocation") and *samā'* ("rhythmical whirling and modes"), and in gatherings in *khanaqāhs* ("Sufi hospices").[3] Several Islamic mystics of Iran and Central Asia, also in this period, found their way to the ideas and worldview of one of the most important and influential schools of Islamic mysticism; that of the Master Maximus Shaykh al-Akbar Muḥyiddin Ibn 'Arabī (d. A.H. 638/1240 CE), who "is probably the most influential author of works on Sufism in Islamic history."[4] With a list of more than

1. See Lloyd Ridgeon, *'Azīz Nasafī* (Richmond: Curzon Press, 1998), xi and 1.

2. 'Alā al-Dīn 'Atā al-Malik Jūvainī, *The History of the World Conqueror*, cited in Ridgeon, *'Azīz Nasafī*, 2.

3. See Ridgeon, *'Azīz Nasafī*, 5.

4. William C. Chittick, "Ibn 'Arabī and His School," in *Islamic Spirituality*, ed. Seyyed Hossein Nasr (New Delhi: Oxford University Press, 1990), vol. 2, 49.

800 works attributed to him,[5] Ibn 'Arabī is also considered one of the most prolific authors in the Islamic world.

As one contemporary scholar has stated, "in the Islamic world itself, probably no one has exercised deeper and more pervasive influence over the intellectual life of the community during the past seven hundred years"[6] than Ibn 'Arabī. This exceptional and multidimensional influence, which perhaps was mainly the result of his extraordinary and comprehensive approach to spiritual concepts, through use of his unique linguistic skills in formation of an array of creative terms and expressions, earned him the title of Shaykh al-Akbar (the greatest master). His "family was descended from one of the oldest Arab lineages in Muslim Spain. His ancestors, Arabs from the Yemen, emigrated toward the Iberian Peninsula…where [they were] listed among the "great Arab families"…living in Andalusia…They belong to the *khaṣṣa*, the ruling class that occupied the highest offices in the administration and the army."[7]

Ibn 'Arabī's Life

Ibn 'Arabī was born in the city of Murcia in the year 560/1165. His father "Alī ibn al-'Arabī, was clearly a man of standing and influence…It is possible that he was the *wazīr* of Ibn Mardanīsh, but this is not certain."[8] Among Ibn 'Arabī's close family members, some are reported to have had an interest in spiritual devotions. Ibn 'Arabī mentions his father's brother, and also two of his mother's brothers, Abū Muslim al-Khawlānī and Yaḥyā b. Yūghān, as Sufis.[9] "After the downfall of Ibn Mardanīsh and the occupation of Murcia by the Almohads, Ibn 'Arabī's family moved to Seville,"[10] where he began his "dogmatic and intellectual training."[11] This was the year 578/1183 which "coincided with the renewal of the religious and

5. For fuller details of Ibn 'Arabī's works, see Osmān Yaḥiā, *Histoire et Classification de l'oeuvre d'Ibn 'Arabī* (Damascus: Institute Français de Damas, 1964).

6. William C. Chittick, *Ibn 'Arabī Metaphysics of Imagination: The Sufi Path of Knowledge* (Albany: State University of New York Press, 1989), x.

7. Claude Addas, *Ibn 'Arabī: The Voyage of No Return*, trans. from French by David Streight (Cambridge, England: Islamic Text Society, 2000), 11-12.

8. R. W. J. Austin, *Sufis of Andalusia: The Rūḥ al-Quds and al-Durrat al-Fākhirah of Ibn 'Arabī* (Los Angeles: University of California Press, 1971), 21.

9. See ibid.

10. Ibid., 22.

11. See Claude Addas, *Quest for the Red Sulphur: The Life of Ibn 'Arabī*, trans. Peter Kingsley (Cambridge: Islamic Text Society, 2000), 95.

literary disciplines—especially Qur'ānic learning."[12]

Among his family members with spiritual inclinations Ibn 'Arabī also mentions his wife, whom he married while he was in Seville.[13] He refers to her as "my saintly wife" and describes her mystical vision as follows:

> My saintly wife, Maryam bint Muḥammad b. 'Abdūn, said, "I have seen in my sleep someone whom I have never seen in the flesh, but who appears to me in my moments of ecstacy. He asked me whether I was aspiring to the Way, to which that I replied that I was, but that I did not know by what means to arrive at it. He then told me that I would come to it through five things, trust, certainty, patience, resolution, and veracity." Thus she offered her vision to me (for my consideration) and I told her that that was indeed the method of the Folk."[14]

Ibn 'Arabī "was raised in the great cultural centers of Islamic Spain, where his extraordinary spiritual gifts were already apparent by his adoslescence; traveled and encountered innumerable spiritual teachers…throughout Spain and North Africa in his youth; and left that area definitely for the Hajj; which brought him to Mecca."[15] His journey to Mecca resulted in the compilation of his magnum opus *al-Futūḥāt al-Makkiyyah* ("The Meccan Openings") which began in the year 598/1202. During his residence in Mecca, Ibn 'Arabī also "completed four works; a collection of Traditions called *Mishkāt al-Anwār*, a treatise on Sufi virtues, *Ḥilyat al-Abdāl*, a treatise on visions, *Tāj al-Rasā'il* and the *Rūḥ al-Quds*."[16]

Regarding the significance of *Futūḥāt*, which was completed shortly before the author's death,[17] Ibn 'Arabī affirms: "the essence of what is included in this work comes from what God inspired in me while I was fulfilling my circumambulations of His Temple [the *Ka'ba*, *bayt Allāh*], or while I was contemplating it while seated in its holy precincts."[18] He also testifies to the total conformity of the

12. ibid.

13. See Austin, *Sufis of Andalusia*, 22.

14. *Futūḥāt* II, cited in ibid., 22-23.

15. James Morris, preface to *The Meccan Revelation*, vol. 1, by Ibn al-'Arabī, ed. Michel Chodkiewicz, trans., William C. Chittick and James W. Morris (New York: Pir Press, 2002), 6.

16. See Austin, *Sufis of Andalusia*, 38.

17. Ibid., 8.

18. Ibid.

content of the *Futūḥāt* with *imlā' ilāhī* ("Divine dictation") through *ilqā' rabbānī* ("casting by God").[19] The first part of the work's title (i.e., the *Futūḥāt*) pertains to a key element in the whole compendium of the Shaykh al-Akbar's writings. The term *futūḥ* "is a near synonym for several other terms, such as unveiling, tasting, witnessing, divine effusion, divine self-disclosure, and insight."[20] In other words, this term which represents the partial title of the Shaykh al-Akbar's longest and encyclopedic work, reveals a combination of the elements critical to Ibn 'Arabī's worldview.

We might state that in the view of Ibn 'Arabī, the genuine medium through which an audacious wayfarer arrives at a more comprehensive level of knowing/realizing *wujūd* ("existence"), which is nothing but one *tajallī* ("self-disclosure/manifestation") of the Absolute, and thus manifests His *waḥdah* ("Unity"), is the way of *kashf* ("unveiling"), *shuhūd* ("witnessing") and *dhawq* ("tasting"). The Absolute becomes unveiled to the mystic through His constant self-disclosures. In each of these everlasting mystical experiences, he witnesses a new effusion of the Absolute. This "method of knowing" which perhaps for Ibn 'Arabī, is the preferred pathway for approaching the Real, distinguishes the most exceptional seekers of the way (i.e., Perfect Human Beings) from the rest of wayfarers. Ibn 'Arabī confirms that "the prophets and friends among the Folk of Allah have no knowledge of God derived from reflection. God has purified them from that. Rather they possess the opening of unveiling through the Real."[21] The book of *Futūḥāt*, which is the longest literary exercise of Ibn 'Arabī within its 560 chapters, appears as "the vast encyclopedia of the Islamic sciences within the context of *tawḥīd*, the profession of God's Unity that forms the core of Islam."[22] This theme (i.e., *tawḥīd*) which is perhaps the most important doctrinal ground for Ibn 'Arabī's entire *Weltanschauung*, leaves its substantial mark on all of his technical terms and expressions, and also binds together his whole realization of existence.

Shaykh al-Akbar's "years of maturity were spent in travel and the inroads of the Crusaders and ongoing conquests of the Mongol hordes."[23] He traveled to Konya and then, "after criss-crossing

19. See *Futūḥāt* II, cited in ibid.
20. Chittick, *The Sufi Path of Knowledge*, xii.
21. *Futūḥāt* III, cited in ibid.
22. Chittick, *The Sufi Path of Knowledge*, xi.
23. Ibid.

the East for a period of twenty years Ibn 'Arabī – now aged sixty – decided to settle in Syria."[24] He remained there until his death (638/1240) in Damascus "except for his brief visit to Aleppo in 628/1231."[25]

In the year 580/1184, which has been considered by scholars such as Osmān Yaḥiā as the year in which Ibn 'Arabī entered the spiritual path,[26] a meeting occurred between Ibn 'Arabī and Ibn Rushd, better known in the West as Averroes (d.594/1198). William Chittick considers this meeting as the sign of Ibn 'Arabī's remarkable influence:"The significance of Ibn 'Arabī's extraordinary influence on Islamic thinking is suggested by a frequently quoted passage in which he recalls his meeting, as a youth of perhaps fifteen, with a famous philosopher Averroes, when the latter would have been fifty five. Averroes perceived in the young Ibn 'Arabī the wisdom for which he had been searching all his life. In cryptic language, the boy informed him that rational investigation was not sufficient to attain complete knowledge of God and the world."[27]

During his life, Ibn 'Arabī "studied with many Sufi Shaykhs… and with numerous masters of the Islamic sciences. In one document, he mentions the names of seventy teachers in fields like *hadīth* (sayings of the Prophet), Qur'ān recitations, Qur'ān commentary, and jurisprudence."[28] Shaykh al-Akbar composed two major references, *Rūḥ al-Quds* and *al-Durrat al-Fākhirah*, in which he refers to the names of great men and women of spiritual virtue, many of whom were his teachers on the Path.[29] His masters on the Path were of different social classes representing varaieties of elevated spiritual characteristics. Ibn 'Arabī's account of these masters' spiritual eminence manifests the rich and flourishing spiritual environment of his time in which he, himself, became one of the most accomplished masters of Sufism. For example, on one occasion, he writes on the spiritual states of his master Shaykh

24. Addas, *Quest for the Red Sulphur*, 259.

25. Austin, *Sufis of Andalusia*, 45.

26. See Addas, *Quest for the Red Sulphur*, 34. Addas seems to disagree with O. Yaḥiā in this regard: "However, the account in question contains certain details which appear to contradict such an assumption."

27. William C. Chittick, *Imaginal World: Ibn 'Arabī and the Problem of Religious Diversity* (New York: State University of New York Press, 1994), 1.

28. William C. Chittick, *Ibn 'Arabī: Heir to the Prophets* (Oxford: One World, 2005), 5.

29. See Austin, *Sufis of Andalusia*.

Abū Ja'far al-'Uraynī, whom 'Ibn 'Arabī met at the beginning of his dedication to the spiritual path.

> This master came to Seville when I was just beginning to acquire knowledge of the Way. I was one of those who visited him. When I met him for the first time I found him to be one devoted to the practice of Invocation. He knew, immediately he met me, the spiritual need that had brought me to see him. He asked me, 'Are you firmly resolved to follow God's way?' I replied, 'The servant may resolve, but it is God who decides the issue.' Then he said to me, 'If you will shut out the world from you, sever all ties and take the Bounteous alone as your companion, He will speak with you without the need of any intermediary.' I then pursued this course until I had succeeded. Although he was an illiterate countryman, unable to write or use figures, one had only to hear his expositions on the doctrine of Unity to appreciate his spiritual standing. By means of his spiritual power he was able to control men's thoughts, and by his words he could overcome the obstacles of existence. He was always to be found in a state of ritual purity, his face towards the *qiblah* and continuously invoking God's Names.[30]

In another instance, he mentions the spiritual characteristics of the Shaykh al-Kumī. In his description of the Shaykh al-Kumī, Ibn 'Arabī also refers to one of the most celebrated spiritual masters of his time, Abū Madyan who left an undying effect on him.[31] Ibn 'Arabī also mentions his close companion Badr al-Ḥabashī in the text. He explains the spiritual qualities of Shaykh al-Kumī as follows:

> This Shaikh had been one of the companions of Abū Madyan and had met many of the most prominent Sufis of this land. For a time he had lived in Egypt and had married in Alexandria. … On one occasion he was offered the governorship of Fez, but he

30. Ibid., 63.

31. See ibid., 69, footnote. On the importance of Abū Madyan among Ibn 'Arabī's masters, Addas states in *Ibn 'Arabī: The Voyage of No Return*, page 51, "Of all his spiritual masters, the name that occurs most in the writings of the Shaykh al-Akbar is, paradoxically, a being that he never 'physically' met: Abū Madyan. Called 'Master of all masters' during his life time, this illustrious Andalusian saint has enjoyed tremendous popularity in the Maghreb throughout the centuries, even up to the present day."

> refused. He was one of those who are well established on the Way. Abū Madyan, who was the spokesman of our order and the one who revived it in the West, said of Abū Ya'qūb [i.e., Shaykh al-Kumī], that he was as a safe anchorage is to a ship. He was much given to private devotions and always gave alms in secret. He honoured the poor and humbled the rich, ministering in person to the needs of the destitute. While I was in his charge he instructed me and looked after me most excellently. My companion, 'Abdallāh Badr al-Ḥabashī, knew him well and the Shaikh died at his house. He used to say of the Shaikh that he could, if he wished, raise the postulant from the lowest depth to the highest spiritual height in a moment. His powers of concentration were considerable…I saw him in a dream on one occasion and his breast seemed to be cleft asunder and a light like that of the sun shone out from it. In the dream he called out to me to come to him. I came to him with some large white bowls which he proceeded to fill to the brim with milk. I drank the milk from the bowls at fast as he filled them. Wonderful indeed is the spiritual grace I have received from him...[32]

Ibn 'Arabī also speaks of one of his favorite masters in Seville, an old lady of eminent spiritual virtues by the name Nunah Fāṭimah bint ibn al-Muthannā, who as he reports, testified to Ibn 'Arabī's unique spiritual devotion to the Path.

> She lived at Seville. When I met her she was in her nineties and only ate the scraps left by people at their doors. Although she was so old and ate so little, I was almost ashamed to look at her face when I sat with her, it was so rosy and soft. Her own special chapter of the Qur'ān was 'The Opening.' She once said to me 'I was given "The Opening" and I can wield its power in any matter I wish." I, together with two of my companions, built a hut of reeds for her to live in. She used to say 'Of those who come to see me, I admire none more than Ibn Al-'Arabī.' On being asked the reason for this she replied, 'The rest of you come to me with part of yourselves, leaving the other part of you occupied with your other concerns, while Ibn 'Arabī is a consolation to me, for he comes to me with all of himself. When he rises up it is with all of himself and when he sits it is with his whole self, leaving nothing of himself elsewhere. That

32. Ibid., 69-70, brackets added.

> is how it should be on the Way.' Although God offered to her His Kingdom, she refused, saying, 'You are all, all else is inauspicious for me.' Her devotion to God was profound. Looking at her in a purely superficial way one might have thought she was a simpleton, to which she would have replied that he who knows not his Lord is the real simpleton. She was indeed a mercy to the world.[33]

The Divine inspiration, through which Ibn 'Arabī claims the birth of the *Futūḥāt*, also appears to be the source of his most celebrated work, *Fuṣūṣ al-Ḥikam* ("Bezels of Wisdom"), which was compiled during the year 627/1230 in Damascus.[34] He elaborates upon the event which resulted in compilation of this book as follows:

> I saw the Apostle of God in a visitation granted to me during the latter part of the month of Muharram in the year 627, in the city of Damascus. He had in his hand a book and he said to me "This is the book of the Bezels of Wisdom; take it and bring it to men that they might benefit from it." I replied, "All obedience is due to God and His Apostle; it shall be as we are commanded." I therefore carried out the wish, made pure my intention, and devoted my purpose to the publishing of this book, just as the Apostle had laid down, without any addition or subtraction."[35]

In each of 27 chapters of the book, Ibn 'Arabī discusses the role and place of one of his chosen Prophets on the spiritual path of perfection, beginning with Ādam and ending with the Prophet Muḥammad. The spiritual characteristics of each of these prophets, who represent the eminent examples of the *al-insān al-kāmil* ("Perfect Man") are discussed in their correlation with one of the Absolute's *ḥikam* ("wisdoms"). It seems that Ibn 'Arabī sees the prophets as envoys of the Absolute's collected *ḥikam* ("wisdoms") as they manifest *asmā' al-ḥusnā* ("most beautiful Divine Names") in their most elevated appearances. Therefore, in Ibn 'Arabī's worldview, the Prophets who have become one with the *ḥikam* ("wisdoms") they represent emerge as *fuṣūṣ* ("ringstones") through which God's

---

33. Ibid., 143-144.

34. Austin, introduction to *The Bezels of Wisdom*, by Ibn 'Arabī, trans. R. W. J. Austin (New York: Paulist Press, 1980), 17.

35. Ibid.

Wisdoms (or Names) find their most perfect and lucid expressions.

Among Shaykh al-Akbar's long list of works, *Fuṣūṣ*, with more than one hundered commentaries written on it,[36] finds a revered and unique place. This book has been considered as "a most important resume' or synopsis of Ibn 'Arabī's principal themes."[37]

Generally speaking, most of Ibn 'Arabī works, due to their involvement with a vast array of creative expressions and original interpretations of mystical subjects, are not comprehensible to the general public. Shaykh al-Akbar, himself, confirms the complex and extraordinary nature of his works when referring to the *Futūḥāt*: "neither this book nor my other books have been composed in the manner of ordinary books, and I do not write in the way authors normally do."[38] This characteristic of the Shaykh's works along with the controversial nature of his mystical interpretations persuaded him to write a commentary on his own work, the well-known collection of Arabic poetry, *Tarjumān al-Ashwāq*. In his commentary, a response to the criticism made by some of the "religious scholars" of his time, who interpreted his poems as "being too sensuous and worldly,"[39] Ibn 'Arabī explains his encounter with a lady of eminent beauty and elevated spiritual virtues whom he met during his residence in Mecca. She became the source of Ibn 'Arabī's inspiration for reciting the collection of his poems in this book.

> When I stayed in Mecca in the year 599 I met there many men and women of great worth, culture and piety, none of whom were self-engrossed, despite their virtues, men like…Abū Shajā' Zāhir b. Abū Rajā' al-Isfahānī and his sister, Bint Rustam, a learned old lady, a shining example among women…. This Shaikh had a virgin daughter, a slender child who captivated one who looked upon her, whose presence gave luster to gatherings, who amazed all she was with and ravished the senses of all who beheld her. Her name was Niẓām (Harmony) and her surname 'Ain al-Shams (Eye of the Sun). She was religious, learned, ascetic, a sage among the sages of the Holy Places.[40]

Ibn 'Arabī's genuine creativity in raising the vast array of sub-

36. See Chittick, "Ibn 'Arabī and His Schools," 52.
37. Austin, introduction to *The Bezels of Wisdom*, 18.
38. Ibn al-'Arabī, *The Meccan Revelations*, vol. 1, 8.
39. Austin, *Sufis of Andalusia*, 36.
40. *Tarjūman al-Ashwāq*, cited in ibid.

jects and expressions pertinent to different Islamic sciences such as philosophy, *kalām* ("Islamic theology"), *tafsīr* ("Qur'ānic exegesis"), *ḥadīth* and *fiqh* ("Islamic jurisprudence"), to their eminent level of spiritual functionality, projects the limitless competence of Islamic mysticism as the *essential medium* through which Islamic worldviews interact with their unifying essence. As William Chittick rightly puts it: "Ibn 'Arabī helped bring the teachings of Sufism into the mainstream of Islamic intellectuality which in any case was moving toward philosophy rather than Kalām."[41]

Chittick also refers to the tendency of Islamic intellectuality towards "synthesis" in which Ibn 'Arabī played a monumental role in the field of Islamic mysticism:

> From the 7th/13th century onward, Islamic intellectuality tends towards synthesis. Many authors contributed to the harmonization of divergent intellectual perspectives, such as Suhrawardī al-Maqtūl (d. 587/1191), the founder of the "Illuminationist" school of philosophy, and Naṣir al-Dīn Tūsī (d.672/1274), the first systematic Shi'ite theologian and the great revivifier of the teaching of Avicenna. It was only logical that Sufism should play a major role in this harmonization of different intellectual streams. Al-Ghazālī (d.505/1111) had begun this task long before Ibn 'Arabī, and Ibn 'Arabī contributed to it by employing the terminology of all the intellectual perspectives.[42]

Other contemporary scholars have also identified the synthetic role that Ibn 'Arabī played in building a bridge between the early Sufi tradition and the mystics who followed him. This role often has been interpreted as the basis for Ibn 'Arabī's claim for being the *khātam al-wilāyah al-Muḥammadiyyah* ("Seal of Muḥammadan Sainthood"):

> Ibn 'Arabī gave expression to the teaching and insights of the generations of Sufis who preceded him, recording for the first time, systematically and in detail, the vast fund of Sufi experience and oral tradition, by drawing on a treasury of technical terms and symbols...This is partly the significance of his claim to have been the Seal of Muḥammadan Sainthood in so far as he may be said to have been the last to re-

41. Chittick, *The Sufi Path of Knowledge*, xviii.
42. Ibid.

ceive directly the, so to speak, unformulated teachings of the Way, while all who came after him received it through the filter of his systematic expression."[43]

As mentioned above, Ibn 'Arabī's *Futūḥāt* and *Fuṣūṣ* manifest the layout of this synthetic role more extensively than any of his other works. The *Fuṣūṣ al-Ḥikam* is considered to be Ibn 'Arabī's most widely read work, which has "played a central role in Islamic intellectual tradition."[44] The first prominent member of Ibn 'Arabī's school, and his stepson, the great Persian thinker, Ṣadr al-Dīn Qūnawī (d. 673/1273-4), wrote the first commentary on the *Fuṣūṣ*, "although he discusses only the general themes of each chapter."[45]

Qūnawī's father, Majd al-Dīn Isḥāq, a Sufi scholar from Malatya in present day Turkey, met Ibn 'Arabī on his journey to Mecca for a pilgrimage in the year 600/1204.[46] Two years later they went to Malatya together, and later on, after Majd al-Dīn passed away, Ibn 'Arabī married Qūnawī's mother.[47] This event seems to have played a very important role in Shaykh al-Akbar's life as well as in the popularization of his worldview.[48] The prominent biographer of Ibn 'Arabī, Claude Addas has criticized Asín Palacíos (1871-1944) for ignoring this event in his well-known book.[49] Regarding the significance of this episode of the Shaykh's life, Addas asserts, "As a matter of fact this event in the private life of the Shaikh al-Akbar was to have very important consequences for the diffusion of his thought in the Islamic world."[50]

---

43. Austin, *Sufis of Andalusia*, 48.

44. ibid., xvii.

45. Chittick, "Ibn 'Arabī and His School," 53. Some of the contemporary scholars believe that the earliest commentary on the *Fuṣūṣ* was written by Ibn 'Arabī's disciple 'Afīf al-Dīn Talmasānī. For example, see Jane Clark, "Best Sellers in the Akbarian Tradition The Dissemination of Ibn 'Arabī's Teaching Through Ṣadr al-Dīn al-Qūnawī," *Journal of Muḥyiddīn Ibn 'Arabī Society* 33 (2003), 48.

46. See William C. Chittick, "Rūmī and Waḥdat al-Wujūd," in *Poetry and Mysticism in Islam: The Heritage of Rūmī*, ed. Amīn Banānī, Richard Houanisian and George Sabagh (Los Angeles: University of California Press, 1994), 77.

47. See ibid.

48. See Addas, *Quest for the Red Sulphur*, 4.

49. Here Addas refers to Palacios' *El Islam Cristianizado*: *estudio del "sufismo" a través de las obras de Abenarabi de Murcia* (Madrid: Editorial Plutarco, 1931).

50. Addas, *Quest for the Red Sulphur*, 4.

The Influence of Ibn 'Arabī

Other scholars also refer to Ibn 'Arabī's visit to Konya as the important event through which the essential "link between Eastern and Western Sufism"[51] was foumulated. This link "was forged ... during Ibn 'Arabī's visit to Konya in 607/1210, when he took as his disciple Ṣadr al-Dīn al-Qūnawī."[52] It was through Qūnawī's "link with some of the most eminent Persian Sufis that Ibn 'Arabī's teaching reached the East."[53]

The author of 25 books,[54] Qunawī in his commentary on the *Fuṣūṣ*, explains the spiritual mode through which he shared the inspiration and knowledge of the *Fuṣūṣ* with Ibn 'Arabī.

> I only asked for an explanation of the preface (*khuṭba*) – nothing else – of this book from its author (may God be pleased with him). But it was [directly] from God to me, through His grace, that He granted me the [privilege] of sharing with him (Ibn 'Arabī) in realizing which was revealed to him, and of taking from God without causal intermediary but rather from the purity of Divine providence and essential binding which protects me from the effects which may come from the properties of intermediaries and the characteristics of [secondary] causes, conditions and ties.[55]

Under the spiritual teaching and guidance of his stepfather Ibn 'Arabī, Qūnawī became his "most influential disciple."[56] After Ibn 'Arabī's death (638/1240), Qūnawī "returned to Anatolia and settled in Konya."[57] Ṣadr al-Dīn "directed a flourishing center in Konya where he was a close friend of Rūmī, though he represents a very different mode of formulating Sufi teachings."[58] As an essential figure who played the most fundamental role in advocating Ibn 'Arabī's thought, Qūnawī trained and guided several disciples

---

51. Austin, *Sufis of Andalusia*, 49.
52. Ibid.
53. Ibid.
54. See William C. Chittick, "The Last Will and Testament of Ibn 'Arabī's Foremost Disciple, and Some Notes on its Author," *Sophia Perennis* 4, no. 1 (1978):47.
55. Ṣadr al-Dīn Qūnawī, *al-Fukūk*, cited in Jane Clark, "Best Sellers in the Akbarian Tradition," 30.
56. Chittick, "Rūmī and Waḥdat al-Wujūd," 77.
57. Ibid.
58. Chittick, "Ibn Arabī and His School," 55.

who became very important masters in the school of Ibn ʻArabī and the Islamic world.

As Claude Addas confirms in her examination of Qūnawī's role in the school of Ibn ʻArabī: "He was also a spiritual master, an Akbarian heir (*wārith akbarī*) and as such, a transmitter of the *rūḥaniyya* or spiritual influence of the Shaikh al-Akbar."[59] Addas also states that "it was perhaps chiefly through the intermediary of his Iranian disciples who studied the works of Ibn ʻArabī under his direction that Ṣadr al-Dīn contributed to the propagation of Ibn ʻArabī's ideas in Iran and Turkey."[60]

Qūnawī's exceptional place in the intellectual world of Islam brought him the title of *Shaykh al-Kabīr* ("the great shaykh"). Chittick also refers to the central importance of what he calls "the circle of of Ibn ʻArabī's step son Ṣadr al-Dīn Qunawī"[61] in "the development of Sufism in the Persianate world from the thirteenth century onward."[62] Chittick also reiterates the great role which Ṣadr al-Dīn and his followers played in dissemination of Ibn ʻArabī's thought where he expands the geographical spectrum of their influence to "everywhere" in the world of Sufism: "In Anatolia, Persia, India, and wherever the theoretical expression of Sufi teachings has had any role to play, Qūnawī and his followers were key intermediaries for the interpretation and diffusion of Ibn ʻArabī's positions."[63]

Qūnawī's desciples ʻAfīf al-Dīn Tilmisānī (d.690/1291), and Mu'ayyd al-Dīn Jandī (d. 700/1300) also wrote important commentaries on the *Fuṣuṣ*. The latter figure is considered to be among "the most influential commentators" on the *Fuṣūṣ*.[64] Contemporary scholars believe that all commentators of Ibn ʻArabī's works depended on Jandī's work.[65] ʻAbd al-Razzāq Kashānī [or Kamāl al-

59. Addas, *Quest for the Red Sulphur*, 233.

60. Ibid.

61. See William C. Chittick, "Spectrum of Islamic Thought: Sa'd al-Dīn Fargahānī on the Implications of Oneness and Manyness," in *The Heritage of Sufism*, vol. II, ed. Leonard Lewisohn (Oxford: One world Publications, 1999), 206.

62. Ibid.

63. Ibid.

64. See Chittick, "Ibn ʻArabī and His School," 53.

65. For example, see Muḥammad Khwājawī, *Du Ṣadr al-Dīn yā du Owj-i Shuhūd wa Andishah dar Jahān-ī Islām: Ṣadr al-Dīn Qūnawī Shaykh-i Kabīr, Ṣadr al-Dīn Shirāzī Mullā Ṣadrā* (Tehran: Intisharāt-i Mowlā, 1378/1999), 62, and Chittick, "Rūmī and Waḥdat al-Wujūd," 79.

Dīn Kāshī or Qāshānī][66] (d. 730/1330), a disciple of Jandī, wrote another well-known commentary on Ibn 'Arabī's most celebrated work. Kāshānī is also considered to be "one of the foremost practitioners of the science and art of *ta'wīl* in the Sufi sense."[67] His well-known "*Ta'wīl al-Qur'ān* has been mistakenly attributed to Ibn 'Arabī."[68]

The renowned Sufi master, Fakhr al-Dīn Irāqī (d. 688/1289) was among Qūnawī's major students. 'Irāqī's *Lama'āt al-Ilāhiyyah* ("Divine Flashes") "was inspired by his study of *Fuṣūṣ al-Ḥikam*."[69] One of the prominent advocates of Ibn 'Arabī was Nūr al-Dīn 'Abd al-Raḥmān Jāmī (d. 898/1492), who wrote a well-known commentary on the *Fuṣūṣ* and also compiled an important commentary on Irāqī's *Lama'āt*. He states that "his [i.e., Jandī's] commentary is the basis for other commentaries on *Fuṣūṣ*."[70] Jāmī also considers Sa'd al-Dīn Farghānī (d. 700/1300), Qūnawī's disciple who wrote a commentary on Ibn Fāriḍ's well-known *Tā'iyyat al-Kubrā*, as one of the most important students of Qūnawī.[71] Farghānī first wrote a Persian commentary on the *Tā'iyya* which was called *Mashāriq al-Darārī*. Then he compiled a more expansive version of his Persian commentary in Arabic under title of *Muntahā al-Madārik*.[72] Qūnawī himself wrote an introduction to *Mashāriq al-Darārī*. In this introduction, *Shaykh al-Kabīr* explains how this book was compiled based on his lectures on the complex concepts of *Tā'iyya*. Qūnawī "...says that in the year 643/1245-1246 (five years after Ibn 'Arabī's death) he traveled from Syria to Egypt with a group of learned and spiritually advanced Sufis. During this journey and upon his return to Anatolia, he read and explained the "Poems of the Way" to his companions, who took notes with the aim of compiling commentaries

---

66. See Mūḥammad Khwājawī, introduction to *Iṣtilāḥāt al-Ṣūfiyyah* by Shaykh 'Abd al-Razzāq Kāshānī, trans., Muḥammad Khwājawī (Tehran: Intishārāt-i Mowlā, 1387/2008), 23.

67. See Sachiko Murata, *The Tao of Islam*, 226.

68. Ibid.

69. Addas, *Quest for the Red Sulphur*, 233.

70. 'Abd al-Raḥmān Jāmī, *Nafaḥāt al-Uns min Ḥaẓarāt al-Quds*, ed. Maḥmūd 'Ābidī (Tehran: Intishārāt-i Iṭṭilā'āt, 1382/2003), 556. In Jāmī's words: *"wa ma'khaz-i sāyir-i shurūḥ-i Fuṣūṣ wey ast."*

71. See William C. Chittick, "The Perfect Man in Sufism of Jāmī," *Studia Islamica*, XLIX: 141.

72. See Chittick, "Rūmī and Waḥdat al-Wujūd," 80.

on difficult passages; only Farghānī succeeded in this goal."[73] Both Kāshānī and his disciple Da'ūd Qayṣarī (d.761/1359), who wrote well-known commentaries on the *Fuṣūs*, were influenced by Jandī and Farghānī.[74] Contemporary scholars also trace the influence of Qūnawī in all of these commentaries.[75]

Qūnawī's essential tendency in systematizing Ibn 'Arabī's teachings[76] is also reflected in the writings and efforts of his disciples and later commentators on the *Fuṣūṣ*. Qūnawī's more extensive knowledge of philosophy compared to his master Ibn 'Arabī,[77] encouraged him to lay "emphasis upon those dimensions of his thought which could easily be reconciled with the philosophical approach."[78] As a result, Qūnawī's attempt to systematize Ibn 'Arabī's worldview, brought "the discussion of *wujūd* (being/existence) to the forefront"[79] of Ibn 'Arabī studies.

Among well-know commentaries written on the *Fuṣūṣ*, "more influential in Iran and the eastern land of Islam,"[80] with the author's considerable focus on the concept of *wujūd*, is Qayṣarī's *Sharḥ*. As Chittick states, "many of the Persian commentaries on the *Fūṣūṣ* are deeply indebted to Qayṣarī."[81] The first Persian commentary on the *Fuṣūṣ* was written by Bābā Rukn al-Dīn Shirāzī (d.769/1367) who "studied with both al-Kāshānī and al-Qaysārī."[82] Contemporary scholars suggest that "Qaysarī was also the founder of Akbarian teachings for the Ottoman state, for the second Ottoman Sultan, Orhan Ghāẓī, invited him to set up the first Ottoman-sponsored *madrasa* in the newly conquered town of Iznik."[83]

Tāj al-Dīn Ḥusayn Khwārazmī (d. 840/1436) also wrote a Persian commentary that "is simply a translation of Qayṣarī's work."[84] Another prominent member of the Akbarian school, Sayyid Ḥaydar

73. Ibid.
74. See Addas, *Quest for the Red Sulphur*, 233.
75. See Chittick, *The Sufi Path of Knowledge*, xviii. Chittick states that "in the case of Qayṣarī, even the Arabic style reflects Qūnawī's work."
76. Ibid.
77. See ibid.
78. Ibid.
79. Ibid.
80. Chittick, "Ibn 'Arabī and His School," 53.
81. Chittick, "Spectrum of Islamic Thought," 207 (footnotes)
82. Ibid.
83. Clark, "Early Best Sellers in the Akbarian Tradition," 50.
84. Ibid.

Āmulī (d.786/1384), in his commentary "integrated the *Fūṣūṣ* into the context of Shī'ite gnosis."[85] Shaykh Maḥmūd Shabistarī (d. 720/1320) another outstanding Akbarian, was deeply influenced by the writings of Ibn 'Arabī. His well-known *Gulshan-i Rāz* is referred to by the contemporary scholars as "the culmination in Persian of Ibn 'Arabī's teachings."[86] In the following account he manifests his vivid interest in teachings of the *Futūḥāt* and the *Fuṣūṣ* in his quest for the "science of Divine Unity."

> I spent a long part of my life studying the science of Divine Unity, traveling through Egypt, Turkey and Arabia, day after day, night after night. Year in and out, for month on end, like time itself, I trekked through town and country...I took pains in the study of the *Futūḥāt* and the *Fuṣūṣ al-Ḥikam*, neglecting no minute detail in either book. Despite these exertions in scholarship, my heart still felt restless. I was puzzling over this disquiet and anxiety when a hidden voice seemed to cry out within me, saying: These words are written in the language of the heart; seek their meaning from the heart. Do not follow every quest and call; knock not upon every door."[87]

'Abd al-Raḥmān Jāmī, as mentioned earlier, was another well-known Akbarian. This prominent commentator on the *Fūṣūṣ*, made "active and conscious use of all the major figures of the school back to Qūnawī."[88] Another key advocate of this school, 'Abd al-Karīm Jīlī (d.832/1428), a prolific author, dedicated his famous work, *al-Insān al-Kāmil* to the central Akbarian notion of the "Pefect Man." It has been suggested by contemporary scholars that "in contrast to most authors of this school, he shows relatively little influence from al-Qūnawī and represents an independent reinterpretation and revivification of Ibn 'Arabī's teachings."[89]

Ṣā'in al-Dīn 'Alī ibn Muḥammad Turkah Isfahānī (d. 836/1432) a well-known philosopher and mystic also wrote a notable Arabic

85. Chittick, "Ibn 'Arabī and His School," 53.

86. Leonard Lewisohn, "The Transcendental Unity of Polytheism and Monotheism in the Sufism of Shabistarī," in Medieval Persian Sufism, cited in Clark, "Early Best Sellers in Islamic Tradition," 47.

87. Ibid.

88. Chittick, "Spectrum of Islamic Thought," 207 (footnotes).

89. Chittick, "Ibn 'Arabī and His School," 56.

commentary on the *Fūṣūṣ*.[90] His contemporary Muḥammad ibn Ḥamzah Fanārī (d.834/1430) produced the book of *Miṣbāḥ al-Uns*, an important commentary on Qūnawī's *Miftāḥ al-Ghayb*.[91] Both of these two figures were greatly influenced by Ibn 'Arabī's worldview. Turkah, in his *Nafkhat al-Maṣdūr*, in objection to the *fuqahā* ("jurists") of the city of Yazd (in Iran) who were opposed to the teachings of Ibn 'Arabī, and while describing the highly revered status of Fanārī in the Islamic world of his time, mentions that Fanārī has been teaching source books of Sufism (such as the *Fuṣūṣ*) for the last twenty years.[92]

Some of the noted contemporary scholars also considered the well-known 13th century philosopher Ibn Sab'īn (d.669/1270), a contemporary of Qūnawī, among those whose writings manifest considerable influence by Ibn 'Arabī.[93] Ibn Sab'īn's follower Awḥad al-Dīn Balyānī (d. 686/1287-8), has utilized such Akbarian expressions as *waḥdat al-wujūd* ("unity of existence") in his writings.[94] His *Risālat al-Aḥadiyyah* seems to suggest his interest in the ideas of Shaykh al-Akbar.[95]

The eminent Persian philosopher and mystic, Ṣadr al-Muti'allihīn Shirāzī, better known as Mullā Ṣadrā (d.1051/1641), the founder of *ḥikmat al-muta'āliyah* ("transcendent theosophy") was also influenced by Ibn 'Arabī's worldview.[96] His turn from the philosophical position of *aṣālat al-māhiyyah* ("primacy of quiddity"), which was the foundational and dominant idea of the illuminationists school of the celebrated Shihāb al-Dīn Suhrawardī

90. See Ṣā'in al-Dīn 'Alī ibn Muḥammad al-Turkah Iṣfahānī, *Sharḥ-ī Fuṣūṣ al-Ḥikam*, ed. Mūḥsin Bīdārfar (Qum: Intishārāt-i Bīdār, 1378).

91. See Ḥamza Fanārī, *Miṣbāḥ al-Uns*, ed. and trans. into Persian, Muḥammad Khwājawī (Tehran: Intishārāt-i Mowlā, 1384).

92. See ibid., 73 (introduction).

93. See Chittick, "Rūmī and Waḥdat al-Wujūd," 82. Chittick confirms that: "Although A. F. Mehren and L. Massignon count Ibn Sab'īn as the last representative of the Arab peripatetic school…One has to agree with Michel Chodkiewicz that Ibn Sab'īn was thoroughly influenced by the perspectives of Ibn 'Arabī."

94. See ibid., 83.

95. Referring to Balyānī's *Treatise on Unity,* Chittick states: "Until recently this work was usually attributed to Ibn 'Arabī himself, but Michel Chodkiewicz has shown that it is by Balyānī and that it does not present a balanced statement of Ibn 'Arabī" (ibid).

96. For Ibn 'Arabī's influence on Mullā Ṣadrā's worldview see, for example, Feresteh Nadrī Abyānah, *Ta'th īrāt-i Ibn 'Arabī bar Ḥikmat-ī Muta'āliyah* (Tehran: Intishārat-i Bonyād-i Ḥikmat-i Ṣadrā, 1386/2007).

(d. 587/1191), to *aṣālat al-wujūd* ("primacy of existence"), put the concept of *wujūd* in the vanguard of his ingenious theosophy.[97] This change of position occurred through "spiritual inspiration rather than a rationalistic discourse and logical investigation"[98] Mullā Ṣadrā refers to the significance of this inspiration in his remark, "until my God guided me and showed me this proof."[99] In his innovative effort to build his theosophy on the basis of primacy of existence, he is "considered by many philosophers within the Islamic tradition to have achieved a successful synthesis of the three truth claims of revelation (*waḥy*), the rational demonstration (*burhān aqlī*) and discursive conclusions of the philosophers and illuminative knowledge (*ma'rifah*) of the Sufis."[100]

Contemporary scholars believe that the influence of figures such as Ibn 'Arabī was of paramount importance in Ṣadrā's turn to the concept of primacy of existence.[101] Among his many works, his voluminous *al-Ḥikmat al-Muta'āliyah fi'l Asfār al-'Aqliyyah al-'Arba'ah* which elaborates creatively and in synthetic detail the doctrinal basis of his theosophy, seems to manifest the influence of Ibn 'Arabī and his school more than any other of Ṣadrā's works. In searching for Ibn 'Arabī's influence on Ṣadrā and also his tendency to create a synthetic analysis of the two peripatetic and illuminationst schools of philosophy, one needs to take into account the influence and role of his precursors in the great *maktab-i Shirāz* ("school of Shirāz") in the field of philosophy and mysticism. This school has been considered by the contemporary scholars as the most essential school of philosophy in the Islamic world during the 8th/14th to the

97. On the subject of Ṣadrā's turn from primacy of quiddity to the primacy of existence, see, for example, Muḥammad Kamāl, *Mullā Ṣadrā's Transcendental Philosophy* (Vermont: Ashgate Publishing Company, 2006). Kamāl states in his book (pp. 2-4) that "Shahāb al-Dīn Suhrawardī...believed that knowledge of an object in the world came only through revealing its essence or quiddity. The Being of the object, unlike its essence, was a mental concept and had no external reality...Mullā Ṣadrā's criticism of Suhrawardī's metaphysics became explicit in his philosophical turn when he formed the contrary philosophical view that Being was not a mental property but an objective reality outside the domain of rational thinking."

98. Kamāl, *Mullā Ṣadrā's Transcendental Philosophy*, 2.

99. ibid.

100. Zailan Morris, *Revelation, Intellectual Intuition and Reason in the Philosophy of Mullā Ṣadrā: An Analysis of the al-Ḥikmat al-'Arshiyyah* (London: Routledge/Curzon, 2003), 2.

101. For example, see Kamāl, *Mullā Ṣadrā's Transcendent Philosophy*, 2

11th/17th centuries.[102] For example, Ghiāth al-Dīn Manṣūr Dashtakī Shirāzī (d.928/1521), one of the most notable members of the school of Shirāz, has shown a considerable influence of Ibn 'Arabī in his works.[103] On many occasions in his writings Ṣadrā referred to and discussed the ideas of several members of this school.[104] One might be able to claim that the prominent scholars who followed the theosophy of Mullā Ṣadrā, such as Mullā Muḥsin Fayḍ Kāshānī (d. 1091/1680), Ḥāj Mullā Hādī Sabziwārī (d.1290/1873), Mullā 'Alī Nūrī (d.1246/1830-1) and Sayyid Muḥammad Kāẓim Aṣṣār (d.1396/1975), came under the influence of Ibn 'Arabī and his school through teachings of Ṣadrā.

Criticism of Ibn 'Arabī's Teachings

The teachings of Ibn 'Arabī, as popular and admired among his followers and advocates as they were, were also attacked and criticized by a group of critics. Perhaps the most aggressive among them was the well-known jurist, Ibn Taymiyyah (d.728/1328). His "systematic attacks"[105] on Ibn 'Arabī, designed to prove the association of his thought with *kufr* ("disbelief"), mainly targeted the Akbarian concept of *waḥdat al-wujūd* ("unity of existence"), which Ibn Taymiyyah held as equal to *ittiḥād* ("unificationism") and *ḥulūl* ("incarnationism").[106]

Looking at most of the works compiled by Ibn 'Arabī's critics who were primarily inspired by Ibn Taymiyyah and his harsh attacks, such as Burhān al-Dīn Biqā'ī (d.885/1480), and also those who criticized Ibn 'Arabī less aggressively and with more balanced approaches, one can discern a tradition of criticizing Shaykh al-Akbar based mostly on the same concept: *wahdat al-wujūd*. Chittick explains the reason for the controversial nature of *waḥdat al-wujūd*: "Those who criticized the expression had certain meanings in mind,

---

102. See Qāsim Kākā'ī, *Ghiāth al-Dīn Manṣūr Dashtakī wa Falsafa-yi Irfān* (Tehran: Farhangistan-i Honar-i Jumhūry-i Islāmī, 1378/1999), 279.

103. See ibid., 97-98.

104. See ibid., 24.

105. The term used by Claude Addas in her book *Ibn 'Arabī: The Voyage of No Return* (p.7): "The systematic attacks against Ibn 'Arabī and his school did not get into full swing until the early part of fourtheenth century when a doctor of the Law (*faqīh*) by the name of Ibn Taymiyyah (d.1328) set about attempting to demonstrate the heretical nature of his teachings."

106. See Chittick, "Rūmī and Waḥdat al-Wujūd," 85-91.

and those who defended the expression typically had other meanings in mind. When any of these authors said that Ibn 'Arabī believed in *waḥdat al-wujūd*, they were attributing to him a doctrine that he did not necessarily hold. This is the key point, and it helps explain why the expression remains controversial."[107]

Shaykh Aḥmad Sirhindī (d.1034/1624), known as *mujaddid-i alf-i thānī* ("Reviver of the Second Millenium"), who is considered to be the second most important person in the Naqshbandī order of Sufism,[108] also found the concept of *waḥdat al-wujūd* to be controversial. He "was born at Sirhind, now in the state of Punjab northwest of Delhi…in a family with a long scholarly tradition…He received his early education from his father Shaykh 'Abd al-Aḥad (927/1521-1007/1598) and memorized Qur'ān."[109] In continuation of his education Sirhindī "learned logic, philosophy and theology from Mullā Kamāl Kashmīrī…a renowned scholar of rational disciplines; studied ḥadīth with Shaykh Ya'qūb Ṣarfī (d.1003/1594), the author of a commentary on the *Ṣaḥīḥ* of al-Bukhārī and a Sufi of the Kubrawīyah order; and read some advanced texts of *tafsīr* and ḥadīth with Qāḍī Bahlūl Badakhshānī. Sirhindī completed his education at the age of seveteen and returned home."[110]

Later on "he left for Agra, the capital of the great Mongol Emperor Akbar (963/1556-1014/1605) and established contact with the scholars of the court."[111] Sirhindī's first awareness of the concept of *waḥdat al-wujūd* perhaps took place through his father's teaching.

> At an early age Shaykh 'Abd al-Aḥad had sought to be initiated into Sufism by the great Chishtī saint, Shaykh 'Abd'l Quddūs of Gangoh (d.991/1583), famous for his ecstasies and his faith in *waḥdat'l-wujūd*. But the Shaykh advised him first to study the *Sharī'ah* and the *ḥadīth*. Shaykh 'Abd'l Aḥad returned, took up study, visited various scholars and traveled to a number of

---

107. William C. Chittick, "Central Point-Qūnawī's Role in the School of Ibn 'Arabī," *Muḥyiddīn Ibn 'Arabī Society* XXXV (2004), http://www.ibnarabisociety.org/articles/centralpoint.html.

108. See Hamid Algar, "The Naqshbandī Order: a Preliminary Survey of Its History and Significance," *Studia Islamica* XLIV (1976):143.

109. Muḥammad 'Abdul Ḥaq Anṣārī, *Sufism and Sharī'ah: A Study of Shaykh Aḥmad Sirhindī's Effort to Reform Sufism* (Leicester: The Islamic Foundation, 1986), 11.

110. Ibid.

111. Ibid.

places. When he came back the master had died, and his son Shaykh Rukn al-Dīn who was also highly ecstatic and a firm believer in *waḥdat'l-wujūd* guided him in Qādirī and Chishtī *tarīqahs* and awarded him *khirqah*.[112]

Sirhindī studied important texts of Sufism such as the *Fuṣūs al-Ḥikam* under his father's supervision.[113] His father "believed in *waḥdat'l-wujūd*, but as Sirhindī says, [he] was not a blind follower of the doctrine. Some of its concepts, he interpreted in his own way."[114]

In the year 1007/1597-8 Sirhindī met Khwājah 'Abd al-Bāqī, better known as Bāqī Billāh (d.1012/1603), in Delhī.[115] Under Bāqī Billāh's guidance, after a short period of time Sirhindī became fascinated with the teachings of Naqshbandī *tariqah* and dedicated himself to spiritual wayfaring in a way pertinent to these teachings.[116] Perhaps, one of the reasons for Sirhindī's fascination with the Naqshbandī *tarīqah* was the fact that "Naqshbandīs were noted for comparatively stricter adherence to the *Sharī'ah* in their *sulūk*."[117] As Bāqī Billāh discerned "great spiritual powers"[118] in Sirhindī and hoped that "he will be in future a lamp which will illuminate the world,"[119] Sirhindī became one of the most essential figures of Naqshbandī *tarīqah*.

Most proponents of Sirhindī's role as the *mujaddid* ("vivifier") of Islam in India and subcontinent and beyond have described his social and religious environment as un-orthodox with a set of particular characteristics such as disregard for the role of *Shari'ah*. Sirhindī made efforts, reflected in his writings such as *Maktūbāt*, to begin an intended reform by propagating the concept of "following the example of the Holy Prophet, and to bring the people back to the folds of *Sharī'at*."[120] The distinguished place of Sirhindī in Naqshbandī

112. Ibid., 12.

113. See ibid.

114. Ibid.

115. See Ibid., 13.

116. See ibid.

117. Ibid.

118. See Bāqī Billāh's letter to a friend in which he mentions Sirhindī's spiritual capabilities, cited in ibid.

119. Ibid.

120. Burhān Aḥmad Fārūqī, *The Mujaddid Conception of Tawḥīd: Study of Shaykh Aḥmad Sirhindī's Doctrine of Unity* (Lahore: Institute of Islamic Culture, 1989), 9.

order of Sufism, brought a bout a well known and popular branch of this order named after his title, known as Mujaddadīyya.

Although at the beginning of his initiation to the spiritual path, Sirhindī was in conformity with the concept of *waḥdat al-wujūd*, he gradually diverged from it and perhaps as a part of his reform in the mysticism of his time, developed an alternative understanding of *tawḥid*, known as *waḥdat al-shuhūd* ("unity of witnessing").[121] He has been considered as one of the well-known critics of Ibn 'Arabī, mostly on the basis of his systematic differentiation between the two concepts of *shuhūd* and *wujūd* in his approach to unity. On the other hand, some of the contemporary scholars believe that although Sirhindī "criticized Ibn 'Arabī on certain points, he supported him on many others and must be considered an adherent of his school."[122] In fact, by looking at some of the concepts critical to Sirhindī's worldview and his reform, such as *mutāba'at* (imitating/following the Prophet Muḥammd) with various designated degrees of imitation[123] and Ibn 'Arabī's focal concept of *al-insān al-kāmil* ("Perfect Man"), elaborated in different categories of perfection that finds its ultimate example in the person of the Prophet Muḥammad, one is able to find similar affinities between their worldviews.

The well-known mystic and the prolific writer of Delhi, Shāh Walī Allāh (d. 1176/1762) who "at least before 1732...seems to have had an unmistakable preference for the Mujaddadīyya-Naqshbandīyya order,"[124] showed an eminent respect for Ibn 'Arabī. He tried to reconcile Sirhindī's *waḥdat al-shuhūd* and Ibn 'Arabī's *waḥdat al-wujūd*.[125] In his treatise, *Faiṣalat Waḥdat al-Wujūd wa al-Shuhūd*, Shāh Walī Allāh suggested that there is no essential difference between these two approaches.[126] In general, most Naqshbandī masters following Sirhindī revered Ibn 'Arabī and man-

121. See Sirhindī's *Maktūbāt*, vol. I:31 and 160, cited in Anṣārī, *Sufism and Sharī'ah*, 14-15.

122. Chittick, "Ibn 'Arabī and His School," 57.

123. See J. G. J ter Haar, *Follower and Heir of the Propthet: Shaykh Aḥmad Sirhindī (1564-1624) as Mystic* (Leiden: Het Oosters Institut, 1992), 55-57.

124. J. M. S Baljon, *Religion and Thought of Shāh Walī Allāh Dihlawī 1703-1762* (Leiden: E. J. Brill, 1986), 85.

125. See ibid., 61-63.

126. See 'Abd al-Ḥussain ZarrīnKūb, *Dunbāla-yi Jostojū dar Taṣawwuf-i Irān* (Tehran: Amīr Kabīr, 1362/1983), 214.

ifested considerable awareness of Ibn 'Arabī's works.[127] In their widespread presence in the Islamic world, "Ibn 'Arabī's ideas were transmitted…to the Mughal courts of northern India, where by the seventeenth century we find Akbarian commentaries upon Hindu texts"[128]

Ibn 'Arabī's worldview exerted a multi-dimensional influence on the Islamic world "from Black Africa and the Balkans to Indonesia and China."[129] As William Chittick states, "They paid attention to him because he offered powerful proofs drawn from the whole repertoire of Islamic knowledge to demonstrate the correctness of his views. Many of these scholars adopted his basic perspectives and a good deal of his terminology, and many also criticized some of his teachings or made sweeping condemnations. But no reputable scholar could simply ignore him."[130]

One might be surprised to find some evidence for the high status of *Shaykh al-Akbar* even in the writings of his most fierce critics. For example, his cardinal adversary, Ibn Taymiyyah, who condemned Ibn 'Arabī in his *fatāwā* as *kāfir* ("disbeliever"),[131] and wrote a book in refutation of *Fuṣūṣ al-Ḥikam*,[132] describes Ibn 'Arabī in his *al-Rasā'il wa'l Masā'il as aqrabuhum il-al-Islām* or the closest to Islam among believers in *waḥdat al-wujūd*, (or as in Ibn Taymiyyah's expression, *al-ittihādīyyah* "unificationists"), who "has the best opinions [among unificationists] in many occasions" (*wa aḥsanu kalāman fī mawāẓi'in kathīrah*).[133] One of Ibn Taymiyyah's followers, Burhān al-Dīn Biqā'ī, who wrote two books condemning Ibn 'Arabī[134] and considered him a *kāfir* (disbeliever), refers to him

127. See Suleyman Uludag, *Ibn 'Arabī*, trans., into Persian, Daūd Wafā'ī (Tehran: Nashr-ī Markaz, 1387/2008), 149.

128. Clark, "Early Best Sellers in the Akbarian Tradition," 47.

129. See Chittick, *Ibn 'Arabī: Heir to the Prophets*, 2.

130. Ibid., 3.

131. Kāzim Muḥammadī, *Ibn 'Arabī Bozorg-i 'Ālam-i Irfān-i Naẓarī* (Tehran: Intishārāt-i Najm-i Kubrā, 1386/2007), 128.

132. The title of his book is *Al-Radd al-Aqwam 'alā mā fī Fuṣūṣ al-Ḥikam.*

133. *Majmū'at al-Rasā'īl wa'l Masā'īl*, vol. 1, 176, cited in Muḥsin Jahāngīrī, *Ibn 'Arabī Chehra-yi Barjasta-yi Irfān-i Islāmī* (Tehran: Tehran University Press, 1361/1982), 200.

134. In his *Tanbīh al-Ghabī ilā Takfīr Ibn 'Arabī*, Biqā'ī attempted to prove Ibn 'Arabī's disbelief. In his another book, *Taḥdhīr al-'Ibād min Ahl al-'Inād bi Bid'at al-Ittiḥād,* he discusses both Ibn Fāriḍ and Ibn 'Arabī. For more information on Biqā'ī's criticism of Ibn 'Arabī, see Alenxander Knysh, *Ibn 'Arabī in the Later*

as "the one with vast knowledge in many fields." (*wa lahu 'ilmun kathīr fī funūnun kathīrah*).[135] Also, Ibn Taymiyyah's student, al-Dhahabī (d.748/1348) who "frequently stated his opposition to Ibn 'Arabī,"[136] and found signs of *kufr* in Ibn 'Arabī's *Fuṣūṣ*,[137] conceded Ibn 'Arabī's spiritual status: "As far as I am concerned, this man [that is, Ibn 'Arabī] may have been a saint."[138] On the other hand, referring to Ibn 'Arabī's teachings, al-Dhahabī states, "By God, it is better that a Muslim live behind his cows in ignorance [...] than possess this gnosis and subtle knowledge!"[139] Claude Addas, however, maintains that al-Dhahabī, "is not condemning the doctrine of Ibn 'Arabī as much as its diffusion among the 'mass of believers' (*āmma*),"[140] Addas's position appears to be the most balanced statement regarding Ibn Taymiyyah and most of his cohorts.

The fear of Ibn 'Arabī's popularity might be also the reason for the "extreme" nature of his condemnation by this group of critics, as reflected in their insistence on declaring him a *kāfir* ("disbeliever'), which perhaps they thought to be more effective on the public than a balanced criticism of his worldviews.

The Kubrawīyyah Order

Among the major Sufi orders that flourished in the 6th /12th and 7th /13th centuries was the Kubrawīyyah order. The Kubrawīyyah, which originated in Central Asia, is named after its founder, Najm al-Dīn Kubrā (d. 618/1221), who is also known as the *shaykh-i walī tarāsh* (saint-producer shaykh), given that many of his major disciples themselves became great masters (shaykhs).[141] "Foremost

---

Islamic Tradition: The Making of a Polemical Image in Medieval Islam (New York: State University of New York Press, 1999), 209-222.

135. Biqā'ī's *Taḥdhir al-'Ibād*, cited in Muḥammadī, *Ibn 'Arabī Bozorg-i 'Ālam-i Irfān-i Naẓarī*, 131.

136. Addas, *Ibn 'Arabī: The Voyage of No Return*, 7.

137. See Kynsh, *Ibn 'Arabī in the Later Islamic Tradition*, 115.

138. Al-Dhahabī, *Mīẓān al-I'tīdāl*, vol. 3, 660, cited in Addas, *Ibn 'Arabī: The Voyage of No Return*, 7.

139. Ibid., 8.

140. Ibid.

141. ZarrīnKūb, *Donbāla-yi Jostojū dar Taṣawwuf-i Irān*, 89. See also Hamid Algar, "Kobrawiya: The Eponym," *Encyclopedia Iranica*, and Muḥammad 'Isā Waley, "Najm al-Dīn Kubrā and the Cental Asian School of Sufism (The Kubrawiyyah)," in *Islamic Spirituality: Manifestations* ed. Seyyed Hossein Nasr (New York: Crossroad Publishing Company, 1991), 81.

among them were Majd al-Dīn Baghdādī (d.1219), Raẓī al-Dīn Alī Lālā (d.1244), Sa'd al-Dīn Hammū'ī/Hammūya (d.1253), Jamāl al-Dīn Jīlī (d.1258), Sayf al-Dīn Bākharzī (d.1261), Najm al-Dīn Dāya Rāzī (d.1256), and Bābā Kamāl Jandī (d.1273)."[142] Kubrā has been considered one of the greatest masters of Persian Sufism.[143] He was also called *al-ṭāmmat al-kubrā* ("the greatest calamity") due to his cleverness in argument.[144] Some of his followers referred to him as *āyat al-kubrā* ("God's supreme sign") which was later abbreviated as Kubrā.[145] In Alexandria, in a visionary event, he received the *kunya* ("nickname") of *Abul Jannāb* from the Prophet.[146] He interpreted this *kunya* as "the one who shuns this world and the next."[147]

> Najm al-Dīn's first master was Isma'īl al-Qaṣrī (d.589/1193), at Dizful in western Persia. But after he had spent only a short while there, Ismā'īl advised him to go to 'Ammar ibn Yāsir al-Bidlīsī...Kubrā underwent spiritual retreats (*khalwah*) with both Qaṣrī and Bidlīsī, and his writings include accounts of some experiences with them. Next Kubrā returned to Egypt on the orders of 'Ammār; here Rūzbihān al-Miṣrī continued Najm al-Dīn's training until he pronounced him qualified to initiate and instruct disciples of his own...Probably between 581/1185 and 586/1190, Rūzbihān sent Najm al-Dīn back to Khwarazm. The remainder of Kubrā's life was devoted to the spiritual path and the training of disciples.[148]

As 'Abd al-Raḥmān Jāmī recorded in his *Nafaḥāt al-Uns*, when the army of the Mongols reached the city of Khwārazm, some of Kubrā's disciples asked him to leave the city, but he refused, stayed in the city and fought with the Mongols and was killed during the confrontation. Jāmī refers to the year 618/1221 as the date of his *shahādat* (martyrdom).[149]

Among several writings of the great Kubrawī shaykh, his most

---

142. Algar, "Kobrawiya: The Eponym."

143. See 'Abd al-Rafī' Ḥaqīqat, *Sitāra-yi Bozorg-i Irfān Shaykh Najm al-Dīn Kubrā dar Qarn-i Shishum wa Haftum-i Hijrī* (Tehran: Golshan, 1385/2006), 96.

144. See Jāmī, *Nafaḥāt al-Uns*, 422.

145. See Algar, "Kobrawiya: The Eponym."

146. See ibid.

147. Ibid.

148. Waley, "Najm al-Dīn Kubrā and the Central Asian School of Sufism," 81-82.

149. See Jāmī, *Nafaḥāt al-Uns*, 426-427.

fully doctrinal work, *Fawā'iḥ al-Jamāl wa Fawātiḥ al-Jalāl*, is of the essential importance. This book represents Kubrā's methodological approach to the foundations and expressions of spiritual wayfaring:

> In it Kobrā discusses visions of heavenly bodies (the sun, the moon, the stars, the signs of zodiac and the stations of the moon) categorized by him as "supernal" (*a'lā*), as well as earthly entities (*adnā*) such as forms, colors, fire, deserts, fields and pits. The precise fashion in which any of these or other objects are seen determines their meaning: thus to dream one is traversing an ocean while submerged in it is an indication that he is being divested of water, one of the four elements that make up man's being as the microcosm; to dream of calm seas in which suns, lights or fires have been immersed is to observe the seas of gnosis; and to dream of rainfall is to witness its descent from the divine mercy to revive the barren soil of dead hearts...As for lights, they are twofold: those that ascend from the human heart, and those that descend from the divine throne; once the veil between heart and throne is removed and a gate to the throne is opened for the heart, the two yearning for each other, the ascending and descending lights merge...Lights may be glimpsed in varying colors: green, red, yellow and blue; these, too, are of significance. Green light, for example, betokens the vitality of the heart.[150]

The aforementioned themes such as systematic categories of colors/lights, their substantial affinities, the role of the "heart" as a major reservoir and the subtle organ of mystical experience that later became central to the Kubrawī understanding of *laṭā'if* as the manifold mediums of mystical experience, and the importance of visionary experiences were elaborated and expanded on by the followers of Kubrā's worldview. Kubrā also paid substantial attention to the "Eight Principles laid down in the third/ninth century by Junayd of Baqdād"[151] as the "disciplinary rules"[152] of Kubrawīs. The rules of Junayd were also pursued and put into practice by the followers of Kubrā.[153]

---

150. Algar, "Kobrawiya: The Eponym."
151. Waley, "Najm al-Dīn Kubrā and the Central Asian School of Sufism," 82.
152. Ibid.
153. See ibid.

As transmitted by Kubrā himself, the first five rules of Junayd prescribe constant observance of the following: ritual purity (*wuḍū'*), fasting (*ṣawm*), silence (*ṣamt*), seclusion (*khalwah*), and invocation or recollection (*dhikr*) of God using the formula *lā ilāha illa' Llah.* Sixth: the disciple must keep his heart forever fixed upon the shaykh, abandoning his own will entirely, and refer to him for interpretation and guidance concerning any spiritual experiences he may have. Seventh: all thoughts and mental impulses (*khawāṭir*) are to be put aside the moment they occur. Finally, the disciple must surrender entirely to the Will of God and never refuse what He imposes upon him; and he must neither pray to be granted paradise nor spared from hell.[154]

Kubrā annexed two other rules to those of Junayd, which appear with his commentary on those rules in the two of his important works, *Risālat al-Hā'im al-Khā'if min Lawmat al-Lā'im* and *al-Uṣūl al-'Asharah.*[155] "The two additional rules are to take the bare minimum of sleep and to observe moderation in eating and drinking when breaking the (daytime) fast."[156]

"Prior to the Mongol invasion of Iran, followers of Najm al-Dīn Kubrā moved from Asia Minor to Iran. Meanwhile, Ibn 'Arabī moved from the West (Andalusia) to the East."[157] Some contemporary scholars believe that this was the socio-historical ground on which the Akbarian and Kubrawī schools of thought met.[158]

The influence of Ibn 'Arabī's school of thought is visible in the writings of major followers of the Kubrawiyyah order, who were particularly influential in transmitting Ibn 'Arabī's worldview to the Persian speaking world.[159]

Diffusion of Ibn 'Arabī's Worldview by the Kubrawī Mystics

Some of the contemporaries of Ṣadr al-Dīn Qūnawī (d. 673/1273-4), Ibn 'Arabī's chief disciple and commentator, were

154. Ibid., 82-83.
155. See ibid., 83.
156. Ibid.
157. See Alī Asghar Mīr Bāqirī Fard, introduction to *Bayān al-Tanzīl* by 'Azīz ibn Muḥammad Nasafī (Tehran: Anjoman-i Āthār wa Mafākhir-i Farhangī, 1379/2000), 6.
158. See ibid.
159. See William Chittick, "Ebn al-'Arabī," http://www.uga.edu/islam/ibnarab.html.

important in making Ibn Arabi's teaching accessible to the Persian speaking world.[160] Among them, the Kubrawī master, Sa'd al-Dīn Ḥamūyah (d. 649/1252), a Persian disciple of Najm al-Dīn Kubrā, "corresponded with Ibn 'Arabī"[161] and spent several years in Damascus, where he conversed with both Ibn 'Arabī and Qūnawī.[162] Among other important figures with whom he had conversed were Shīhab al-Dīn 'Umar Suhrawardī and Jalal al-Dīn Rūmī.[163] "He was born at Bahrābād near Jovayn in Khurāsān in 1191 to a long-established family renowned for both formal learning and the practice of Sufism. He studied Ḥadīth and theology (*kalām*) in various locations in Khurāsān."[164]

His long list of works in Persian and Arabic are often difficult because of Ḥamūyah's fascination with the symbolism of letters, which appears in his work, *al-Miṣbāḥ fī al-Taṣawwuf*, and perhaps represents a partial influence of Ibn 'Arabī.[165] As Hamid Algar states, "It is in general with S'ad al-Dīn that Kobrawī attention to *waḥdat al-wojūd* (the unicity of being) and related concepts and terms associtated with Ebn 'Arabī originates"[166] Ḥamūyah also manifested his interest in other important Akbarian concepts such as *wilāyah* ("sainthood").[167]

It has been reported that Qūnawī once did not grasp the meaning of Ḥamūyah's words when he was elaborating upon a concept, and asked Ibn 'Arabī for elucidation on them.[168] Jāmī in his *Nafaḥāt al-Uns* refers to the complexity of Ḥamūyah's works: "He has many works…full of symbolic speech, difficult words, numbers, diagrams, and circles. The eye of reason and reflection is incapable of understanding and deciphering them. Until the eye of insight is opened with the light of unveiling, it is impossible to perceive

160. See Chittick, "Ibn 'Arabī and His School," 519-521.

161. Ibid., 519.

162. See Algar, "Kobrawiya: The Order," *Ecnyclopedia Iranica*. See also Chittick, "Ibn 'Arabī and His School," 519, and Najīb Māyil Heravī's, introduction to *al-Miṣbāḥ fil-Taṣawwuf* by Sa'd al-Dīn Ḥamūyah, ed. Najīb Māyil Heravī (Tehran: Intishārat-i Mowlā, 1362/1983), 42-43, and for a list of Hamūyah's works see pp. 9-22.

163. See Hamūyah, *al-Miṣbāḥ*, 21-22.

164. Algar, "Kobrawiya: The Order."

165. Chittick, "Ibn 'Arabī and His School," 519.

166. Algar, "Kobrawiya: The Order."

167. See ibid.

168. *Mashāriq al-Darārī*, cited in Heravī, introduction to *al-Miṣbāḥ*, 21.

their meaning."[169] Hamūyah refers to Ibn 'Arabī, Najm al-Dīn Kubrā, and Shihāb al-Dīn Suhrawardī "as the three most important Sufī figures of the previous generation."[170] Hamūyah's meeting with Ibn 'Arabī had a significant effect on him, and when he left Ibn 'Arabī in Damascus, he was asked by his followers "whom did you leave?" Reffering to Ibn 'Arabī, he answered, "I left there a sea without a shore."[171] Ibn 'Arabī also revered Ḥamūyah and described him as *kanzun lā yanfad* ("a never ending treasure").[172] In 617/1220 Ḥamūyah received a *khirqah* from Najm al-Dīn Kubrā and a persmission to guide his disciples to the Path.[173] Perhaps because of his spiritual attainments, Kubrā referred to him as *Ṭāyir* ("*bird*").[174] On one occasion, Jāmī quotes Ḥamūyah's account of his own mystical experience through which his soul remained out of his body for thritheen days.[175] In 642/1245 Ḥamūyah accepted 'Alā al-Dīn Muḥammad Khwārazm Shāh's offer to teach in school of Sulṭāniyyah in Nīshābūr, where he himself studied earlier.[176] He taught in Nishābūr briefly and then left for Baḥrābād, where he repaired his *khāniqāh* ("Sufi hospice"),[177] which later became his place of burial.[178]

Ḥamūyah's disciple, 'Azīz al-Dīn Nasafī (d. 700/1300), was also responsible for spreading Ibn 'Arabī's ideas and making some of his technical expressions well-known.[179] "Despite the popularity of Nasafi's writings, historical sources afford very little reliable information about his life, which accordingly must be outlined from indications in his own works."[180] His birthplace, Nasaf, was home

169. Jāmī, *Nafaḥāt al-Uns*, cited in Chittick, "Ibn 'Arabī and His School," 519.

170. Jamal Elias, *The Throne Carrier of God: The Life and Thought of 'Alā al-Dawlah Simnānī* (Albany: State University of New York Press, 1995), 44 (footnotes).

171. See Heravī, introduction to *al-Miṣbāḥ*, 20.

172. See ibid.

173. See Khwājah Ghiāth al-Dīn Abu'l Fatḥ, *Murād al-Murīdin*, cited in Heravī's introduction to *al-Miṣbāḥ*, 19.

174. See ibid.

175. See Jāmī, *Nafaḥāt al-Uns*, cited in Ḥeravī's introduction to *al-Miṣbāḥ*, 24.

176. See ibid., 15.

177. See ibid.

178. See Mīr Bāqirī Fard, introduction to *Bayān al-Tanzīl*, 4.

179. See Chittick, "Ibn 'Arabī and His School," 519.

180. Herman Landolt, "Nasafī," www.iranica.com/newsite/articles/unicode/sup/Nasafi_Aziz.html.

to many scholars and mystics.[181] In order to study he traveled to Bukhāra,[182] one of the most important places of education in the Islamic world of his time.[183] "During his youth, he studied medicine in addition to the religious sciences, and the acquaintance with philosophy that this entailed gave a distinctive coloring to his writings on Sufism. He joined the following of Sa'd al-Dīn in Baḥrābād some time after 1243-44."[184] Nasafī was influenced by Ḥamūyah, frequently mentioned and revered him in his writings, interpreted his views, and usually preferred his views.[185] After Ḥamūyah passed away, he returned to Bukhāra[186] "where he continued his work on *Kitāb-i Tanzīl*,"[187] which he had begun to compile in Nasaf.[188] He remained in Bukhārā until 671/1273, when he was forced to leave due to the Mongol invasion of the city.[189] Nasafī describes the events which led to his departure as follows:

> In that year the infidel armies came to Transoxania and they destroyed the province, and at that time this helpless one was in the city of Bukhārā with community of dervishes. At dawn on Friday, at the beginning of the month of Rajab, we left the city – or should I say, that they forced us to make an exit – and we passed the waters of Khurāsān and arrived at the cities of Khurāsān. From that time onwards, each day we were in one location and each night at another, having no security anywhere.[190]

As a result of this atrocious invasion in which "the religious schools and books were burned and as many as 50,000 people were killed,"[191] Nasafī, after visiting Ḥamūyah's burial place in Bahrābād,[192] "moved southwards, and composed works at Kirmān,

181. See Mīr Bāqirī Fard, introduction to *Bayān al-Tanzīl*, 1.
182. See ibid.
183. See Ridgeon, *'Azīẓ Nasafī*, 1.
184. Algar, "Kobrawiya: The Order."
185. See Mīr Bāqirī Fard, introduction to *Bayān al-Tanzīl*, 3-4.
186. Ibid., 4.
187. Ridgeon, *'Azīz Nasafī*, 8.
188. See ibid.
189. See Mīr Bāqirī Fard, introduction to *Bayān al-Tanzīl*, 4.
190. Nasafī, *Kitāb-ī Tanzīl*, cited in Ridgeon, *'Azīẓ Nasafī*, 8.
191. Ibid.
192. See ibid.

Shirāz, Iṣfahān and Abarqūh."[193] He "died and buried in Abarqūh"[194]

In his famous book, *al-Insān al-Kāmil*, as well as in his other writings, such as *al-Maqṣad al-Aqṣā*, *Kashf al-Ḥaqā'iq*, *Zubdat al-Ḥaqā'iq*, and *Kitāb al-Tanzīl* Nasafī reflects on some of the major tenets found in Ibn 'Arabī's thought, such as *al-insān al-kāmil* and *waḥdat al-wujūd*, which is partially manifested in his constant mentioning of *ahl-i waḥdat* ("people of unity") and their beliefs and ideas throughout his aforementioned works. Contemporary scholars have approached the affinities between Nasafī and Ibn 'Arabī's worldviews in different modes. For example, Chittick discusses both Ḥamūyah and his disciple Nasafī under the heading of "other members of Ibn 'Arabī's school"[195] who "deserve mention as important conduits of Ibn 'Arabī's teachings."[196] He also confirms that Nasafī "was more important than Ḥamūyah…in the dissemination of Ibn 'Arabī's teaching"[197] Reffering to Nasafī, Chittick also adds that "he makes no claims to represent Ibn 'Arabī's teachings, but he uses terms such as *waḥdat al-wujūd* and "perfect human being," and explains them in ways that are not unconnected with discussions found in Ibn 'Arabī's writings."[198]

On the other hand, Herman Landolt considers Nasafī neither a representative of Kubrawīs nor of the Akbarians[199]: "he cannot really be considered a representative of "Kobraviya Sufism"…, despite his personal attachment to the figure of Ḥamū'ī. He certainly did not share the...Islamic ideology which was adopted by famous Kobraviya Sufis before and during the Mongol domination, and his *ahl-e waḥdat* even include certain forms of Indian spirituality, for which he in fact showed greatest admiration."[200] Although, Landolt believes in making a vivid differentiation between Nasafī and school of Ibn 'Arabī, he admits that "their influence is certainly perceptible in many ways in his [i.e., Nasafī's] works."[201]

'Abd al-Ḥusain ZarrīnKūb considers both Nasafī and Abu'l MafākhirYaḥyā Bākharzī (d.658/1260) as the Kubrawī masters who

193. Ibid.
194. Landolt, "Nasafī."
195. See Chittick, "Ibn 'Arabī and His School," 519.
196. Ibid.
197. Ibid.
198. Ibid.
199. See Landolt, "Nasafī."
200. Ibid.
201. Ibid., brackets added.

have provided "a sort of connection (*payvand gūna-īy*)" between Kubra's teachings and "some (*chīzī*) teachings of the school of Ibn ʻArabī."[202] Having stated that, ZarrīnKūb also points to the fact that "Nasafī who left a considerable heritage of mysticism and *taṣawwuf* intermeshed with *ḥikmat*...manifests a type of vastness in his way of thinking and an intellectual openmindedness which were rare to find among torchbearers of intellectual investigation in topics related to Islamic belief, particularly in the field of Sufism."[203] As seen above, although contemporary scholars approached Nasafī's worldview from different persepctives, there seems to be a consensus among them, on the perceptibility of the influence of Ibn ʻArabī and his school on Nasafī's thought.

As ZarrīnKūb mentions, the formation of the aforementioned connection between Kubrā's teachings and Ibn ʻArabī's world-view seemed to be postponed for some time by the criticisms of Ibn ʻArabī made by another well-known Kubrawī master, ʻAlā' ad-Dawlah Simnānī (d. 736/1337).[204] Simnānī was born in Biyābānak, a village near Simnān in Iran in the year 659/1261 in an old, well-known, revered and wealthy family.[205] His family, known as *mulūk* ("landlords"), were the second largest landholders in Simnān.[206] Several of his family members including his father held important government offices during the Khārazmīd and Mongol periods.[207] Following his family tradition of holding government positions, "at the age of fifteen (674/1275-76) and with the encouragement of his paternal uncle, Simnānī joined the court of Arghūn (reigned 683/1284-691/1292)."[208]

As Simnānī mentions himself, while he was serving at court, his knowledge consisted of some court regulations which he refer to as *faḍliyāt*, limited familiarity with *ʻulūm-i ʻaqlī wa naqlī* ("rational and transmitted sciences") and a few memorized Qur'ānic verses.[209] The depth of Simnānī's dedication to the service of Arghūn some-

---

202. ZarrīnKūb, *Dunbāla-yi Jostojū dar Taṣawwuf*, 160

203. Ibid.

204. See ibid.

205. See ʻAlā ad-Dawlah Simnānī, *Chihil Majlis yā Risāla-yi Iqbāliyyah* (Tehran: Shirkat-i Mua'liffān wa Mutarjimān, 1358/1980), 15.

206. See Elias, *The Throne Carrier of God*, 15.

207. See ibid., 15-16.

208. Ibid., 18.

209. See Najīb Māyil Heravī, introduction to *Moṣannafāt-i Fārsī* by ʻAlā Addawlah Simnānī (Tehran: Intishārāt-i ʻIlmī wa Farhangī, 1383/2004), 8-9.

times made him neglectful of his daily prayers, and also left him no time for improving his knowledge.[210] Around 24-25 years of age, in the year 683/1284[211] Simnānī experienced a life changing event in a battle. He was in the company of Arhgūn in a battle against "'Alīnāq, the general and son-in-law of Aḥmad Takūdār (reigned 681/1282 to 683/1284)."[212] As Simnānī confirms, when the army of Arghūn reached Sulṭān Aḥmad's army in the proximity of Qazwīn, he shouted *takbīr* to begin attacking the crowd of enemies.[213] Simnānī describes the event as follows: "When I was busy saying the *takbīr*, God (may He be praised and exalted) removed the veil of this world from in front of these blind eyes and revealed the beauty of the world to come."[214]

After this event, he was bewildered and not able to participate in the battle.[215] Simnānī's spiritual state continued until the next day when the entrusted *zājir-i ḥaqqānī*[216] (or the true luring/awakening medium of his unveiling experience) left him, leaving its permenant effect on him.[217] After this life changing experience, "Simnānī then consciously began to compensate for neglected religious duties by adopting an ascetic life, saying ten days' worth of prayer each night to make up for the prayers forfeited in his youth and memorizing five verses from the Qur'ān each night."[218] Through this strict practice of *tawbah* ("repentance") from his past life, Simnānī came across other visions of spiritual nature in his dream, went through a physical sickness[219], and finally in the year 685/1286[220] "asked persmission to return to Simnān, and was allowed to do so by Arghūn."[221] "When he traveled only a short distance from Tabrīz,"[222] in Ūjān, he found his sickness healed, which he interpreted as the result of

210. See ibid., 10.
211. Simnān's autobiography, cited in ibid.
212. Elias, *The Throne Carrier of God*, 18-19.
213. See Heravī, introduction to *Moṣannafāt-i Fārsī*
214. Elias, *The Throne Carrier of God*, 19.
215. See Heravī, introduction to *Moṣannafāt-i Fārsī*, 10.
216. See ibid.
217. See ibid.
218. Elias, *The Throne Carrier of God*, 20.
219. Heravī, introduction to *Moṣannafāt-i Fārsī*, 10.
220. See ibid., 11. See also Elias, *The Throne Carrier of God*, 20.
221. Elias, *The Throne Carrier of God*, 20.
222. Ibid., 20-21.

leaving Arghūn and his courtly life.[223] In Simnān, 'Alā' ad-Dawlah dedicated his time to religious education and study of Sufi teachings based on Abu Ṭālib Makkī's *Qūt al-Qulūb*[224] and other well-known works such as Ghazālī's *Iḥyā'Ulūm ad-Dīn.*[225] He also reconstructed the *Khānaqāh-i Sakkākiyyah* which was built by Shaykh Ḥasan Sakkākī, one of Abū Sa'īd Ab al-Khayr's contemporaries.[226] "At some point he also built a large *Khānaqah* ("hospice") of his own called *Ṣūfīyābād-i Khudādād* outside his ancestoral home of Biyābānak."[227]

Through his keenness to find an ideal guide on the Path, he finally found his supreme master in the person of Nūr al-Dīn 'Abd al-Raḥmān Isfarāyinī Kasirqī (d. 717/1317). Simnānī became familiar with Isfarāyinī's method of wayfaring through one of his disciples, Sharaf al-Dīn Sa'd Allāh ibn Ḥanawayh in Simnān.[228] Simnānī's meeting with Isfarāyinī in the town of Baghdādak where he taught his disciples[229] was postponed for some time, because of Arghūn's disapproval of this trip.[230] Finally, without Arghun's knowledge,[231] in the year 688/1289[232] Simnānī went to meet his preferred master in Baghdādak.

Isfarāyinī himself learned the first methods of wayfarying in a form of *dhikr* from Shaykh Aḥmad Jūrpānī [Gūrpānī] who himself entered the Path through Raẓi al-Dīn Alī Lālā (d.649/1244) who himself was associated to both Kubrā and Majd al-Dīn Baghdādī.[233] Isfarāyinī in his writings, which manifest the influence of Kubrawī masters such as Baghdādī and the well-known author of *Mirṣād al-'Ibād*, Najm al-Dīn Razī,[234] described Kubrā as *shaykh-i shaykh-*

223. See Heravī, introduction to *Moṣannafāt-i Farsī*, 11.

224. See ibid.

225. See 'Abd al-Rafī' Ḥaqīqat, introduction to *Khomkhāna-yi Waḥdat* by 'Alā ad-Dawlah Simnānī (Tehran: Ṭahūrī, 1362/1983), 29.

226. See ibid.

227. Elias, *The Throne Carrier of God*, 28.

228. See 'Alā Addawlah Simnānī, *al-'Urwah li Ahl al-Khalwah wa'l Jalwah*, ed. Najīb Māyil Heravī (Tehran: Intishārāt-i Mowlā, 1362/1983), 314-319

229. See ibid., 319.

230. See ibid., 320.

231. See ibid., 323.

232. See Elias, *The Throne Carrier of God*, 27.

233. See Herman Landolt, introduction to *Kāshif al-Asrār* by Nūr al-Din 'Abd al-Raḥmān Isfarāyenī (Tehran: Mu'assisa-yi Muṭāli'āt-i Islāmī-i Dānishgāh-i Tehrān/McGill University, 1383/2004), 15.

234. See ibid.

i shaykh-i mā ("the master of master of our master") and refered to Baqdādī as *shaykh-i mā wa sulṭān-i mā* ("our master and our *sulṭān*").[235] Simnānī also came under Baghdādī's influence.[236] Contemporary scholars seem to vary in describing the role played by Simnānī's masters in his life. For example, Landolt states that Simnānī venerated Baghdādī more than any other master,[237] but Elias confirms that "Isfarāyenī was indubitably the most influential mystical guide in Simnānī's life."[238] Simnānī gave him the title of *quṭb al-irshād fi-zamānihī* ("the Pole of Guidance in his time").[239] Simnānī's companionship with his master Isfarāyinī, seems to have lasted, although not without interruption, until the year 719/1319.[240]

Simnānī and his master Isfarāyinī, exchanged many letters (known as the *Mukātibāt*) for almost four decades.[241] The *Mukātibāt* brings to light some of the common themes also expounded by Ibn 'Arabī, such as the notion of *wilāyah* ("sainthood") and the *shaykh* ("Sufi master") as a source of spiritual inspiration as well as the concept of *waḥdat al-wujūd*.

Simnānī left a large corpus of writings, perhaps as many as 300 works.[242] His doctrinal work, *Al-'Urwah li-Ahl al-Khalwah wa'l Jalwah*, which was originally written in Arabic and translated into Persian later,[243] has often been considered as Simnānī's most notable writing.[244] Some of the contemporary scholars believe that "the most important part of Simnānī's literary and doctrinal legacy is contained in his esoteric commentary on the Qur'ān."[245] In his work on the Qur'ān, Simnānī completed a commentary which was originally begun by Najm al-Dīn Kubrā, and was later continued

---

235. See ibid, 16.

236. For example, see Elias, *The Throne Carrier of God*, 44, 123, 119.

237. See Landolt, introduction to *Kāshif al-Asrār*, 16.

238. Elias, *The Throne Carrier of God*, 37.

239. See ibid.

240. See Ḥaqīqat, introduction to *Chihil Majlīs*, 21.

241. See *Mukātibāt Correspondence spirituelle échangée entre Nurodīn Esfarāyenī et son disciple 'Alā'oddawleh Semnānī*, ed. Herman Landolt (Teheran: Department D'inranologie De L'Institut Franco-Iranien, 1351/1972).

242. See Ḥaqīqat, introduction to *Chihil Majlīs*, 73, quoted from Dhahabī's *al-Durar al-Kāminah*.

243. See Heravī, introduction to *al-'Urwah*, 46.

244. See ibid., 27.

245. Waley, "Najm al-Dīn Kubrā and the Central Asian School of Sufism," 97.

by Najm al-Dīn Rāzī.[246] In Simnānī's works, the favorite Kubrawī concept of *laṭā'if* and its relevant colors were expanded, categorized and methodologically discussed and elaborated.[247]

A meeting between Simnānī's disciple, Amīr Iqbāl Sistānī, who wrote down his master's *Chihil Majlīs*, and the aforementioned celebrated *shāriḥ* of Ibn 'Arabī's *Fuṣūṣ*, Kamāl al-Dīn 'Abd al-Razzāq Kāshānī, seems to have triggered correspondence between the two Kubrawī and Akbarian masters.[248] After addressing Simnānī with considerable reverence, and referring to him with titles such as *Shaykh al-Islām* ("the shaykh whose being represents Islam") and *qudwah arbāb al-tarīqah* ("the torchbearer of the masters of the Path"), Kāshānī continues his letter with criticism of Simnānī's *al-'Urwah*, while quoting Sistānī's words regarding Simnānī's disapproval of Ibn 'Arabī's approach to *tawḥīd*.[249] Kāshānī also quotes Isfarāyinī's agreement with Ibn 'Arabī's methodology.[250] On the other hand, Simnānī's response shows a considerable aggressiveness toward and resentment of both Kashānī and Ibn 'Arabī.[251] He also denies Isfarāyinī's positive attitdue towards Ibn 'Arabī, referring to his proscription of teaching the *Fuṣūṣ*.[252]

'Alā'ad-Dawlah Simnānī, although he criticized Ibn 'Arabī', "adopted much of his terminology and his worldview."[253] Although he opposed certain tenets of Ibn 'Arabī's teaching, such as *waḥdat al-wujūd* ("unity of existence"), as projected in his criticism of Ibn 'Arabī's *al-wujūd al-muṭlaq* ("Absolute Existence"), Simnānī gave him the title of *al-'ārif al-ḥaqqānī* ("the true/or divinely inspired mystic"), and refer to him as *al-walī* ("saint"), *al-ṣiddīq* ("very honest/close friend"), and *al-muqarrab* ("the one drawn close to God").[254] On another occasion, he confirms that Ibn'Arabī was for-

---

246. See ibid., 97-98. For a fuller analysis of this subject see Henry Corbin, *Man of Light in Iranian Sufism*, trans., Nancy Pearson (Boulder: Shambhala, 1978).

247. See ibid., 98. On the concept of *laṭā'if* 'see Elias, *The Throne Carrier of God*.

248. See Jāmī, *Nafaḥāt al-Uns*, 483.

249. See ibid., 484. See also Herman Landolt, "Der Briefwechsel zwischen Kāšanī und Simnānī über *Waḥdat al-Wuğud*," *Der Islam* 50 (1973): 29-81.

250. Ibid., 488.

251. See ibid., 489-492.

252. See ibid., 489.

253. Chittick, "Ebn al-'Arabī."

254. See Jāmī, *Nafaḥāt al-Uns*, 553. Jāmī quotes Simnānī's words regarding Ibn 'Arabī as follows: "*ayyuh al-ṣiddīq, wa ayyuh al-muqarrab wa ayyuh al-walī wa ayyuh al-'ārif al-haqqānī*."

given by God for his approach to *al-wujūd al-muṭlaq*, because of his original intention to prove the concepts of *waḥdat dar kathrat* ("unity in multiplicity") and God's *waḥdāniyyat* ("God's unity").[255] A commentary on *Fuṣūṣ al-Ḥikam* also has been listed among Simnānī's works.[256]

Simnānī's attempt to find an alternative solution to Ibn 'Arabī's *waḥdat al-wujūd* resulted in his focus on *shuhūdī* ("witnessing") methodology,[257] through a systematic approach to concepts such as *tajallī* ("God's theophany"),[258] which is also an important element of the Akbarian worldview. "It was only several centuries later, in socio-political and religious circumstances similar to those of Ilkhānid Iran, that Aḥmad Sirhindī turned to Simnānī's writings and found inspiration for his own ideas."[259] As a result of this influence, "Simnānī's concept that the ultimate mystical state is that of being a witness of God's essence, attributes, acts and effects was further elaborated by Sirhindī in the doctrine of oneness of witnessing"[260] or *waḥdat al-shuhūd*.

Sayyid Muḥammad al-Ḥusaynī, also known as Gisūdirāz (d.825/1422), a prominent figure of Chishtī order of Sufism in India, and one of the critics of Ibn 'Arabī, also manifested Simnānī's influence. His ancestors, originally from Khurāsān, were referred to as *sādāt-i dirāz gisū* (sayyids with long-locks),[261] and his father was "a disciple of Shaykh Nizām al-Dīn Awliyā'."[262] A few years after his father passed away, Gisūdiraz along with his brother underwent spiritual training by Shaykh Awliyā's successor, Shaykh Nasīr al-Dīn Maḥmūd (d.757/1356) known as Chirāgh-i Delhī.[263] Gisūdirāz

255. See Jāmī, *Nafaḥāt al-Uns*, 553-554.

256. See Ḥaqīqat, introduction to *Chihil Majlīs*, 79.

257. See Heravī, introduction to *al-'Urwah*, 36. See also Elias, *The Throne Carrier of God*, 2-56.

258. See Elias, *The Throne Carrier of God*, 2, 61-77. See also Herman Landolt, "Simnānī on Waḥdat al-Wujūd," in *Collected Papers on Islamic Philosophy and Mysticism*, ed. Mehdī Moḥaqqiq and Herman Landolt (Tehran: The Institute of Islamic Studies McGill University, Tehran Branch, 1971), 100.

259. Elias, *The Throne Carrier of God*, 57.

260. Ibid., 162.

261. See Syed Shāh Khusro Ḥussainī, *Sayyīd Muḥammad al-Ḥusaynī-i Gisūdirāz: on Sufism* (Delhi: Idārah-i Adabiyāt-i Delhī, 1983), 11.

262. Ibid.

263. See ibid., 11-12.

himself succeeded Shaykh Maḥmūd after his death.[264] Although critical of Ibn 'Arabī, Gisūdirāz manifested the influence of Shaykh al-Akbar in his works.[265] Simnānī's disciple, Sayyid Ashraf Jahāngīr Simnānī (d. 829/1425) met with the Chishtī master in Gulbarga where he found himself learning from Gisūdirāz, and also perhaps, as mentioned in Sayyid Ashraf's letter, tried to convince Gisūdirāz in Ibn 'Arabī's favour.[266] Some of the contemporary scholars have referred to the possible influence of Simnānī's writings, such as *al-'Urwah*, and also his teachings, on Gisūdirāz, as were advocated by Simnānī's disciples in their meetings with the Chishtī figure.[267] In any case, contemporary scholars found Gisūdirāz's views very close to Simnānī's *shuhūdī* thought.[268]

The later followers of Ibn 'Arabī did not find the criticisms of most of his Sufi critics such as Gisūdirāz and Shaykh Aḥmad Sirhindī very credible.[269] Sayyid Ashraf Jahāngīr Simnānī, a disciple of 'Alā' al-Dawlah Simnānī,[270] who was "an intermediary in the correspondence between Simnānī and...Kashānī,"[271] later "sided with Kāshānī in the dispute over Ibn 'Arabī,"[272] and became his disciple.[273] Sayyid Ashraf's conclusion is that Simnānī's assessment of Ibn 'Arabī's ideas had been incorrect and that he himself had withdrawn his criticisms before he passed away.[274] 'Alā' al-Dawlah Simnānī's approach to the "prophets" as the resemblances of *ḥaqā'iq* ("spiritual realities") reminds us of Ibn 'Arabī's similar approach in his *Fuṣūṣ al-Ḥikam*. Simnānī's considerable work on the Qur'ānic esoteric interpretation also provides another opportunity for comparative study.

Most of the Persian commentaries on Ibn 'Arabī's major work,

---

264. See ibid., 12.

265. See ibid., 43-109. See also William C. Chittick, "The School of Ibn 'Arabī" in *History of Islamic Philosophy*, Part I, ed. Seyyed Ḥossein Nasr and Oliver Leaman (New York: Routledge, 1996), 520.

266. See ibid., 18.

267. See ibid., 17. The author refers to S. A. A. Riẓvī as the one who hold this opinion.

268. See ibid.

269. See Chittick, "Ebn al-'Arabī."

270. See Elias, *The Throne Carrier of God*, 15.

271. Ibid., 48.

272. Chittick, "The School of Ibn 'Arabī," 520.

273. See Elias, *The Throne Carrier of God*, 15.

274. See Chittick, "Ebn al-'Arabī."

Fuṣuṣ al-Ḥikam, were influenced by the well known Arabic commentary (*Sharḥ)* written by Kāshānī's disciple Da'ūd Qayṣarī (d. 751/1350).[275] Among more than ten Persian commentaries on *Fuṣūṣ*,[276] the commentary of another well-known *Kubrawī* master, Sayyid 'Alī Hamadānī (d. 786/1385), entitled *Ḥall al-Fuṣūṣ*, is indicative of this influence and is considered one of the most important Persian commentaries. This commentary has been mistakenly attributed to one of the Naqshbandī Sufi masters by contemporary scholars.[277] Hamadānī is known with titles such as *'Alī-i thānī* ("the second 'Alī") and *shāh-i Hamadān* ("king of Hamadān").[278] He "was allegedly Simnānī's nephew by his sister Fāṭima."[279] He first began his training under supervision of Simnānī himself.[280] "Hamadānī was descended from Zayn al-'Ābidīn, the Fourth Imām of Shī'ah, and was the disciple of two *khalīfahs* of 'Alā' al-Dawlah Simnānī."[281] Through Hamadānī's many ventures in the Islamic world of his time, "his initiatic line was perpetuated in a number of places that he visited."[282]

Upon his arrival in Kashmīr in the year782/1380,[283] "for some six years he propagated Islam and the Kubrawī Way to great effect in Kashmir and in neighboring Badakhshān, accmumlating a large following."[284] Besides his aforementioned commentary of Ibn 'Arabī's *Fuṣūṣ*, Hamadānī "has been credited with more than a hundred treatises, primarily in Persian, on various topics of theoretical and practical Sufism and *fotowwa*, as well as a respectable body of verse."[285] Hamadanī left an important and long lasting lineage of

275. See ibid.

276. See ibid.

277. See ibid. See also Algar, "Kobrawiya: The Order." This commentary has been attributed to the Naqshbandī master Khwājah Muḥammad Parsā. See Khwājah Muḥammad Parsā, *Sharḥ-i Fusūṣ al-Ḥikam*, ed. Jalīl Misgar Nijād (Tehran: Markaz-ī Nashr-i Dānishgāhī, 1366/1987).

278. See Muḥammad Riyāḍ, *Aḥwāl wa Āthār wa Ashār-i Mīr Sayyīd 'Alī Hamadānī* (Islamabad: Markaz-i Taḥqīqāt-i Fārsī-yi Irān wa Pākistān, 1985), 3.

279. Elias, *The Throne Carrier of God*, 49.

280. See ibid., 49-50.

281. Waley, "Najm al-Dīn Kubrā and the Central Asian School of Sufism," 102.

282. Algar, "Kobrawiya: The Order."

283. See Waley, "Najm al-Dīn Kubrā and the Central Asian School of Sufism," 102.

284. Ibid.

285. Algar, "Kobrawiya: The Order."

the Kubrawī order which is known as Hamadāniyya.[286] In shaping "Hamadānī's broad posthumous influence,"[287] his vast corpus of writngs played an important role.[288] For example, his "*Awrād-e Fatḥiya*...is still rectied today as far west as Bosnia by Sufis of various allegiances, particularly Naqshbandīs who have incorporated it into their devotional manuals."[289] Besides his commentary on *Fuṣūṣ*, his other works such as *Asrār al-Nuqtah*, *Mashārib al-Adhwāq*, and also his *Risālat al-Sab'īn fī Faḍā'il-i Amīr al-Mu'minīn* which is dedictated to the personality of the first Shī'ī Imām, also manifest Hamadānī's wide interest in the essential Akbarian concepts such as *waḥdat al-wujūd*, *al-insān al-kāmil* and *wilāyah* ("sainthood").

Contemporary scholars have referred to the status of Hamadānī in India as a great *muṣliḥ* (reviver/reformer) who played a major role in spreading Islam, popularizing Arabic and Persian languages, and building libraries, *khānaqāhs*, mosques and religious schools, and reviving Islamic and Persian art, and local skills and trades in Kashmir.[290] Hamadanī also trained many disciples and *murīds* including some of the royal figures of his time.[291] Hamadānī's prominent role as a reformer in Kashmīr has been also highly commended by the well-known Pakistani poet, Iqbāl Lahūrī.[292] "Numerous followers of Hamadānī continuted his work in Kashmir after his departure."[293] Among these followers was Hamadānī's son Mīr Muḥammad whose advent in Kashmir (in 796/1393) initiated what is known as the second phase of the Kubrawī presence in that region.[294] The above mentioned Kubrawī branch of Hamadāniyyah "also had lasting offshoots of Shī'ite persuasions."[295] Nūrbakhshiyyah and Dhahabīyyah branches of Hamadāniyyah were born after the execution of Hamadānī's *khalīfah*, Ishāq Khuttalānī (d.826/1423); the lat-

286. See Waley, "Najm al-Dīn Kubrā and the Central Asian School of Sufism," 102.

287. Algar, 'Kobrawiya: The Order."

288. See ibid.

289. Ibid.

290. See, for example, Riyāḍ, *Aḥwāl wa Athār*, 43-76. See also Muḥammad Yūsuf Nayyerī, introduction to *Risālat al-Sab'īn fī Faḍā'il Amīr al-Mu'minīn* (Shiraz: Navīd Publishers, 1375/1996), 33.

291. See ibid., 81.

292. See ibid., 53.

293. Algar, "Kobrawiya: The Order."

294. See ibid.

295. Waley, "Najm al-Dīn Kubra and the Central Asian School of Sufism," 102.

ter branch being still practiced in Iran today.[296] Generally speaking, the Kubrawī order seems to continue to exist through its different branches in several parts of the world such as Iran, Central Asia, and China.[297]

The Aim of the Present Manuscript

Despite the important works of prominent members of the Kubrawīs and their contribution in spreading the ideas of Ibn 'Arabī and his followers, there is no major study available on this topic. The present manuscript is a study of major Kubrawī works and the manner in which the Kubrawīs adopted, supported and occasionally criticized Ibn 'Arabī's ideas.

I will conduct a study of the major concepts in the school of Ibn 'Arabī, such as *waḥdat al-wujūd* ("unity of existence"), *al-insān al-kāmil* ("Perfect Man") and *asmā' wa ṣifāt* (("God's Names and Attributes"), in order to provide an analysis of their reception by the prominent Kubrawī masters, especially Najm al-Dīn Kubrā, founder of the order, Sa'd al-Dīn Ḥamūyah, 'Aziz al-Dīn Nasafī, 'Alā' al-Dawlah Simnānī and Sayyid 'Alī Hamadānī..

Considering the principal importance of the concept of *wahdat al-wujūd* in Ibn 'Arabī's worldview, which appears as the foundation of his teachings, and also the tendency of the Kubrawī masters in approaching this concept (in its different relevant manifestations), more than any other concept in the Akbarian thought, I will dedicate the first chapter to the Akbarian/Kubrawī approaches to this concept. Because of the aforementioned centrality of *waḥdat al-wujūd*, both in discussion of Ibn 'Arabī's worldview and his school, as well as the Kubrawī approaches to this school, I have relied on this concept as the main foundational ground for the entire discussions provided in this work.

In the second chapter, I will discuss the criticism of Ibn 'Arabī and his school by Simnānī, and the other two main figures, Sirhindī and Gisūdirāz, who have been inspired by his *shuhūdī* approach. I will refer to the views and criticism of Ibn 'Arabī by these three figures under the title of "*shuhūdī* triangle."

The third and last chapter is an attempt to look at another central Akbarian concept, *al-insān al-kāmil* in both schools of Akbarians

296. See ibid.

297. See ibid., 102-103. See also Algar, "Kobrawiya: The Order."

and Kubrawīs. This of course will be done with focus on the affinities and correlations between the concepts of *insān al-kāmil* and *waḥdat al-wujūd*, as projected in both worldviews.

Throughout this work, I will rely largely on the original works written by the founders and members of the Akbarian and Kubrawī schools of Islamic mysticism, both in published form and original manuscripts, as well as commentaries, books and articles written by contemporary scholars in this field.

Abbreviations for libraries holding manuscripts referred to in footnotes and bibliography:

Library of Āstān Quds Razavi (Mashhad/Iran): Āstān
Library of Ḥaram-i Moṭahhar-i Aḥmad ibn Mūsā Shāh Chirāgh (Shiraz/Iran): Shiraz
Library of Āyatollāh al-ʻUẓmā Marʻashī Najafī (Qum/Iran): Marʻashī
Malek Library (Tehran/Iran): Malek

Chapter One

Waḥdat al-Wujūd ("Unity of Existence"): A Comparison of the Akbarian and Kubrawī Approaches

Waḥdat al-wujūd is one of the most important concepts in the school of thought associated with Ibn 'Arabī and his followers. This term encapsulates the *nature* of the interrelationship between the Absolute and the universe. Although the notion of *waḥdat al-wujūd* is attributed to Ibn 'Arabī, the term itself does not appear in his writings.[1] In the works of Sufis who predate Ibn 'Arabī we find numerous expressions in which the centrality of *tawḥīd* as the very foundation of the mystical path is emphasized. Yet here again the precise term, *waḥdat al-wujūd* does not appear or at least did not become the most important term to express a prominent meaning of *tawḥīd*.[2]

The Concept of waḥdah Among Islamic Mystics: A Review

Biographical and hagiographical accounts such as *Tadkirat al-Awliyā'* of Shaykh Farīd al-Dīn 'Aṭṭār Nishābūrī (d.672/1274) contain the reports of numerous and varied expressions, indicating *tawḥīd* as the core of the spiritual attainment in the experiences of early Sufi masters. Such utterances are also noticeable in the writings and sayings of Sufi figures with recorded *shaṭḥiyyāt* ("theopathic locutions")[3]. The Ninth century well-known controversial

1. See Chittick, "Rūmī and Waḥdat al-Wujūd," 72, and "Ibn 'Arabī" in *History of Islamic Philosophy*, 504.

2. See ibid., 70-71.

3. See Annemarie Schimmel, *The Mystical Dimensions of Islam* (Chapel Hill: The University of North Carolina Press, 1985), 41.

mystic, Ḥusayn ibn Manṣūr al-Ḥallāj (d.310/922), considers *tafrīd* ("singleness") as the first step in realization of *tawḥīd*.[4] Also a distinct understanding of *tawḥīd*, intertwined with annihilation (*fanā'*) and lifting the veil of realization, is indicated in his poetry, in such lines as, "I saw my Lord through His eyes, I asked: who are you?, He responded: you."[5] It is worth mentioning that the French scholar Massingnon interprets the *'ayn* ("eye") in the above poetry as the Absolute's Essence: Je vis mas Seigneur avec l'æil (= l'essence) de mon Seigneur.[6]

Another controversial mystic, the renowned Bāyazīd Basṭāmī (d.260/874), stated, "I came forth from Bāyazīd-ness as a snake from its skin."[7] As Chittick points out: "Ma'rūf al-Karkhī (d.200/815-816) is said to have been the first to reexpress the *shahāda* in the form often heard in later centuries, 'There is nothing in *wujūd* but God.'"[8] Chittick also mentions another mystic: "Abul-'Abbas Qassab (fl. 4th/10th century) used similar terms: 'There is nothing in the two worlds except my Lord. The existent things (*mawjūdāt*) — all things except His *wujūd* – are nonexistent (*ma'dūm*).'"[9]

From the standpoint of *waḥdat al-wujūd*, "existence (*wujūd*) is something that is one single reality (*haqīqah*) and that has many divergent manifestation-forms (*maẓāhir*). This position is established upon the fundamental vision of the act of "existence," which is the one absolute reality, running through, or flowing through, all things in the universe."[10]

The term *ahl al-waḥdah* [or *ahl-i waḥdat*] has been utilized to refer to the followers of Ibn 'Arabī by both Ibn-Taymiyyah, the fierce opponent of Ibn 'Arabī and also 'Aziz al-Dīn Nasafī,[11] one of the ardent advocates of Ibn 'Arabī among Kubrawīs, pejoratively by the former and sympathetically by the latter.

---

4. See ibid., 69.

5. See Abu'l Mughīth al-Ḥussain ibn Manṣūr al-Ḥallāj al-Bayḍāwī al-Baqdādī, *Kitāb aṭ-Ṭawāsīn*, ed. Louis Massignon (Paris: Puaul Geuthner, 1913), 167.

6. Ibid.

7. Murtaḍā Muṭahharī, *Understanding Islamic Sciences* (London: Sāqī Books, 2002), 55.

8. Chittick, "Rūmī and Waḥdat al-Wujūd," 71.

9. Ibid.

10. Toshihiko Izutsu, *The Concept and Reality of Existence* (Tokyo: Keio Institute of Cultural and Linguistic Studies, 1971), 47.

11. See Chittick, "Rūmī and Waḥdat al-Wujūd," 84.

School of Ibn 'Arabī and waḥdat al-wujūd (Unity of Existence)

The Aspects of Bātin and Ẓāhir ("exterior and interior")

In his *Kitāb al-Ma'rifah,*[12] Ibn 'Arabī distinguishes between *marātib* ("levels") and *majālī* ("loci of manifestations"). *Marātib* includes six stages beginning with *al-ḥadrat al-aḥadiyyah* ("the presence of exclusive unity"), while *majālī* commences with the stage of *ḥaḍrat al-waḥdāniyyah* ("the presence of Oneness/inclusive unity").[13]

Ibn Arabī utilizes various terms to refer to the numerous aspects of the Absolute's Self-manifestations. For example, in many occasions, he makes use of such terms as *ḥaḍarāt* (presences), *nasha'āt* ("configurations"),[14] *ta'ayyunāt* ("entifications"),[15] *tanazzulāt* ("descending stages"), *shu'ūn* ("levels or loci of manifestations"), *tajallīyāt* ("manifestations"), *aḥkām* ("properties"),[16] *wujūh* ("aspects"), *a'dād* ("numbers"), and *al-a'yān al-thābitah* ("immutable entities")[17].

As the late Toshihiko Izutsu rightly puts it: "One of the basic points on which all thinkers of the *waḥdat al-wujūd* school are in perfect agreement with each other is that the Absolute itself has two aspects…*bāṭin* and *ẓāhir*, i.e., 'interior' and 'exterior.'"[18] These two aspects belong to the One and Only Real Reality.[19] *Bāṭin*, or the inner aspect, represents the Self-hidden dimension of the Absolute that is exemplified in the well-known Divine tradition (*ḥadīth-i qudsī*): *kuntu kanzan makhfiyyā*: "I was a hidden treasure," while *ẓāhir*, or the outer aspect, is His Self-unveiling presence as the continuation of the same *ḥadīth* reveals: *faḥbabtu an u'raf fa khalaqtu'l khalq li-kay 'uraf* – "then I loved to be known, therefore I created

12. See Ibn 'Arabī, *Kitāb al-Ma'rifah*, ed. Sa'īd Abu'l Fattāḥ (Beirūt: Dār al-Mutanabbī, 1993), 79.
13. See ibid.
14. See Chittick, *The Sufi Path of Knowledge*, 68.
15. Ibid., 83.
16. Ibid., 39.
17. Ibid., 7.
18. See Izutsu, *The Concept*, 47.
19. See ibid.

the creatures to be known."[20]

Bāṭin is *terra incognita* – "absolute Unknown-Unknowable."[21] It is the perpetual "mystery of mysteries"[22] or *Ghayb al-ghuyūb*[23] in the expressions of several members of Ibn ʻArabī's school.[24] In the aspect of *ẓāhir* or exterior, which might be referred to as *terra manifesta*, through the act of *tajallī* ("manifestation"), the Absolute manifests Himself to the entire existence.

Regarding popular expressions such as *wujūd-i iʻtibārī* ("fictitious existence") and *wujūd-i majāzī* ("metaphorical existence"), used in the school of Ibn ʻArabī to refer to the "tangible existence," Izutsu states, "These and other similar expressions simply mean that the things of the empirical world are sheer nothing if considered in isolation from the underlying unity of existence."[25]

The prominent philosopher/mystic Mullā Ṣadrā of Shīrāz whose thought and ideas were influenced by Ibn ʻArabī "calls the things of the empirical world "sheer connections," that is, sheer relations…For in this particular context, "relation" means "illuminative relation" (*iḍāfah ishrāqīyah*). That is to say, the things of the empirical world are established as partial realities only through the illuminative or self-manifesting act of the one Absolute Reality."[26]

Ibn ʻArabī addresses the unity of *wujūd* on numerous occasions. For example, in *Rasāʼil*, he claims that "nothing has become manifest in *wujūd* through *wujūd* except the Real (*al-Ḥaqq*), since *wujūd* is the Real, and He is one."[27] He also confirms that "the en-

20. See ibid., 47 and 51. For Ibn ʻArabi's approach to this *ḥadīth-i qudsī*, see, for example, Jaakko Hämeen-Anttila, "The Immutable Entities and Time." *Journal of the Muhyiddin Ibn ʻArabi Society*, XXXIX (2006): 15-32. For an example of Kubrawī approach to the above quoted *ḥadīth*, see Najm al-Dīn Abu Bakr Muḥammad ibn Shāhāwar Asadī Rāzī Dāyah, *Manārāt al-Sāyirīn*, MS. Malek, Tehran.

21. See ibid., 47.

22. See ibid., 49.

23. Ibid.

24. For example, see Tāj al-Dīn Ḥussain ibn Ḥassan Khwārazmī, *Sharḥ-i Fuṣūṣ al-Ḥikam*, ed. Najīb Māyīl Heravī (Tehrān: Intishārāt-i Mowlā, 1368/1989), 11, 13, 56 and 647. See also other expressions such as *Ghayb-i Muṭlaq-i Awwal* ("The First non-delimited Unseen"), *Ghayb-i Kulli-yi Rabbānī* ("The Universal Unseen Divine") in Ṣadr al-Dīn Qūnawī, *Nafaḥāt al-Ilāhiyyah*, trans., Muḥammad Khwājawī (Tehran: Intishārāt-i Mowlā, 1375/1996), 3, 13 and 24.

25. See Izutsu, *The Concept*, 44.

26. Ibid.

27. Chittick, "Rūmī and Waḥdat al-Wujūd," 78.

tity (*'ayn*) of *wujūd* is one, but its properties (*aḥkām*) are diverse."[28] Moreover, "all of *wujūd* is one in reality; there is nothing along with it."[29]

As it appears, Ibn 'Arabī's discussion of the Absolute's Unity contains both dimensions of *tanzīh* ("Absolute's peerlessness") and *tashbīh* ("Absoslute's similarity").

To understand the correlation between the *kathrat/takaththur* ("multiplicity/manyness") and the *waḥdah* ("unity"), we should pay attention to the manner in which Ibn 'Arabī and his followers have clarified the different presences or planes of existence. Perhaps every one of these presences – which Ibn 'Arabī refers to, by employing such terms as as *haḍarāt* ("presences"), *nasha'āt* ("configurations"), *ta 'ayyunāt* ("entifications"), *tanazzulāt* ("descending stages"), or *tajallīyāt* ("manifestations") – is discussed to make the reciprocity of the *manyness-oneness* imaginable.. Each of the Absolute's *tajallīyāt* ("manifestations") is a portrayal of such ties.

Ṣadr al-Dīn Qūnawī

Ibn 'Arabī's most well-known 13th century disciple and interpreter of his works was Ṣadr al-Dīn Qūnawī. He "stresses the centrality of *wujūd* to all discussion."[30] As Chittick maintains, one of the reasons for which this cardinal disciple of Ibn 'Arabī was more severely attacked by Ibn Taymiyyah than his master was Qūnawī's reliance on philosophy in his works.[31] Qūnawī utilizes the exact expression of *waḥdat al-wujūd* on a few occasions, and he does not regard the expression of *waḥdat al-wujūd* as a precise statement of unity of existence.[32]

For both Ibn 'Arabī and Qūnawī, notions such as *wahdah* ("unity") and numerous discussions of the nature and reality of *wujūd* ("existence") point to the fact that there is only one true existence; the *wujūd* of the Absolute. Qūnawī, and his master, Ibn 'Arabī, viewed the concept of unity of existence to refer to the fact that this *waḥdah* does not in any way foreclose, oppose, or contradict the multiplicity of its self manifestations.[33]

---

28. Ibid.
29. Ibid.
30. Ibid.
31. Ibid.
32. See ibid.
33. See ibid., 79.

Qūnawī mentions in his *Miftāḥ al-Ghayb* ("Key to the Unseen") that "Though there is nothing but one *wujūd*, it manifests itself as diverse, multiple, and plural because of the diversity of the realities of the receptacles. Nevertheless, in itself and in respect of its disengagement...does not become plural or multiple."[34]

In Ibn 'Arabī's approach only those mystics with "both eyes" or *dhul 'aynayn* are able to overcome the deficiency of the one dimensional approach to the Absolute.[35] Perhaps developing the notion of *waḥdat al-wujūd* was considered by followers of Ibn 'Arabī's school as the comprehensive solution to provide the *sālikīn* ("wayfarers") with a more advanced perspective of the Path and their ties with the Absolute. Ibn 'Arabī refers to the realization of the Absolute as *huwa-lā-huwa* ("He/not He") i.e., realizing the two dimensions of God's peerlessness, and comparability at once.[36]

The terms *aḥadīyyat al-jam'* ("comprehensive unity") and *aḥadīyyat al-jam'iyah* ("collective-comprehensive unity") represent stages of the "all-comprehensiveness of the Absolute's exclusive unity" and they may refer to the complementarity of both *tashbīh* and *tanzīh* in the *jam'iyah* ("comprehensive view") of *waḥdat al-wujūd.* In this regard, the proponents of *waḥdat al-wujūd* have elaborated on the complicated nature of the ties between God and man.[37]

Qūnawī states in his *Nafaḥāt al-Ilāhiyyah* that the Absolute's *shu'ūn* ("loci of manifestation") are not apart from Him[38]; however, because "they are the realities of the entities,"[39] they bring *kathra* ("multiplicity") to the notion of *waḥdah* ("unity").[40] Therefore, based on this *munāsibah* ("consideration of their ties with

34. Ibid.

35. See Chittick, "Ibn 'Arabī," 501.

36. See Chittick, "Ibn 'Arabī," 504-505. Among many examples, also see Muḥyīddīn Ibn 'Arabī, *Dīwān* (Beirūt: Dār al-Rashīd, 1412), 45, in his praise of the Absolute in his statement *kuntu ana huwa al-shuhūd*, and his answer to Ḥakīm Tirmidhī's question in chapter 73 of *Futūḥāt*, and question 115, on "*subuḥāt al-wajh*" in Ibn al-'Arabī, *The Meccan Revelations*, vol. I, ed. Michel Chodkiewicz, trans., William C. Chittick & James Morris (New York: Pir Press, 2002), 45-47.

37. For example, see Sa'īd al-Dīn Farghānī, *Mashāriq al-Darārī*, ed. Sayyid Jalāl al-Dīn Āshtiyānī (Qum: Daftar-i Tabliqāt-i Islāmī-yi Hawza-yi 'Ilmiyya-yi Qum, 1379/2000), 512.

38. See Chittick, "Rūmī and Waḥdat al-Wujūd," 79.

39. Ibid.

40. See ibid.

the Absolute") they ought to be called *siwā* ('separate") or *ghayr* ("other").[41]

Although the complementarity of these two dimensions constitutes the very foundation of the notion of *waḥdat al-wujūd*, this has been ignored by some of its major critics.[42] For example, Ibn Taymiyyah (d.728/1328) identifies *waḥdat al-wujūd* with *ittiḥād* ("union with God"), and *ḥulūl* ("incarnation").[43] In his *Rasā'il*, Ibn Taymiyyah asserts that those who believe in the unity of existence "…have no faith in God, in His prophets, or in the Last Day,"[44] and they believe that God's "*wujūd* is identical with the *wujūd* of the cosmos and that the cosmos has no other maker than the cosmos itself."[45] He also claims that advocates of unity of existence believe that "the necessary *wujūd* that belongs to the Creator is the same as the possible *wujūd* that belongs to the creature."[46] As Chittick confirms, Ibn Taymiyyah ignored the dimension of *lā-huwa* ("not He") or *tanzīh*, the complementary aspect of *huwa* ("He, the Absolute") or *tashbīh* in the teachings of Ibn 'Arabī, and, therefore, overlooked the comprehensive realization of the idea of *waḥdat al-wujūd*.[47]

'Abd al-Karīm Jīlī and Sayyid Ḥaydar Āmulī

Using cognitive metaphors, some other members of the school of Ibn 'Arabī have elaborated on the nature of the ties between the Absolute and creation. In his book, *al-Insān al-Kāmil* ("Perfect Man"), the prominent mystic 'Abd al-Karīm Jīlī (d.827/1421) explains these two dimensions in the connection between *Ḥaqq* ("the Real") and *khalq* ("creation").[48] He states that "to call the things of

41. See ibid. See also Ṣadr al-Dīn Qūnawī, *Nafaḥāt al-Ilāhiyyah*, trans., Muḥammad Khwājawī (Tehran: Intishārāt-i Mowlā, 1375/1996), 31, 58-59. Qūnawī refers to the confined forms of the entities (*ṣūrat-i juz'ī*) as the manifestation of the un-delimited Universal Knowledge (*ṣūrat-i 'ilm-i Kullī*). In his elaborations on the realities of entities (*ḥaqā'iq-i ashyā'*) which he calls *furū'* (sub-branches), Qūnawī refers to their ties with the Absolute *Wujūd* as the *aṣl* (Source).

42. See ibid., 86.

43. See ibid., 85.

44. Ibid.

45. Ibid.

46. Ibid., 86.

47. See ibid. For a different approach to the concepts of *ittīḥād* (union with the Absolute) and *tawḥīd* (oneness of the Absolute) with that of Ibn Taymiyyah, see, for example, 'Azīz al-Dīn Nasafī, *Ittīḥād wa Waḥdat, Kufr wa Tawḥīd*, MS. 405/13, Malek, Tehran.

48. See Izustu, *The Concept*, 45.

this world "creatures" or "created things" is simply to call them by a "borrowed" name."[49] In other words, "God "lends"[50] the attribute of *khalqiyyah* ("createdness")[51] "to His own attributes in so far as they appear in the empirical world."[52] Thus, Jilī mentions that "the Absolute (*ḥaqq*) is, as it were, the prime matter of this world. The world in this sense is comparable to ice...The congealed mass of water is called "ice," which is but a borrowed name; its true name is water."[53]

The 14th century Sufi master, Sayyid Ḥaydar Āmulī (d.787/1385), in his *Jāmi' al-Asrār* ("The Compendium of Secrets"), utilizes the metaphor of the relation between *ink* and *letters*:[54] "Ink structurally corresponds to the all-pervasive unique reality of existence while the letters written with it corresponds to the "quiddities" (*māhiyyāt*) as actualized in the forms of the various things in the empirical world."[55]

Also in the introduction to his commentary on Ibn 'Arabī's *Fuṣūṣ al-Ḥikam* ("Bezels of Wisdom"), *Naṣṣ al-Nuṣūṣ fī Sharḥ al-Fuṣūṣ*, Āmulī reiterates the focal aspects of the concept of *waḥdat al-wujūd* through his elaborations on the categories of the Absolute's manifestations (*tajallī*).[56] He mentions the presence of the *aḥadiyyat* ("Absolute's exclusive unity") as the first manifestation, which he refers to as the manifestation of the Absolute's Essence or *tajallī al-dhātī*.[57] In describing the characteristics of this manifestation, Āmulī speaks of a certain *waḥdat* ("unity"), which borrows its entire validity and essence from the very nature of Absolute's *Dhāt* (Essence). The key to this type of unity, according to Āmulī's explanation, seems to be the fact that the unity of the Essence, which is the sheer existence of the Truth (*Ḥaqq*), is exactly the same (*'ayn*) as the Essence Itself.[58] This is also the category

49. Ibid.
50. Ibid.
51. See ibid.
52. Ibid.
53. Ibid.
54. See ibid., 46.
55. Ibid.
56. Shaykh Sayyīd Ḥaydar Amulī, *Naṣṣ al-Nuṣūṣ fī Sharḥ al-Fuṣūṣ*, trnas., into Persian by Muḥammad Riḍā Jawzī (Tehran: Chapkhāna-yi Intishārāt-i 'Ilmī wa Farhangī, 1375/1996), 399.
57. See ibid.
58. Ibid.

which Āmulī refers to as *wujūd bimā huwa wujūd* (i.e., the existence from the standpoint of being sheer existence and not being with/or manifesting any other characteristics). He calls the Essence the *Ghayb al-ghuyūb* ("Unseen of the Unseen").[59] He also provides us with an example to make the conceptuality of this first category better imaginable. He states that "the reality of the creatures in the Essence of *aḥadiyyat* ("the exclusive unity") is like a tree in the seed."[60]

Āmulī believes that *waḥdat al-dhāt* ("the unity of the Essence") is the source of both *aḥadiyyat* and *wāḥidiyyat* ("exclusive and inclusive unity"). The latter of these two Āmulī considers, to be the second category of the Absolute's manifestation (*tajallī*), which he also calls *tajllī-yi asmā'ī* ("manifestation of the Names"), and also "the first entification, with attributes of knowledge and receptivity (*ta'ayyun-i awwal bi-ṣifat-i 'ālimiyyat wa qābiliyyat*)."[61]

By elaborating upon this type of *tajallī*, Āmulī employs an interesting set of expressions. He mentions that the immutable entities (or possible entities) are the first *ma'lūmāt* ("known content") of the Absolute's Essence.[62]

These known contents, Āmulī believes, are the receptacles of *tajllī-yi shuhūdī* ("the perceptible manifestation"). Through what he calls *tajallī-yi shuhūdī*, because of the active function of the Names in their reciprocity with each other (*nisab-i asmāī*), the Absolute causes His manifestations to descend from *aḥadiyyat* ("exclusive unity") to *wāḥidiyyat* ("inclusive unity").[63]

The usage of expressions such as *tajllī-yi shuhūdī* and *tajllī-yi shuhūdī-yi fi'lī* ("active-perceptible manifestation") for the second manifestation of the Absolute seems to be the outcome of Āmulī's extensive knowledge of Sufi texts along with his own creativity.

Employing the same expression, he calls the third category of the Absolute's manifestation, *tajallī al-wujūdi al-shuhūdī* ("manifestation of perceptible existence"). This type of manifestation is referred to by Āmulī as the appearance of *wujūd* through the function of the Absolute's Name *Nūr* ("Light"). In this category of *tajallī*, the Absolute, through His Names, manifests Himself as the

59. Ibid.
60. Ibid.
61. Ibid.
62. Ibid.
63. Ibid., 39-40.

ṣuwar ("forms").[64]

By elaborating upon these three categories of manifestations, Āmulī connects the three concepts of the Absolute's *'ilm* ("knowledge"), the Absolute's *qudrah* ("power"), and the Absolute's *irādah* ("will") to the Absolute's *Dhāt* ("Essence"), the Absolute's *ṣifāt* ("attributes"), and the Absolute's *af'āl* ("actions") respectively.[65] Using the well-known expression *haḍrah* ("presence") used by Ibn 'Arabī, Āmulī provides us with another set of expressions to make his triple categories more comprehensible. He indicates that in the first *tajallī*, the known content (*ma'lūmāt*), is manifested through the *ḥaḍrat 'ilmiyyah* ("Presence of the Absolute's knowledge"). By the second manifestation (or manifestation of the Names), the existent beings enter the *ḥaḍrat rūḥāniyya al-ghaybiyyah* ("Presence of the Unseen Spirit"), and finally by the third manifestation (manifestation of perceptible existence *or* manifestation of perceptible act), they face the *ḥaḍrat jismāniyyah shahādiyyah* ("Presence of the physical realm").[66]

Other creative and systematic sets of triple expressions in Āmulī's *Sharḥ*, include *aḥadiyyah* ("exclusive unity"), *wāḥidiyyah* ("inclusive unity"), *rubūbiyyah* ("Divinity'), and also *jabarūt* ("realm of Omnipotence"), *malakūt* ('realm of Sovereignty"), *mulk* or *nasūt* ("the corporeal realm").[67]

Using these categorical expressions, Āmulī points to different stages of *'urūj* ("arc of ascent"), *tanazzulāt* ("arc of descent"), and also the aspects of *ẓawāhir* ("manifest") and *bawāṭin* ("non-manifest") regarding the Absolute Reality.[68] Expressions such as these seem to play the role of creative mediums, by which, members of Ibn 'Arabī's school attempted to describe the concept of *waḥdat al-wujūd.*

Sa'd al-Dīn Farghānī

Another of Qūnawī's disciples, Sa'd al-Dīn Farghānī (d.700/1300), applied the concept of *waḥdat al-wujūd* more systematically. This is supported by his more methodical way of dealing with the *Fuṣūṣ* in his *sharḥ*. He explains the notion of *kathrat*

64. Ibid.
65. Ibid.
66. Ibid.
67. Ibid., 40-41.
68. See ibid.

(multiplicity) through *kathrat al-'ilm,* or multiple manifestations of the Absolute's knowledge.[69] In his *Mashāriq al-Darārī* (the Persian version of his Arabic work, *Muntahā al-Madārik*), Farghānī expands the discussion of *waḥdat al-wujūd* in a symmetrical pattern with the notion of *kathrat al-'ilm.*[70]

He states that the multiplicity of this particular "attribute" of the Absolute (His knowledge, i.e. Absolute as *al-'Ālim al-Muṭlaq*-the Absolute Knower) is indistinguishable from the "unity of existence" in the stage of *aḥadīyyat al-jam'* ("the comprehensiveness of the exclusive unity").[71] Although he believes that these two stages ought to be distinguished from each other in the stage of *ilāhiyyah*,[72] he confirms that "both the oneness of *wujūd* and the manyness of knowledge…are attributes of the Essence."[73]

Among several examples in *Mashāriq al-Darāri* are where he elaborates upon such terms as *tajallīy-i dhātī-yi aḥadī-yi jam'ī*[74] ("the comprehensive manifestation of the Essence"), *waḥdat wa jam'īyyat-i wujūd* [75] ("the unity and comprehensiveness of existence"), and *āftāb-i tajallī-yi dhāti-yi jam'ī*[76] ("Sunshine of the Essential and comprehensive manifestation").

Commenting on one of the poems of the well-known Ibn Fāriḍ (d.633/1235), Farghānī explains four categories that manifest the concept of *waḥdat al-wujūd.* He calls them, the categories of *maḥw wa fanā'* ("fading and annihilation").[77] The first three are *maqām-i kullī* ("general stations") and are related to *'umūm-i anbiyā' wa awliyā'* ("all prophets and saints").[78] The first is the annihilation of *nafs wa ṣifāt-i ū* ("the self and its characteristics"). In this type of annihilation, according to Farghānī, one is able to witness *waḥdat al-wujūd*, because in *āyina-yi kathrat* ("the mirror of multiplicities") the realities of knowledge and its characteristics are reflected. When the mirror is fully covered with such reflected content, the

---

69. See Chittick, "Rūmī and Waḥdat al-Wujūd," 80, and also "Ibn 'Arabī" 505.
70. See ibid.
71. See ibid., 107 (footnotes).
72. See ibid.
73. Ibid., 81.
74. See, for example, *Mashāriq al-Darārī*, 619 and 765.
75. See, for example, ibid., 245 and 530.
76. See, for example, ibid., 765.
77. Ibid., 512.
78. Ibid., 513.

reality and its characteristics become manifested in the mirror.[79]

The second is the annihilation of *ruḥ wa ṣifāt-i ū* ("soul and its characteristics"). In this station, the wayfarer is able to witness the multiplicity of realities that are manifested in the mirror of *waḥdat al-wujūd* – such as *bāṭin-i rūḥ* ("the very kernel of the spirit"). Therefore, *waḥdat* ("unity"), which is the *mirror* itself, is *nā-payda* ("invisible"), while multiplicities or the *munṭabi'* ("reflected or manifested realities") are *paydā* ("visible").[80]

The third station, according to Farghānī, is the annihilation of any *taqayyud* ("limitation"), or attachment to either of the two previous states in their singularity, and combining them both (*jam' miyān-i ishān*). The negation of the two previous stations in their singular form seems to lead to the *ibqāy-i ḥukm-i mughāyīrat miyān-i in waḥdat wa kathrat* ("continuing contradiction between unity and multiplicity"). According to Farghānī, the third state is the state in which, combination of unity and multiplicity takes place (*taḥaqquq-i jam'īyyat*).[81]

By combining the two seemingly *mughāyir* (contradictory) concepts of unity and multiplicity, in the third station, the *sālīk* reaches the state of *jam'* or collectedness/comprehensiveness. In this station neither *waḥdat* nor *kathrat* should be considered separate from the other, for both concepts become annihilated in the totality of one collected and comprehensive view, or *aḥadīyyat al-jam'*. By employing the word *mughāyir* in explaining the ties between *waḥdat* and *kathrat*, Farghānī seems to refer to the impossibility of considering either of these two concepts separate from the other. Therefore, in Farghānī's view, the third station of *fanā'* ("annihilation") is the realm in which both unity and multiplicity are entirely combined. With this notion, Farghānī reminds us of the concept of *dhul 'aynayn* – having two eyes – a concept Ibn 'Arabī elaborated upon in order to view both unity [He] and multiplicity [not He] at once.[82] In other words, realization of either of these two by itself, and without the other, does not lead to a comprehensive view of existence. The fourth station of annihilation, which belongs exclusively to the Prophet of Islam, is the state of

79. Ibid.
80. Ibid.
81. Ibid.
82. See Chittick, "Rūmī and Waḥdat al-Wujūd," 81.

waḥdat-i ḥaqīqī ("the real unity").[83]

Farghānī's approach to the concept of *mughāyirat* ("contradiction") of unity and multiplicity, in order to constitute the validity and possibility of the state of *aḥadīyyat al-jam'*, exhibits striking similarity to the approach of Ibn 'Arabī in his *Fuṣūṣ al-Hikam,* where he delves into the "Wisdom of the Unity" in the *Fass* of Hūd.[84]

In explaining the state of *jam'*, Farghānī employs an example from a well-known Sufi of the early period, Abū Sa'īd Kharrāz (d. 277/890), who was asked about his personal knowledge of God.

> Shaykh Abū Sa'īd Kharrāz, who had reached this state of *jam'* (comprehensive collectedness), was asked: by which (concept/medium) did you know God? He responded: by the way God combines the contraries together! (*Bi jam'ī-hi bayn al-aḍdād*), then he recited this verse: "He is the First and the Last, and the Manifest and the Non-Manifest...." Therefore, he affirmed the contradiction (*mughāyirat*)...in this station by the affirmation of the (station) of comprehensive collectedness (*jam'īyyat*).[85]

Reading Ibn 'Arabī's elaboration upon the function of the *al-nafas al-raḥmān* ("Breath of the Merciful), leads us to the source from which Farghānī borrows the basic elements of his argument of *mughāyirat* ("contradiction"), annihilation and fading (*fanā' wa maḥw*) and their ties to the concept of *waḥdat al-wujūd*. Ibn 'Arabī states:

> He relates the Breath to the Merciful, because by it He had mercy [assented] on the demand of the divine Modes for the creation of the forms of the Cosmos, which are the manifest Reality, He being the Manifest. He is also their inner Essence, being also the Unmanifest. He is the First, since He was when they were not, and also the Last, since in their manifestation He is their Essence; the Last is the Manifest and the First is the Unmanifest. Thus, *He knows all things*, as knowing Himself."[86]

83. See *Mashāriq al-Darārī*, 513.
84. See Austin, *Bezels of Wisdom*, 135-136.
85. *Mashāriq al-Darārī*, 513.
86. Austin, *Bezels of Wisdom*, 135-136.

Turkah Iṣfahānī

Similar to the approaches of Ibn 'Arabī and Farghānī, is one by another member of this school. A 14th century advocate of Ibn 'Arabī's school and one of the well-known commentators on *Fuṣūṣ al-Hikam*, Ṣa'in al-Dīn 'Alī ibn Mūḥammad al-Turkah Iṣfahānī (d.835/1431) employs the concepts of *taghāyur*, *jam'* ("collectedness") and *waḥdat* in his definition of *iṭlāq* (non-delimitation). Under the heading of *towshiḥ-i tafḍīlī 'alā 'urf al-Ṣūfiyyah* (defining elucidations on the terminology of Sufis), in his commentary on Ibn 'Arabī's *Fuṣūṣ al-Hikam*, he writes the following:

> First [among these terms] (is) the meaning of delimitation (*iṭlāq*), and that is the non-consideration (*'adam-i luḥūẓ*) of an entity (*shay'*) when it leaves its domain of unity and becomes multiple through its divisions and relations (*bi wujūh al-qismah wa l-nisbah*)...and this is called "the presence of exclusive Oneness" (*al-ḥaḍrah al-aḥadiyyah*), and the presence of collectedness and existence (*ḥaḍrah al-jam' wa'l-wujūd*) and the First entification (*ta'yyun al-awwal*), and its manifestation (*tajallīhi*) and the Muḥammadan Reality (*al-haqīqah al-Mūhammadiyah*)....The second: what it belongs to this meaning [i.e., the meaning of *iṭlāq*], and that is the comprehensiveness of unity in all aspects, and this is the differentiation of unity from multiplicity and the affirmation of contradiction (*taghāyur*) and opposition (*taqābul*) and this is called: the presence of inclusive oneness (*ḥaḍrah al-waḥdāniyyah),* the Breath of the Merciful (*nafas al-raḥman*), the second entification (*ta'ayyun al-thanī*) and its manifestation (*tajallīhi)* and the comprehensive isthmus (*al-barzakh al-jāmi'*), and the reality of being human (*al-haqīqah al-ādamiyyah*)...and the presence of the Names (*ḥaḍrat al-asmā'*)...and the foundation for spiritual knowledge (*mustanad al-ma'rifah*).[87]

The usage of *taghāyur* and *taqābul* by Turkah Iṣfahānī, and *mughāyirat* and *muqābalah* by Farghānī seem to manifest the same result through different methods. In the words of Farghānī, *mughāyirat* ("contradiction") of unity and multiplicity, in an elevated state of *fanā'* (annihilation) portrays a genuine vision of *waḥdat*

87. 'Alī ibn Muḥammad Turkah Iṣfahānī, *Sharḥ-i Fuṣūṣ al-Ḥikam*, vol. 1, (Qum: Bīdār Press, 1378/1999), 11.

("unity") which makes the presence of multiplicity fade away. For Turkah, *Taghāyur* ("contradiction") represents a medium by which *iṭlāq* manifests itself, and becomes tantamount to *wāḥidiyyah* ("inclusive oneness"), where all multiplicities are extinguished, and the face of *waḥdat* remains.

Farghānī employs a similar approach towards the Absolute's knowledge in order to understand the concept of *waḥdat al-wujūd* as expounded in the writings of Turkah Iṣfahānī. Turkah explains the above mentioned quotation from Ibn 'Arabī's *Faṣṣ* of Hūd:

> The manifested and non-manifested limitations of the entities are the very nature of the Absolute He-ness (*nafs-i huwiyyat al-Ḥaqq*) and its appearance in the presence of the ultimate Absolute's knowledge (*ḥaḍrat al-'ālīmiyyatih*), and His exclusive He-ness (*huwiyyat al-aḥadiyyah*), which does not differentiate between the known and the knower.[88]

Ibn Sab'īn and Awḥad al-Dīn Balyānī

The prominent philosopher Muḥammad Ibn 'Abd al-Ḥaqq Ibn Sab'īn (d. 669/1270) was influenced by Ibn 'Arabī and is considered one of the proponents of *waḥdah al-wujūd.*[89] In his *Rasā'īl*, he treats the notion of *waḥdat al-wujūd* as the foundation which governs the existence of the elites on the path of proximity towards the Absolute.[90] The multiplicities and accidents (*katharāt* and *a'rāḍ*), in contrast, dictate the life of the common people.[91] For this very reason, the inhabitants of God's Knowledge are steadfast in their knowledge of existence, while those who are prisoners of accidents and multiplicities become the people of negligence and ignorance and, as a result, are deprived of consistency and firmness in their knowledge, and therefore will remain perplexed.[92] As is evident, although using a different approach from Farghānī, Ibn Sab'īn also takes into account the notion of "knowledge" in his discussion of *waḥdat al-wujūd.*[93]

Among the followers of Ibn 'Arabī who also lived close to

88. Ibid., 481.
89. See Chittick, "Rūmī and Waḥdat al-Wujūd," 82.
90. See ibid., 83.
91. See ibid.
92. See ibid.
93. See ibid.

the time of Ibn Sab'īn, was Awḥad al-Dīn Balyānī (d. 687/1288). Balyānī realizes the existence of God's messengers, His word, and His veil "only" through the Absolute.[94] The literal understanding of Balyānī's words in his treatise, *Risālat al-Aḥadiyyah* (Treatise on Unity), seemingly equates the entirety of existence, such as prophets, with the Absolute. He protects us, however, from a careless misunderstanding of his words, when he states that the Absolute "sent Himself with Himself to Himself."[95]

Balyānī's words reminds us of one of the Ibn 'Arabī's *naba'* (news) in his *Shujūn al-Masjūn* where he writes, "Your essence is within you (but) it is concealed from you, and His Essence is from you (but) is concealed within you, therefore He is with you wherever you are, and His proof (of this companionship) for you is your helplessness (*'ajzuka*) in knowing Him (*ma'rifah*)."[96]

Perhaps both of these quotations share one fundamental aspect in particular, i.e., the limitation of our knowledge of the Absolute due to the "veiling multiplicities." The notion of *waḥdat al-wujūd* is perhaps an effort for the possible removal of this veil through elaborating on the nature of the relationship between the only One and the one whose entire being – if any – comes from the One, i.e. between God and *mā-sīwā'* ("the rest").

Ibn 'Arabī mentions in one brief *īḍāḥ* (clarification) of his *Shujūn al-Masjūn,* that "The friends (of God) [*abrār*] refrain from (*yattaqūna*) ignorance (*jahl*), and those elites of the Path who have been brought near (*al-muqarrabūn*), refrain from knowledge (*'ilm*)."[97] This knowledge from which the elite of the Path abstain, is perhaps the "limitation" of their understanding, which deserves to be dissolved in the "limitless" Unity of the Absolute's Presence.

We may now be able to attain a better understanding of Farghānī's words on the parallel (identical) nature of the multiplicity of the Absolute's knowledge (His *kathrat al-'ilm*) and the notion of *waḥdat al-wujūd,* in the stage of *aḥadīyyat al-jam'* before reaching the stage of Divinity.

---

94. See ibid.

95. Ibid.

96. Ibn 'Arabī, *Shujūn al-Masjūn wa Funūn al-Maftūn* (Damascus: Dār Sa'd al-Dīn, 1419/1999), 133: "*dhātuka fīk ghaybun 'ank, wa dhātuhu minka ghaybun fīk, fa huwa ma'akum ayna mā kunt, wa burhānuhū 'alayk ajzoka 'ank…*"

97. See ibid., 149: "*al-abrār yattaqūn al-jahl wa'l muqarrabūn yattaqūn al-'ilm.*"

Kubrawī Approach to the Concept of waḥdah ("Unity")

'Azīz al-Dīn Nasafī

One of the renown Kubrawī masters and advocates of *waḥdat al-wujūd*, was Sa'd al-Dīn Ḥamūyah (d. 649/1252). Ḥamūyah's prominent disciple, 'Azīz al-Dīn Nasafī (d. 700/1300), a well-known Kubrawī master, in his *Kashf al-Ḥaqā'īq* (Unveiling Realities) quotes his master, Ḥamūyah, when he was asked to clarify on the realization of existence. He answered that the "The existent [*al-mawjūd*] is God...There is no existent but God."[98]

Words almost identical to those of Ḥamūyah are found in Ibn 'Arabī's *Futūḥāt* where he writes, "There is no existent but God."[99] In his *Misbāḥ fi'l Taṣawwuf* ("the Lamp of Sufism"), Ḥamūyah adds another interesting element to his approach to the concept of "existent," where he states that "whatever you see other than oneness is imagination."[100]

As Chittick states, Nasafī "was probably the first to divide the people of oneness into different groups according to their differing formulations of *waḥdat al-wujūd.* In several instances Nasafī includes his own master Ḥammūya among the people of oneness."[101]

In his book, *Kitāb al-Tanzīl,* while approaching the concepts of *tashbīh* and *tanzīh* (similarity and peerlessness of the Absolute), Nasafī reminds us of Ibn 'Arabī's expression of *huwa/lā-huwa* ("He/not He"). Nasafī believes that everyone including the advanced wayfarers of the spiritual path (such as *awliya'* or Friends of God) as well as the prophets, made their own realizations of the Absolute, in accordance with their *isti'dād* ("readiness"). This readiness refers to their level *of ma'rifah,* or gnosis, which they

---

98. Chittick, "Rūmī and Waḥdat al-Wujūd," 84. See also Shaykh 'Abd al-'Azīz ibn Muḥammad Nasafī, *Kashf al-Ḥaqā'iq*, ed. Aḥmad Mahdawī Damghānī (Tehran: Bongāh-i Tarjoma wa Nashr-i Kitāb, 1344/1965), 153. Ḥamūyah's responses to the above question have been reported as "*al-mawjūd huw-Allāh*" and "*lā mawjūd siwa-Allāh.*"

99. Ibid., 108.

100. Ibid., 85. See also Ḥamūyah's words in his *al-Miṣbāḥ fi'l Taṣawwūf*, ed. Najīb Mayīl Heravī (Tehran: Intishārāt-i Mowla, 1362/1983), 66: "*dar nafs-i waḥdat kathrat muḥāl ast wa har-chī bīnī joz waḥdat khyāl ast.*"

101. Ibid., 84.

could attain (i.e., the level or the limit of their knowledge).[102]

In Nasafī's view, the Absolute's Essence is too elevated to be grasped in Its utter reality. The *nihāyah* ("the utmost level") of knowledge of each man is to reach a true realization of his incapability of knowing the Absolute. Perhaps we can say that in Nasafī's view, *knowledge* and its categories are the instruments/mediums for each wayfarer's realization of *tashbīh* and *tanzīh* ("God's similarity and peerlessness").[103]

The realm in which a wayfarer knows God, is the dimension of *tashbīh* (in which God is knowable for or accessible to that particular *knower*). When a wayfarer reaches the realization of his *'ajz* ("incapacity") in knowing God, he arrives at the realm in which he witnesses the Absoluteness of God's Essence.

In his book, *Kashf al-Ḥaqā'iq*,[104] Nasafī refers to *ahl-i imān* ("the people of faith") in two categories: *ahl-i waḥdat* and *ahl-i kathrat* ("people of unity and people of multiplicity"). He then divides the people of multiplicity into two categories of the *ahl-i sharī'at* ("people adhered to *sharī'ah*") and *ahl-i ḥikmat* ("philosophers"). *Ahl-i Sharī'at* believe in two categories of *wujūd* ("existence"), namely *ḥādith* ("created") and *qadīm* ("uncreated").[105] For this group, the only "uncreated existence" is God, and the created existence is *mā-siwā'* ("the rest of existence"). The philosophers believe in three categories of existence, namely *wājib* ("necessary"), *mumkin* ("possible"), *mumtani'* ("impossible").[106]

Nasafī compares the entire *'ālam* ("world") to a book consists of multiplicities. He does this in a traditional approach to the con-

---

102. See Nasafī, *Bayān al-Tanzīl*. Among several examples, see p. 148, in his discussion of the ties between the wayfarer (*sālik*) and God (*Khudāy*) and p. 146, in his approach to *wujūd* as being both "*khayāl wa nimāyesh*"(imagination and playact) and "*bi ḥaqīqat mawjūd*" (existent in reality).

103. For example, see ibid., 192: "*insān musta'īdd-i iktisāb-i anwār ast*" the human being is capable of receiving knowledge and light, and p. 231 on the concept of *'ilm-i insān-i Kāmil* (knowledge of the Perfect Man), p. 225 "*sukhan-i ahl-i waḥdat dar bayān-i waḥy wa ilhām*," or the opinion of the people of unity regarding revelation and inspiration, p. 209, on "*nūr-i Khudāy*" or the Light of God and *istī'dād-i darīche-hā* or the capacity (vastness) of mystical openings (horizons), and also p. 150, on the interrelationship between *'aks* and *'ilm* or the image and knowledge.

104. See Nasafī, *Kashf al-Ḥaqā'iq*, 149-50. See also his *Risāla-yi Waḥdat-i Wujūd*, MS. 8013/2, Mar'ashī, Qum.

105. Ibid.

106. Ibid. See also Nasafī, *Ikhtilāf-i Madhāhib*, MS. 8013/1, Mar'ashī, Qum.

cept of *waḥdat* ("unity") and *kathrat* ("multiplicity"), in his *Kashf al-Ḥaqā'īq*,[107] and *Insān al-Kāmil*[108] regarding the interpretation of the Quran, 6:59 [...*la raṭbin wa lā yābisin illā fī kitābin mubīn* – "there is not a grain in the darkness (or depths) of the earth, nor anything fresh or dry (green or withered), but is (inscribed) in a record clear (to those who can read)"[109]]. He also makes symbolic correlations between *jins* ("genus") of the nature and each chapter, between each *naw'* ("type") and the verses, and also between each *mawjūd* ("existent") and each *ḥarf* ("letter") of the Qur'ān. He states that God sent the Qur'ān as *kitāb-i ṭabi'at* ("the book of nature") to creatures in order to show them its lines and letters.[110]

In his *Insān al-kāmil*,[111] Nasafī divides *ahl-i waḥdat* ("the people of unity") into two groups of *ahl-i nār* ("people of fire") and *ahl-i nūr* ("people of light"). The former group is also called by Nasafī, as *nāfiān* ("deniers"), and the latter are referred to by him as *muthbitān* ("affirmers"). Although in his *Kashf al-Ḥaqā'iq*, Nasafī confirms his intention to be only a *rāwī* ("narrator") of the other groups' opinions without discussing his personal views, his tendency towards the ideas of the people of *waḥdat* is clear.[112] As Herman Landolt states in his introduction to Nasafī's *Bayān al-Tanzīl*, "Nasafī never tires of repeating that the *ahl-i waḥdat* are those who believe that the Reality is only one, and that Reality called 'existence' (*wujūd*), is identical with God."[113]

In addition to his methodology, which is strongly concerned with the concept of "unity," (*waḥdat*), Nasafī also manifests his

107. Ibid., 218-219.

108. See 'Azīz al-Dīn Nasafī, *Kitāb-i Insān al-Kāmil*, ed. Marijan Molé (Tehran: Intishārāt-i Ṭahūrī, 1377/1998), 373-4 and 404.

109. For the translation of the verse (6:59), I have used Yusuf 'Alī's English translation.

110. Nasafī, *Insān al-Kāmil*, 373-4 and 404. See also Nasafī, *'Aql wa 'Ilm*, MS. 8013/23, Mar'ashī, Qum, on *sukhan-i ahl-i waḥdat dar bayān-i 'ālam wa 'ālamiyān* (the opinion of the people of unity regarding the world and its inhabitants).

111. See Nasafī, *Insān al-Kāmil*, *risāla-yi* 19-21. See also *Kashf al-Ḥaqā'iq*, 190, *Bayān al-Tanzīl*, 162, and *Risāla-yi Waḥdat*.

112. See Nasafī, *Kashf al-Ḥaqā'iq*, 1-2. See also his *Risāla-yi Waḥdat*, in his discussion on the gnosis (*ma'rifah*) of the Absolute Existence (*wujūd al-muṭlaq*), and the opinion of the people of unity (*ahl-i waḥdat*) in dividing everything in the world into three different levels (*martiba*), namely levels of essence (*dhāt*), countenance or face (*wajh*) and self (*nafs*), respectively, and the two forms (*ṣūrat*) of the multiple/scattered (*mutifarriqah*) and the unified/collected (*jāmī'ah*).

113. Landolt, introduction to *Bayān al-Tanzīl*, 11.

unique creativity in expanding, expounding upon, and categorizing this concept. As contemporary scholars suggest, Nasafī paid considerable attention to discussions on the concept of "unity" as found in the school of Ibn 'Arabī as well as the perspectives of mystics/philosophers of *mashā-'ī* ("peripatetic") and *ishrāqī* ("illuminationist") schools.[114] Despite the point that he is perhaps the most ardent interpreter and advocate of Ibn 'Arabī's idea of "unity of existence" among the Kubrawīs, Nasafī never remains a simple imitator or narrator of *Shaykh al-Akbar* or his followers.[115]

In his creative categorization regarding *ahl-i waḥdat*, he refers to *aṣḥāb-i nār* ("the people of fire") [or *nāfiān* "deniers" in his *Bayān al-Tanzīl*] as those whose imaginations (*khayālāt*), doubts and arrogance have been extinguished in the fire of unity.[116] As Nasafī tells us, these wayfarers experience spiritual solace in the stage of selflessness.[117] The *aṣḥāb-i nūr* ("people of light") [or *muthbitān*], the second group among *ahl-i waḥdat*, enjoy the *yaqīn* ("certainty") which emerges from the light of unity. This light gives them the assurance of being in the presence of *Wujūd* (the Existence) with His everlasting Attributes (or manifestations).[118] We may be able to assert that the *nār* ("fire") in Nasafī's usage, is a metaphor for the station of *fanā'* ("spiritual annihilation"). On the other hand, *nūr* (light) may represent the station of *baqā'* ("subsistence"), in which the unity subsides.[119]

---

114. See Mīr Bāqirī Fard, introduction to *Bayān al-Tanzīl*, 32.

115. See, for example, Landolt, "Nasafī." Referring to Nasafī, Landolt confirms that "In all of his writings, he shows a remarkable degree of spiritual independence."

116. See Nasafī, *Bayān al-Tanzīl*, 162.

117. See ibid.

118. Ibid., 165.

119. See ibid., 165. On the characteristics of *ahl-i waḥdat*, see also 'Abd Allāh Naqshbandī Maghribī, *Nūr-i Waḥdat*, MS. 8069/3, Mar'ashī, Qum,. Maghribī utilizes the expression *āftāb-i waḥdat* or "the Sun of Unity" in order to approach the concepts of "nearness and distance" (*qurb wa bu'd*). He believes that in the Light of the Absolute Unity there is no room for discussing the proximity or distance: "*chūn aftāb-i waḥdat ṭulū' nimāyad bu'd wa qurb 'ayn-i waḥdat bāshad* (when the Sun of Unity rises, nearness and distance [to the Absolute Reality] become Unity itself). Perhaps due to this attribute of "unity" (i.e., dissolving distances), Maghribī continues by regarding *ahl-i waḥdat* (people of unity) as those who have no conflict with any other group: "*har firqah ba firqa-yi dīgar dar niẓā' wa jidāl ast magar ahl-i waḥdat ke ishān bā hama yekī-yand agar che hich-kodām ba oū yekī nist*" (every group is in argument and conflict with another, except the *ahl-i waḥdat* who are one with others although neither of those [groups] is [in agreement] with them).

Nasafī also divides the people of *nār* ("fire") or *nāfiān* into two groups. "The first group among the people of fire believes that existence is one and that is God, and there is no *wujūd* ("existence") other than Him. Creatures do not have any real existence; their existence is *khayālī* ("imaginary"). They believe that the *khudāy-i khalq* ("God of creation") is one [Real Being], and *khalq-i khudā* ("God's creation") is another [imaginary being]. God of creation (is) the Real Existence, because He is not subject to *taghyīr wa tabdīl* ("change and transformation") and has no beginning or end. He has always been, and will be, and His Being contains no *kathrat wa ajzā'* ("multiplicity and parts")."[120] Nasafī then describes his reasons for making this distinction. He mentions that God is the *aḥad-i ḥaqīqī* ("the Real One") from all perspectives (*min kull al-wujūh*), but creatures of God have no existence except an imaginary one. The imaginary existence receives the opportunity for appearance only because of the *khāṣiyyat* ("characteristic") of *wujūd-i ḥaqīqī* ("the Real Existence"), i.e, the existence of God.[121] Nasafī states that the creatures are like the beings (as they appear) in a dream, or are reflections in water, or a mirror, and have no existence in reality.[122]

Nasafī considers two categories of *'awāmm* ("non-elite"), and *khawāṣṣ* ("elite") for each of the aforementioned groups of the *ahl-i sharī'at* ("people adhered to *sharī'ah*"), *ahl-i ḥikmat* ("philosophers"), and *ahl-i waḥdat* ("people of unity"),[123] but in the case of *ahl-i sharī'at*, he adds another subdivision, namely *khāṣṣ al-khawāṣṣ* ("the elite of the elites").[124] Although Nasafī provides us with the same three main categories of *ahl-i sharī'at*, *ahl-i ḥikmat* and *ahl-i waḥdat* in his *Bayān al-Tanzīl*, *Zubdat al-Ḥaqā'iq*, and also *Kashf al-Ḥaqā'iq*, the divisions and categories of these three groups are not invariable. In his *Kashf al-Ḥaqā'īq*, these categories are discussed even in more details. In this book, he refers to *ahl-i sharī'at*, as *ahl-i ẓāhir* ("exoteric people") with

120. See ibid., 162.
121. Ibid.
122. Ibid.
123. See, for example, ibid., 143-186 on the views of these groups on several subjects.
124. See ibid., 160.

two sub-categories of Sunnī and Shī'a.[125]

In his *Bayān al-Tanzīl*, in continuation of a section on the "words of the group of *nāfiān* ("deniers") regarding *tawḥīd* ("God's Unity"), he describes the opinions of the *'awāmm* ("non-elite") among the people of unity. This group, according to Nasafī, believes that *'ālam-i khalq* ("the world of creation") and *'ālam-i amr* ("the world of Command") which represent the *'ālam-i jism* ("world of body"), and *'ālam-i rūḥ* ("the world of spirit"), respectively are *khalq-i khudā* ("God's creation") and have no existence except *wujūd-i khayālī* ("an imaginary existence").[126] Then in order to describe the notions which this group (i.e., non-elite among the deniers or *'awāmm-i ṭā'ifa-yi nāfiān*) considers as imaginary and non-existent, Nasafī writes:

> For these people, if (there is) a substance (*jawhar*) or an accident (*'arāḍ*), and if (it) is a body (or) and spirit, and if (there) is knowledge (*'ilm*) or ignorance (*jahl*), and if (there) is faith (*imān*) or disbelief (*kufr*), and if (there) are angels (*malak*) or a Satan (*shayṭān*), all (are considered to be) the imagination, and appearance (*nimāyish*), with no real existence. What is beyond the world of creation (*'ālam-i khalq*) and the world of Command (*'ālam-i amr*) is the Real Existence (*wujūd-i ḥaqīqī*), and...the Real Existence, i.e. the God of creation (*khudāy-i khalq*) has no attribute (*ṣifāt*), act (*fi'l*), and name (*ism*).[127]

Nasafī's description of the opinions of the *khawāṣṣ* ("elite") among *nāfiān* ("deniers") is almost identical with the ideas of non-elite among *ahl-i waḥdat*. There are only slight differences in the combination of terminologies which Nasafī has utilized. For example, he has employed the term *jism-i 'ālam* ("the body of the world") in describing the opinions of *khawāṣṣ* (among *nāfiān*) and the term *'ālam-i jism* ("the world of bodies") in the *faṣl* ("chapter") on the ideas of *'awāmm* (among *ahl-i waḥdat*). Nasafī then begins a chap-

125. See, for example, Nasafī, *Kashf al-Ḥaqā'iq*, 11, his reference to the well-known Sunnī and Shi'ī scholars such as Abū Mansūr Mātarīdī (Ḥanafī), abū Muḥammad Ghazālī (Shāfi'ī), and Abū Ja'far Tūsī (Shī'ī): "*ishān har-se dar madhāhib wa ūṣūl-i madhāhib sukhan bihtar az dīgarān gofte-and*" See also Nasafī, *Ikhtilāf-i Madhāhib*, MS. 8013/1, Mar'ashī, Qum, in which he refers to the opinions of the above mentioned scholars as the most balanced among others.

126. See Nasafī, *Bayān al-Tanzīl*, 162.

127. Ibid., 162-163.

ter on the words of the *muthbitān* (affirmers) among *ahl-i waḥdat.* As mentioned before, Nasafī also calls this group by another name *aṣḥāb-i nūr* ("people of the light"). Here, Nasafī employs a unique terminology in order to make an elaborate distinction between the approach of *khawāṣṣ* ("elite") and *'awāmm* ("non-elite") *of ahl-i waḥdat* ("people of unity") towards the concept of *tawḥīd.*

The term "*yekī kardan*," which Nasafī uses to describe the applicable meaning of *tawḥīd* according to the affirmers among *ahl-i waḥdat*, might refer to "unifying/identifying or defining everything with the concept of *tawḥīd.*" Expatiating upon this term (*yekī kardan*), Nasafī states:

> And it is not possible to make the One (who is innately one), One [again], since bringing an existent thing into existence, and eradicating (*i'dām*) [an entity which is innately] non-existent (*ma'dūm*), and affirming/creating (*ithbāt*) an entity [which is innately] affirmed (or well established) is impossible (*muḥāl*), (and) in the same way, (proving/imposing) unity upon (the One Who is innately/Essentially) One (*aḥad*) [is impossible].[128]

In an immediate sentence on the above description of *tawḥīd*, in a seemingly paradoxical mode, Nasafī differentiates between what he described as the view of *muthbitān*, and his own definition of *tawḥīd*;

> Since you understood that the meaning of *tawḥīd* is making everything one [unified] (*yekī kardan*), and making [an entity who is innately] one, one [again] is impossible, now know that *tawḥīd* is (or means) *making multiple or many things [chizhā-yi bisyār], one.*[129]

Looking at the parallel representation of Nasafī's words, we see that the statement of *yekī rā yekī kardan muḥāl ast* ("making one who is innately one again is impossible") is a refined articulation of the aforementioned aspect of *tanzīh* (a term which refers to "God's peerlessness" in Ibn 'Arabī's school). The uniqueness and incomparability of *yekī* ("the One") or God at the level of His Essence, or the level of *aḥadiyyah* ("exclusive unity"), is beyond comprehension and *ma'rifah* ("gnosis"). By referring to *yekī kardan*

128. Ibid., 163. See also Nasafī, *Asrār al-Tawḥīd*, MS. 8013/9, Mar'ashī, Qum, in which he refers to *yekī shudan miyān-i du chīz* ("unity between two things").

129. Ibid., 165.

and its impossibility, Nasafī perhaps alludes to the impossibility of approaching the Absolute in His Absoluteness, and also to our fractional and incomplete understanding of *tawḥīd* at the level of *tanzīh*.

Nasafī does not remain aloof from the other side of *tawḥīd*, i.e., the aspect of *tashbīh* (God's comparability according to the school of Ibn 'Arabī). He seems to point to this aspect when he states that, "*tawḥīd* is (or means) making multiple things [*chizhā-yi bisyār*], one."[130] In the worldview of Ibn Arabi's school, *tashbīh* occurs (or becomes possible) at the stage of *wāḥidiyyah*, i.e., when *a'yān al-thābitah* ("immutable entities") become manifested and therefore, God's manifestations ("*tajallīyāt*") appear in the corporeal realm.[131]

Yekī kardan ("making multiple things, one,"),[132] in Nasafī's definition of *tawḥīd*, represents the multiple levels of phenomenal beings, that refer to the One. Making multiple phenomenal beings one thing, or journeying from *kathrat* ("multiplicity") towards *waḥdat* ("Unity") or *yekī kardan* is tantamount to practical understanding of *tawḥīd* from the point of view of *tashbīh* ("God's similarity").[133]

Well known Kubrawīs such as Nasafī were fully familiar with the Akbarian expressions. For example, in his *Insān al-kāmil* and *Manāzil al-Sayi'rīn*, Nasafī explains a widely used *Akbarian* expression, namely *a'yān al-thābitah* ("immutable entities"). His words might help us to understand his above definition of *tawḥīd* and its connection with the Akbarian worldview more clearly. Nasafī mentions the approach of Ibn 'Arabī and also that of his own master, Sa'd al-Dīn Ḥamūyah to this concept.

> All substances (*jawāhir*) and accidents (*a'rāḍ*) of the world potentially exist in the world of non-existence at once (*bi-yekbārah*) [and] in general (*bi ṭarīq-i kullī*). Those...are called

130. Ibid.

131. See, for example, Khwārazmī, *Sharḥ-i Fuṣūṣ*, 26: "*mabda'-i ta'yyūnāt haḍrat-i huwiyyat ast wa tajallī-yi awwal... ta'yyunāt-i dhāt dar haḍrat-i aḥadiyyat, ya'nī... tanazzul az huwiyyat bi aḥadiyyat wa tajallī-yi duwwum az aḥadiyyat bi wāhidiyyat*" (The source of entification is the Presence of the Absolute He-ness, and the first manifestation…is the entification of the Essence in the Presence of the exclusive unity which means…descending from the Absolute He-ness to the exclusive unity and the second manifestation (means descending from) the exclusive unity to the inclusive unity).

132. Nasafī, *Bayān al-Tanzīl*, 162.

133. Ibn 'Arabī also refers to the Absolute as *al-Wāḥid al-Kathīr* (One/Many). See Chittick, "Ibn 'Arabī," 505.

quiddities, possibilities, and generalities (*kullīyāt*). All those potential existents (*mawjūdāt*) are things (*ashyā'*), and are all subjects of God's knowledge (*jomle ma'lūm-i Khudāyand*). Ibn 'Arabī calls these things the immutable entities (*a'yan-i thabitah*), and the Master of all masters (*Shaykh al-Mashāyikh*) Sa'd al-Din Hamūyah calls these things the immutable things (*ashyā'-i thābitah*) and this humble one [Nasafī] calls these things the immutable realities (*ḥaqā'iq-i thābitah*).[134]

According to Nasafī, making multiple or many things, one thing, based on the view of *muthbitān* ("affirmers") among *ahl-i waḥdat* ("people of unity"), occurs in two stages. He refers to these two stages as *tawḥīd-i 'ilmī* ("cognitive unity") and *tawḥīd-i 'amalī* ("practical unity").[135] He then describes the latter as "making many things one, through *'amal* ("practice")." A good example of this type of *tawḥīd,* in Nasafī's view, is making different types of *mat'ūmāt* ("edibles"), and *mashrūbāt* ("beverages") one thing. He then explains the other type of *tawḥīd* as follows:

> *Tawḥīd-i 'ilmī* ("cognitive unity") is knowing (recognizing) many things as one, through utilizing knowledge (or cognition), such as knowing many persons (*ashkhāṣ*) by one type (*naw'*) and knowing many types (*anwā'*) by one genus (*jins*), and (knowing) the genera by One Absolute Existent (*mawjūd-i Muṭlaq*).[136]

Nasafī considers subdivisions for the categories of *ahl-i sharī'at* and *ahl-i ḥikmat*, and also makes a distinction between the *'awāmm* ("non-elite") and *khawāṣ* ("elite") among *ahl-i waḥdat* ("the people of unity").[137]

---

134. Nasafī, *Insān al-Kāmil*, 353-54. See also Mīr Sayyid 'Alī Hamadānī, *Risāla-yi Wujūdiyyah*, MS. 780/1, Shirāz. Hamadānī refers to God as *Ḥakīm*, the Absolute Knower, whose *Ḥikmah* ("Eternal Knowledge") brought the *a'yān al-thābitah* ("immutable entities") into existence: "*Ḥakīmī ke ḳamal-i ḥikmatash a'yān-i thābitah rā a'yānī kard.*"

135. Nasafī, *Bayān al-Tanzīl*, 165-166.

136. Ibid.

137. See ibid., 166.

The Absolute's Names and Attributes (Asmā' and Ṣifāt): the Akbarian-Kubrawī Approaches to the Concepts of Unity and Multiplicity

Ibn 'Arabī, Nasafī and Hamadānī

Based on Nasafī's description of ideas of the non-elite among *ahl-i waḥdat*, we might be able to consider the following aspects as their most prominent ideas. They believe that "*wujūd* from the point of view of being *wujūd* [*wujūd min haith al-wujūd,* i.e., without any other characteristics such as being a particular entity such as a human being, etc.], is (only) one existence.., and (in this view of *wujūd*), *dū'ī* ("duality") and *kathrat* ("multiplicity") are impossible."[138] Nasafī then makes a connection between the concept of *iḍāfāt* ("correlations") and *i'tibāriyyāt* ("fictitious appearances"). He states that "*kathrat* ("multiplicity") is nothing but *iḍāfāt* ("correlations"), and *i'tibāriyyāt* ("fictitious appearances")."[139]

In a separate *faṣl* ("chapter"), in which he seems to provide us with his own views by discussing the relevance of *asāmī* ("names") to the concept of *waḥdat*, Nasafī states as follows:

> Know that most of the names (*asāmī*), veiled people's way (*rāh-i mardum*), and made them disbelievers and astray (*mushrik wa sargardān*), since names stand at the door of unity's abode (*ḥaram-i waḥdat*) like a doorkeeper (*darbān*) [to] keep strangers (*mardum-i nā-maḥram*) out of unity's abode.[140]

Nasafī's worldview correlates itself to both Kubrawī and Akbarian schools of Islamic mysticism. His thought brought new perspectives to the lineage of Kubrawīs and made possible a better understanding of the Akbarian ideas

Nasafī spent a great deal of effort elaborating upon the concept of *waḥdat,* as one of the key principles of his thought. In his *Insān al-kāmil* and in a chapter on *ẓāhir wa bāṭin-i wujūd*, the exterior and interior (or manifested and non-manifested) aspects of existence, Nasafī offers another depiction of the "unity of existence." In order to explain the function of *kathrah* ("multiplicity"), while expounding the concept of *waḥdah* ("unity"), Nasafī

138. Ibid.
139. Ibid.
140. Ibid., 167.

employs the symbolism of *nūr* ("light").

> Existence is only one (*wujūd yekī bīsh nīst*), and it consists of the manifest (*ẓāhir*) and the non-manifest (aspects). And the non-manifest (aspect), and existence together are one light. And this light is the spirit (*jān*) of the world. And the world is immersed in that light (*'ālam mālāmāl-i nūr ast*). (This) light is limitless and eternal, and it is (like) a boundless and unceasing ocean. Existence, knowledge, resolution (*irādat*), and the power of creatures (all) stem from this light.... Natural states, characteristics (*khāṣṣiyyāt*), and the acts of creatures are from this light, [but we can even go further and say that], everything is this light (*bal khud hama in nūr ast*)...O dervish! This light desired to see its own beauty (*jamāl*), and (wanted to) witness its own attributes (*ṣifāt*), names and acts. (Therefore this light) manifested itself (*tajallī kard*) and dressed in the attribute of act (*be ṣifāt-i fi'l multabis shud*), and it came from the manifest (*ẓāhir*) to the non-manifest (*bāṭin*), from the unseen [world] (*ghayb*) to the visible [world] (*shahādah*), and from unity (*waḥda*) to multiplicity (*kathrah*).[141]

Nasafī's approach to the Absolute's *ṣifāt* ("attributes") as the prominent representation of the concept of *kathrah*, reminds us of the views of another well-known Kubrawī master regarding this concept. In his *Rasā'il-i Kalāmī* ("Theological Treatises"), another Persian proponent of Ibn Arabī's school, Mīr Sayyid 'Alī Hamadānī, who wrote a commentary on *Fuṣūṣ al-Hikam*, makes similar remarks. In a response to the fifth theological question presented to him, on the reason for the existence of multiplicities, he writes, "[The appearance of] the Attributes (*ṣifāt*) in forms (*ṣūrat*) are multiplicities (*ta'addud wa takaththur*), and the Essence (*dhāt*) is One."[142]

Another striking similarity between Nasafī's approach to the Absolute's Names as the barrier in the Path (which veil people's way and stand at the door of unity as doorkeeper to keep strangers away, in the above quotation) and that of Hamadānī appears in the latter's response to the first question (*su'āl-i awwal*) in his *Rasā'il*. Hamadānī was asked about the nature of the Absolute's concealment, as reported in the above *ḥadīth-i Qudsī*.

141. Nasafī, *Insān al-Kāmil*, 268.

142. Riyāḍ, *Aḥwāl wa Āthar wa Ash'ār-i Mīr Sayyid 'Alī Hamadānī*, 174.

> The first question: it is reported in the Prophetic recorded saying (*ḥadīth*) from God that: "I was a hidden treasure, (then) I wished to be known, so I created all creation in order to be known." From whom the Absolute was hidden?[143]

Using one of the key expressions in the school of Ibn 'Arabī (i.e. *ta'ayyun* or entification), Hamadānī writes, "it means that the Essence (*Dhāt*) was hidden in the veils (*parda hā-yi*) of His Attributes (*ṣifāt*) and His entifications (*ta'ayyunāt*)."[144] Here, Hamadānī seems to point out to the two realms of *aḥadiyyah* and *wāḥidiyyah* in a creative and intertwined stage. In other words, *Dhāt* (as the realm of *aḥadiyyah* or "exclusive unity") becomes both "manifested and hidden" in the realm of *wāhidiyyah* or inclusive unity. The "inner Reality" of *Dhāt* stays inaccessible everlastingly. The Absolute's manifestations cannot divulge this "inner Reality," which remains "hidden" forever. On the other hand, the only way through which this inner Reality's existence can be revealed to the world is through Its manifestations or attributes. In the above elucidation on the well-known *ḥadīth* regarding creation, Hamadānī seems to refer to this seemingly paradoxical nature of the mutual reciprocation between the two concepts of exclusive unity and inclusive unity.

The Absolute's Beauty and Majesty (jalāl and jamāl):

Ibn 'Arabī, Najm al-Dīn Kubrā, Nasafī, Hamadanī and Simnānī

Also in a response to the last (i.e, the tenth) question regarding the nature of the Absolute's *rūḥ* ("Spirit"), Hamadānī provides a similar hint. He maintains that "some people believe that God's Spirit emerges from the Light of His Essence, and some regard it as the *ṣifāt* ("attributes") of His *jamāl* ("Beauty") and His *jalāl* ("Majesty")."[145] Then he mentions a quotation from the founder of the *Kubrawī* order, Najm al-Dīn Kubrā, whom he refers to as the *quṭb al-aqṭāb* ("Pole of the poles").

> The clash (*taṣādama*) happened between the Attributes of Beauty and Majesty and the Spirit was born [from that encoun-

143. Ibid.
144. Ibid., 173. See also Hamadānī, *Bahrāmshāhiyyah*, MS. 8253/4, Mar'ashī, Qum.
145. Ibid., 175.

ter] (*fa-tawallada min-hā al-Rūḥ*.)[146]

Ibn 'Arabī's approach also addresses the question that how a limited being can envisage the Source of Infinity (the Absolute). The medium for this "envisage," as Ibn 'Arabī seems to suggest, is the contemplation of the different Names in order to ponder upon the One Real. Through this medium, *insān* is able to *distinguish* from each other, the manifestations which may seem paradoxical, or even in conflict, at first sight. Therefore, he becomes capable of comprehending the Absolute's *waḥdah* ("Unity"), while witnessing the numerous visions of His *kathrah* ("multiplicity"). Ibn 'Arabī states:

> The Names of God are infinite because they are known by all that derives from them which is infinite, even though they derive ultimately from a [known] number of sources, which are the matrices or abodes of the Names. Certainly, there is but one reality which embraces all these attributions and relations called the Divine Names. This Reality grants that every Name, infinitely manifest, should have its own reality by which to be distinguished from every other Name. This *distinguishing* reality is the essence of the Name [the Name itself], not that which it may have in common [with others]. In the same way every [divine] gift is distinguished from every other by its own individual quality; for even though all derive from a single source, it is evident that one gift is not the same as another.[147] [Emphasis added]

Najm al-Dīn Kubrā's use of the word *taṣādum* ("clash") in the case of God's attributes of *jamāl* ("Beauty") and *jalāl* ("Majesty") is quite close to Ibn 'Arabī' s expression, *tanāzu'* ("conflict").[148] Ibn 'Arabī seems to suggest that this seemingly "quarrel" (for example between God's Mercy and Wrath) is indeed *aḥsan* ("the most beautiful") method of "harmony."[149]

By referring to a Quranic verse (16:25) in which God guides the Prophet to "dispute" with disbelievers in "the most beautiful (or the best) method" (*aḥsan*), Ibn 'Arabī refers to the nature of this

146. Ibid.

147. Austin, *Fuṣūṣ al-Ḥikam*, 68.

148. See Chittick, *The Sufi Path of Knowledge*, 55.

149. See ibid.

method as the embodiment of the quarrel between the Absolute's Attributes of Beauty and Majesty, i.e. a method of dispute that is the most harmonious.[150] His view is reflected in Kubrā's usage of the notion of *taṣādum* ("clash/encounter") between these two sets of attributes which, in Kubrā's view, led to the existence of the *Rūḥ* ("Spirit").

God's Spirit (*Rūḥ*), which in the Qur'ānic understanding, is infused in man (*fa-nafakhtu fihi min rūḥī*, 15:29), represents the source of "all Divine Attributes." Ibn 'Arabī repeatedly regards the Trusteeship of the Spirit in man as *nafas al-Raḥmān* ("Breath of the Merciful").[151]

Ibn 'Arabī's particular approach to the concept of Divine Mercy in the *Fuṣūṣ al-Ḥikam,* provides us with a further understanding of his aforementioned analogy in the *Futūḥāt*. At the beginning of the 21st chapter of his celebrated the *Fuṣūṣ al-Ḥikam* ("Bezels of Wisdom"), Ibn 'Arabī draws our attention to the Absolute's attribute of Mercy.

> Know that the Mercy of God encompasses everything existentially and in principle, and that the Wrath [of God] exists only by virtue of God's Mercy on it. His Mercy has precedence over His Wrath, which is to say that Mercy is attributed to Him before Wrath. Since every [latent] essence has an existence that it seeks from God, His Mercy must embrace every essence, for the Mercy by which He is Merciful accepts the desire of the essence for existence and so creates it. We therefore say that His Mercy encompasses everything existentially and in principle.[152]

Ibn 'Arabī also quotes a *ḥadīth-i Qudsī* ("Divine Saying") in his *Mishkāt al-Anwār*, which conveys the same meaning:

> "God ever mighty and majestic is He, says: Indeed my Mercy and Compassion prevail over My Anger."[153]

In Ibn 'Arabī's understanding, the Breath of the Merciful, which

---

150. See Ibn 'Arabī, *Futūḥāt*, II, cited in Chittick, *The Sufi Path of Knowledge*, 55.

151. See, for examples, *Futūḥāt*, II, cited in Chittick, *The Sufi Path of Knowledge,* 128.

152. Austin, *Fuṣūṣ al-Ḥikam*, 223.

153. Stephen Hertenstein and Martin Notcutt, trans., *Divine Sayings: The Mishkāt al-Anwār of Ibn 'Arabī* (Oxford: 'Anqā Publishing, 2004), 60.

is infused through God's Spirit, is the source of all mercy. God's Mercy (as the source of God's attribute of Beauty) precedes His Wrath (which represents God's attribute of Majesty). As a result, the "conflict" (*tanāzu'*) between these two Attributes, becomes "harmony" because of the precedence of the Beauty (Mercy) which encompasses the entire existence unconditionally. In other words, the "duality" of the above Attributes becomes "unity" by precedence of the Mercy, and this unity represents harmony (in its most beautiful or best way "*aḥsan*").

In the above saying of Najm al-Dīn Kubrā reported by Hamadānī, God's Spirit (*Rūḥ*) is the outcome of the *taṣādum* ("clash/encounter") between God's attributes of Beauty and Majesty. As mentioned before, God's Spirit is the source of all Mercy. Therefore, we might be able to conclude that, although the "meeting" between God's attributes of *jamāl* ("Beauty") and *jalāl* ("Majesty"), brings the Spirit into existence (*tawallada*),[154] such an encounter results in harmony because the Spirit represents unity (of God's attributes) through Mercy. Besides the above words of Najm al-Dīn Kubrā's on God's attributes, there are other examples of the correlations between the God's attributes of *jamāl* and *jalāl*, and the preference of the attribute of Beauty over Majesty in his works.

For example, in his *Fawā'iḥ al-Jamāl wa Fawā'tiḥ al-Jalāl*, Kubrā refers to the "state of being witness to the manifestation of God's *jamāl*" as "being immersed (*mustaghraq*) in intimacy."[155] He also describes the "state of witnessing God's attribute of *jalāl* ("Majesty")," as "being immersed in awe (*hayba*)."[156] Then using one of Ibn 'Arabī's favorite terms, *tajallī* (Absolute's manifestation), he explains the state in which these two attributes are intermingled (*imtizāj*). Here, Kubrā prefers to refer to the Absolute's *Dhāt* ("Essence") instead of the *Rūḥ* ('Spirit"):

> The intermeshing [or blending] (*tamtazij*) of these attributes [of *jamāl* and *jalāl*] occurs when the Essence manifests itself (*tajallat*)...indeed the Essence is the source of the Attributes and their meeting abode (*majma'iha*).[157]

---

154. See Riyāḍ, *Aḥwāl wa Āthar*, 174.

155. See Shaykh Najm al-Dīn Kubrā, *Fawā'iḥ al-Jamāl wa Fawātiḥ al-Jalāl*, ed. Yusuf Zaydān (Cairo: Dar Sa'd al-Ṣabāḥ, 1993), 193.

156. Ibid.

157. Ibid.

One is able to find other similar examples in Kubrā's *Aqrab al-Ṭuruq ila-Allāh* (the Closest Path towards *Allāh*). While discussing the aspects of *dhikr* ("recollection of God's Names"), he approaches the concept of God's attributes and *waḥdat* ("unity").

> The recollection of God's name (*dhikr*) is a spiritual elixir which...cleanses...the heart (which is) the place of the Divine Presence and (is also) the dawning House of the Sun of Oneness (*fardāniyyat*), out of the dust of temporality (*ḥudūth*) and the darkness of multiplicity (*kathrat*)...and through the exaltations of the manifestation of the Unity's Light (*saṭawāt-i ẓuhūr-i nūr-i waḥdat*), the darkness of the temporal being's multiplicity, becomes divulged, until the King of the Spirit...(sitting) on the Throne of Certainty (*sarīr-i īqān*)...manifests His transcendent Beauty (*jamāl-i ba kamāl*)...and the imaginative illusiveness of the recollector's existence (*rusūm-i wujūd-i mawhūm-i dhākir*) becomes vanquished in the flame of the Sun of the Recollected's Existence (*sho'lay-i aftāb-i wujūd-i madhkūr*), and the dust of the recollector's (*dhākir*) existence and the recollection (*dhikr*) [both] become annihilated and the Beauty of the Recollected (*jamāl-i madkhūr*) becomes manifested in the very being of the recollector (*'ayn-i dhākir*), and the [Qur'ānic] point of "He is with you wherever you are (*huwa ma'akum ayna mā kuntum*, 57:4)" proves itself to be right."[158]

In the words of Najm al-Dīn Kubrā, the concept of "unity" seems to take place through annihilation of both *dhākir* ("recollector") and the *dhikr* ("recollection"). The Beauty of the Recollected, which is again preferred by Kubrā over His Majesty, becomes the essential Attribute to define the most intimate Presence of God's manifestations. In other words, the concept of *waḥdat*, is depicted by Kubrā in the manifestation of God's Beauty.

Although here Kubrā does not employ the exact expression of *waḥdat al-wujūd,* his pinpoint to the vanquishing of the *unreal* and imaginative existence of the recollector in the flaming Sun of the Existence, Who is the only Real, seems close to the concept of "unity of existence" as understood by the school of Ibn 'Arabī. Kubrā also employs a Qur'ānic verse (57:4) which has been fre-

158. Shaykh Najm al-Dīn Kubrā, *Aqrab al-Turuq il-Allāh*, trans., Sayyid 'Alī Hamadānī (Tehran: Nashr-i Ṣafā, 1361/1983), 95. See also *Najm al-Dīn Kubrā, al-Sharī'ah Kas-Safīnah wa'l Trarīqah Ka'l Baḥr*, MS. 1626/16, Āstān, Mashhad.

quently referred to by Ibn 'Arabī. For example, in his magnum opus, *al-Futūḥāt al-Makkiyyah*, Ibn 'Arabī utilizes the above-quoted Qur'ānic verse, along with a few others which convey a similar message. He mentions a verse regarding "the All-merciful, the Lord of the Throne" (20:5), as well as another verse that refers to "God as the only Lord of the heavens and the earth" (6:3).[159] Ibn 'Arabī's interpretation suggests that "All of these [attributes] are relationships in keeping with His Majesty without asking "how" (*takyīf*), without declaring Him similar (*tashbīh*) and without conceptualization (*taṣawwur*)."[160]

Ibn 'Arabī, in his brief treatise, *Kitāb al-Jalāl wal-Jamāl* (The book of Majesty and Beauty), refers to an important combination of Attributes, namely the "Majesty of Beauty" (*jalāl al-jamāl*)."

> Majesty, in so far as it is a divine aspect, is a meaning that comes from Him (God) and returns to Him alone, the knowledge of which He has made inaccessible to us. On the other hand, Beauty is a meaning proceeding from Him, but directed towards us, and it is this aspect which allows us to accept the knowledge that we have of Him, making possible the descents, the contemplations and the states which He bestows on us. In its turn, this divine aspect of Beauty manifests itself in us in two ways: either as reverential fear or as intimacy. This is due to the fact that this Beauty has [two forms of manifestations]: 'elevation' and 'proximity.' We call elevation, the *Majesty of Beauty*, and it is to this that the gnostics refer when they talk [simply] about Majesty, since, on its manifesting itself to them, they imagine that it is the first Majesty, which we have mentioned above, that is being discussed, although in reality it is the Majesty of Beauty, which is associated with intimacy, as far as we are concerned. On the other hand, it is with this Beauty, which is the proximity, that reverent fear is associated, as far as we are concerned.[161] [Emphasis added]

'Abd al-Razzāq Kāshānī (d. 731/1330), a well-known advocate of Ibn 'Arabī's worldview, indicates that the Absolute's *jamāl*

---

159. See Ibn 'Arabī, *Futūḥāt*, II, cited in Chittick, *The Sufi Path of Knowledge*, 125

160. See ibid., with added brackets.

161. Pablo Beneito, "On the Divine Love of Beauty," Journal of Muḥyiddīn Ibn „Arabī Society XVIII (1995): 3.

("Beauty") is the manifestation of His Face.[162] This Beauty, Kāshānī suggests, carries a Power that leads everything to be submitted to Him (*taslīm*). He calls that Power the Majesty of Beauty.[163]

This collaborative fusion of *jamāl* and *jalāl* ("Beauty and Majesty") in the Akbarian thought also appears in some of the Kubrawī views. In his *Fawā'iḥ al-Jamāl wa Fawā'tiḥ al-Jalāl*, while explaining the concept of *fanā' al-qalb* ("annihilation of the heart"), Najm al-Dīn Kubrā writes about *istiwā' al-jalālī* ("the absolute domination or superiority of the Absolute's Majesty") and *istiwā' al-jamālī* ("the absolute domination or superiority of the Absolute's Beauty"). Najm al-Dīn's expression, *istiwa'* ("absolute power or domination") brings to mind the concept of *taslīm* ("submission"), referred to by Kāshānī as mentioned above. In other words, we might be able to state that *taslīm* is the outcome of the Absolute's *istiwā'* ("His absolute power and domination").[164]

Kubrā describes the *istiwā'* as the state in which God is the Master of the Throne (*istiwā' 'ala'l-'arsh*)[165], referring to the Quranic verse 6:3, the same verse in which Ibn 'Arabī sees the manifestation of the Absolute's Majesty.[166]

Kubrā regards the Absolute's Majesty as *istiwā' 'ala'l-qulūb* ("the Absolute's power or domination over the hearts").[167] One might see Kubrā's creativity in his utilization of the term *istiwā'* (literally, "settled on"), which he refers to as the Absolute's *absolute Power* and ultimate Mastery over the "heart," i.e., the core cognizant of the *Intimacy*.[168] This seemingly paradoxical parallelism (of the hearts and Majesty) is very close in meaning to Ibn 'Arabī's expression, *jalāl al-jamāl* ("Majesty of Beauty"). Ibn 'Arabī also recognizes the "heart" as the meeting place of all Divine Names: "The heart is His Throne and not delimited by any specific attribute. On the contrary, it brings together all the divine names and attributes, just as the All merciful possesses all the Most Beautiful Names."[169]

162. See Shaykh 'Abd al-Razzāq Kāshānī, *Iṣṭilāḥāt al-Ṣūfiyyah*, trans., into Persian, Muḥammad Khwājawī (Tehran: Intishārāt-i Mowlā, 1387/2008), 21.

163. See ibid.

164. See Kubrā, *Fawā'iḥ*, 200-201.

165. See ibid.

166. See Ibn 'Arabī, *Futūḥāt*, II, cited in Chittick, *The Sufi Path of Knowledge*, 125

167. See Kubrā, *Fawā'iḥ*, 201.

168. See ibid.

169. Ibn 'Arabī, *Futūḥāt*, III, cited in Chittick, *The Sufi Path of Knowledge*, 107.

In order to realize the refined elements of this similarity more clearly, an examination of Kubrā's words in the same text (*Fawā'iḥ*) seems helpful. Kubrā views the Absolute's Names of *al-Raḥmān* ("the Merciful") and *al-Raḥīm* ("the Compassionate") as His absolute domination over the Throne, and His absolute encompassing presence over the hearts, respectively.[170] Kubrā maintains that recollection of and hearing the Name *al-Raḥmān* (the Merciful) provides a taste of all attributes of the Absolute's *Majesty*. On the other hand, recollecting or hearing the Name *al-Raḥīm* (the Compassionate) is like tasting the entire attributes of His *Beauty*.[171]

We know that both of these Names (*al-Raḥmān* and *al-Raḥīm*) have been considered by many mystics as the Names (and/or manifestations) of God's Beauty (*Jamāl*). In a creative approach, Kubrā explains them in terms of the "Majestic dimensions of Beauty."[172]

The well-known interpreter of Rumi's *Mathnawī*, and one of the Kubrawī mystics, Kamāl al-Dīn Ḥussain Khawārazmī (d. 958/1551), who also wrote a commentary on Najm al-Dīn Kubrā's *Aqrab al-Ṭuruq il-Allāh* (the Closest Path towards *Allāh*), provides a similar interpretation regarding these attributes of God. In his comments on *ṣabr* ("patience"), as the eighth *aṣl* ("foundation") in Kubrā's book, he writes as follows:

> There is a bounty (*karam*) accompanied by each pain, a treasure along with each suffering…and *there is a majesty (har jalālī) in each beauty (har jamālī)*."[173]

In his well-known masterpiece, *Kāshif al-Asrār* ("the Revealer of the Secrets"), 'Alā'ad-Dawlah Simnānī's foremost master, the Kubrawī Shaykh Nūr al-Dīn 'Abd al-Raḥmān Isfarāyinī (d. 717/1317) utilizes the combination of *kamāl-i jalāl wa jamāl* ("the perfection of Beauty and Majesty"). Referring to the Absolute, Isfarāyinī indicates that "none of the creatures can reach the very depth of His pre-eternal Existence (*kunh-i qidam*), on the perfec-

170. See Kubrā, *Fawā'iḥ*, 201.

171. See ibid.

172. See ibid. In Kubrā's word: "*fanā al-qalb wa'l 'arsh fil-Ḥaqq wa dhālika 'inda instiwā' al-Ḥaqq 'alayh-i wa istiwā' al-Ḥaqq 'ala' l-'arsh hasab-i istiwā'-uhū fi'l-qulūb illā 'an istiwā'-uhū 'ala'l-'arsh jalāliyyun wa istiwā'-uhū 'al'al-qulūb al-jamālī…wa huwa ma'nā "al-Raḥmān al-Raḥīm" fa'l-Raḥmān huwa al-mustawī 'ala'l-'arsh wa 'l-Raḥīm huwa al-mutajallī fi'l-qalb.* See also Najm al-Dīn Kubrā, *Minhāj al-Sālikīn wa Mi'rāj al-Ṭālibīn*, 4267/3, Āstān, Mashhad.

173. Kubrā, *Aqrab al-Ṭuruq*, 128.

tion of His Beauty and His Majesty (*kamāl-i jalāl wa jamāl*)."[174] Isfarāyinī employs this expression to refer to the practical understanding of *tawḥīd* ("God's Oneness"). He continues as follows:

> So exalted is [the Absolute's] inaccessibility (*izz'*) and Majesty (*jalāl*) and His attributes (*ṣifāt*) that among all creatures none is able to comprehend Your attributes of Essence (*'irfān-i ṣifāt-i dhāt-i tow*) in their totality.[175]

It seems that in Iṣfarāyenī's view, the unique, ultimate and incomprehensible *kamāl* ("perfection") of the Absolute's attributes make Him the "Only" incomparable Essence. Thus, the perfection of His attributes leads us to envisage the perfection of His Essence. To prove his point, Isfarāyinī borrows the well-known Prophetic tradition:

> The ultimate praise is Yours. We have not known You as befits You (*ṣubḥānaka ma 'arafnāk ḥaqqa ma'rifatik*)....The ultimate praise is Yours. We are incapable of worshipping You as You deserve to be worshipped (*ṣubḥānaka ma 'abbadnāka ḥaqqa 'ibādatik*).[176]

In a response to one of Isfarāyinī 's letters, his well-known disciple, 'Alā'ad-Dawlah Simnānī (d. 737/1336) takes a similar but creative stance towards approaching the Absolute's attributes. Utilizing the word *kamāl* ("perfection"), Simnānī views the Absolute's attributes as the testimonies to His Oneness.

> O You! Who saw in Your Beauty, my perfection (*kamāl*), and O You! Who saw in His Perfection my imperfection. When two eyes become one, then the imperfection becomes tantamount to perfection (*'ayn-i kamāl*), and if there are two eyes [i.e., duality], then perfection becomes tantamount to sheer imperfection (*maḥḍ-i nuqṣān*). The double vision of the cross-eyed person is not because of the duality of one, but rather the oneness of two.[177]

Among major Kubrawī figures, Nasafī prefers an uncommon approach towards the attribute of *jamāl* ("Beauty"). By consider-

174. *Kāshif al-Asrār*, 56.
175. Ibid., 56-7.
176. Ibid.
177. *Mukātibāt*, 62.

ing *insān* ("the human being") as the very foundational essence of *'alam-i ṣaghīr* ("microcosm"), Nasafī concludes that the Will of God is to be viewed by His Beauty through multiplicities.

> O dervish, the human seed (*nuṭfa-yi insān*) is the first substance (*jawhar-i awwal*) of the microcosm, and is [also] the essence (*dhāt*) of the lesser world, and is [also] the seed (*tukhm*) of the microcosm. And the world of love (*'ālam-i 'ishq*) is the lesser world. The human seed is in love with itself. It [*nuṭfah*] wants to see its own beauty (*jamāl-i khud*), and its own attributes and names. [Thus] it will be manifested (*tajallī khāhad kard*), and it will be dressed in the attribute of act (*ṣifat-i fi'l*), and will come from the world of brevity (*'ālam-i ijmāl*) to the world of expansion (*'ālam-i tafṣīl*). And it will become visible in different forms (*suwar*), patterns (*ashkāl*), meanings (*ma'ānī*), and lights (*anwār*), until its *beauty* become visible, and [so] its attributes, names and acts [become visible].[178]

Thus, Nasafī focuses on the centrality of *insān* as the essence of *ālam-i ṣaghīr* ("the lesser world"), as well as his crucial place in the manifestation of the Absolute's Names and attributes as the representations of multiplicities. Nasafī's words revolve around the critical importance of *insān* in dealing with *kathrat* ("multiplicity"), without mentioning any other forms of the Absolute's manifestations by their particular names (such as the earth or skies, etc.)

Nasafī's approach might appear unorthodox in the above quotation. He seems to refer to *insān*-in his various forms and stages, such as *nuṭfah*,-as the source from which the *ṣifāt* (attributes), *jamāl* ("beauty"), and the *anwār* ("lights") emerge.

Without mentioning any clear reference to the Absolute, he suggests that the entire "lesser world" is the manifestation of *insān*. Perhaps this is a creative method by which Nasafī intends to explain the crucial place of *insān* as God's manifestation *par excellence*. He seems to refer to different manifestations of *insān* ('human

---

178. Nasafī, *Insān al-Kāmil*, 86. Also see Nasafī, *Lawḥ-i Maḥfūẓ wa Ālam-i Saghīr*, MS. 8013/19, Mar'ashī, Qum, in which he explains that: "*lawḥ-i maḥfūẓ-i ālam-i saghīr nuṭfah ast az jahat-i ānk-i har chīzī ki dar ān paydā miāyad anchīz dar nuṭfah ast hamchūn sa'ādat wa shiqāwat wa diyānat wa khiyānat* (The Preserved Tablet of the lesser world is the human seed, because whatever appears in existence [i.e., the lesser world] such as prosperity, wretchedness, piety, and treason…is to be found in the human seed.)

being") as different manifestations of the "Absolute." As quoted above, Nasafī maintains that, the human being is the essence of the lesser world [the terrestrial world or *nasūt*] and this world is the world of love, in which the human being is in love with himself.

In other words, the Absolute's Love for the human being (which projects itself by the infinite forms of manifestations) appears with an unimaginable extent of intimacy and closeness, placing God and man in a *waḥdat* ("unity"). Nasafī suggests that God is so near to *insān* that it seems that "*insān* is in love with himself" (*nuṭfah* is in love with himself, in Nasafī's word), but in reality, he is in love with God. Thus, in Nasfi's words, God's manifestations seem to be tantamount to the human being's manifestations. As Nasafī suggests above, the manifestations of the human being comes in different forms, patterns, and lights, etc. Therefore, *insān* (in his perfect stage as *insān al-kāmil*) sees his own beauty in "*his own manifestations*" (i.e, "*the entire lesser world*"), and this is the same as seeing God's Beauty in the entire existence.

Ibn 'Arabī, in his short treatise, *Haqīqat al-Haqā'iq* ("The Reality of Realities"), while writing on the critical place of *insān*, employs a similar approach that might have inspired Nasafī's writings on the same subject.

> The existence of the human being is essential in creation, and the existence of [other] creatures is secondary. Because this world has been created for the human being, and he [is] the general purpose, as God Almighty says: "O son of Ādam I created you for Myself and all other things for you," and the general purpose that we mentioned, is the manifestation of the Real (*Ḥaqq*) in the human being, and *God seeing His Names and Attributes is nothing but [seeing] the Perfect Human Being. Whenever Almighty wants to look at the world, He does it through the human being (insān), because the Perfect Human Being (insān al-kāmil) is the eye of God ('ayn Allāh)*"[179]

Ibn 'Arabī suggests that when the Perfect Human Being looks at the world, it is as if God looks at the world. Here, Shaykh al-Akbar depicts the "unity of existence" as the unity of God and the human being, not on the essential plane or the level of *dhāt*, but at the level of *asmā' wa ṣifāt* ("Names and attributes"), i.e. the image of

179. Ibn 'Arabī, *Ḥaqīqat al-Ḥaqā'iq*, trans., into Persian, Najīb Mayil Heravī (Tehran: Instishārāt-i Mowlā, 1382/2003), 11.

the Absolute manifested through/in the human being. God sees the entire world through the Perfect Human Being, because the Perfect Human Being is the essence of existence, or the entirety of existence itself. That is to say that God looks at Himself through Himself.

The Kubrawī master Sayyid Alī Hamadānī also delves into the concept of God's attributes. He refers to a spiritual stage in which the wayfarer reaches the knowledge of *tafrīd* ("singleness"), through the Absolute's attributes of *jamāl* ("Beauty") and *jalāl* ("Majesty"). In one of the passages of his systematic treatise, *Asrār al-Nuqtah* ("Secrets of the Dot"), Hamadānī elaborates upon the six categories of *'ilm al-laṭifah* ("knowledge of the subtlety"). In the last category which he calls *'ilm al-laṭifah al-khafiyyah* ("the knowledge of concealed subtlety"), he mentions a type of knowledge through which the manifestations of the attributes of *jamāl* and *jalāl* lead to the emancipation of the wayfarer from *al-ithnaynīyyah* ("duality") and as a result, he reaches the stage of *tafrīd* ("singleness").[180]

We might state that according to Hamadānī, the annulment of duality and advancement towards *tafrīd* ("singleness"), may not directly point to the concept of *waḥdat al-wujūd* ("unity of existence"), but rather to "the elevated unity of the wayfarer's total consciousness."

Hamadānī in his *Mashārib al-Adhwāq* ("the Fountains of Tastes"), a commentary on the well-known *qaṣīda* ("elegy') of Ibn Fāriḍ, makes a reciprocal connection between the concept of God's *jamāl* and the concept of *waḥdat*. By describing the characteristics of a *ṭā'yifah* ("group"), whom he calls the "elites among *a'yān-i awliyā' wa warithān-i anbīyā'* ("Friends of God and heirs to the prophets"), Hamadānī mentions that these chosen wayfarers "have been nurtured on the thrones of witnessing (*shuhūd*) under the [comfort] shadow of the courtyard of [God's] Beauty (*jamāl*), [and they] have become intoxicated by the wine of love (*maḥabbat*) from the cups of the cup-bearer of nearness (*sāqī-yi taqarrub*)... they have become intoxicated with unity (*waḥdat*) through constant manifestations of the secrets of [God's] Beauty (*jamāl*)."[181]

180. See Mīr Sayyid 'Alī Hamadānī, *Asrār al-Nuqṭah*, trans., into Persian, Muḥammad Khwājawī (Tehran: Intishārāt-i Mowlā, 1382/2003), 81. See also Hamadānī, *Al-Qudsiyyah fī Asrār al-Nuqṭah* (*al-Risālah al-Ḥissiyyah*), MS. 4250/9, Malek, Tehran.

181. See Mīr Sayyid 'Alī Hamadānī, *Mashārib al-Adhwāq*, ed. Muḥammad Khwājawī (Tehran: Intishārāt-i Mowlā, 1384/2005), 32.

In his introduction to this work, Hamadānī creatively expands on his combined discussion of *waḥdat* ("unity') and *kathrat* ("multiplicity') by utilizing the concept of God's Beauty (*jamāl*). He refers to *ḥaḍrat-i jalīl* ("Presence of the Majestic") in his interpretation of the concept of *jamāl* ("Beauty"). Hamadānī also discusses the possibility of melding the two aspects of God's *jamāl* and *jalāl* together as One Source.

By expounding upon the well-known Prophetic *ḥadīth* which states "God is Beautiful and He loves beauty," Hamadānī writes as follows:

> Because Beauty is the eternal Attribute of the Absolute Beautiful (*jamīl-i Muṭlaq*) and absolutely no one deserves the Name of Beauty (*jamīl*) except His Majestic Presence (*ḥaḍrat-i jalīl),* therefore, the Beautiful (*jamīl*) is truly not more than One, *waḥdahū lā sharika lah* – He is One and has no partner – and each goodness (*ḥusn*) and beauty which find the possibility of manifestation on the pages of existence (*wujūd*)...are all the images (*'ukūs*) of the lights of Beauty of that Presence (*ḥaḍrat*) which appear through the loci of manifestations (*majālī*) and loci of abilities.[182]

Hamdanī also, in defining the beauty of existence that is totally borrowed – in its absolute sense – from the Beauty of the Absolute, employs the Akbarian expression of *aḥadiyyah* ("exclusive unity"). Without mentioning the other related Akbarian expression, i.e., *wāḥidiyyah* ("inclusive unity"), Hamadānī describes the appearance of the Absolute's manifestations (or existence) by explaining the affinity between *jamāl* ("Beauty") and the Essence of *aḥadiyyah.* He makes a correlation between *hijāb* ("veil") and multiplicities or manifestations, and also approaches the notion of multiplicity by mentioning the four classical categories of *tawḥīd.*

> The beauty of signs (*āthār*) is one reflection (*'aks*) from the Sun of Beauty of the Essence of Unity (*dhāt-i aḥadiyyat*) which shines through a thousand veils of the Names (*asmā'ī*), Attributes (*ṣifātī*), Acts (*af'āli*) and Signs (*āthārī*).[183]

Hamadānī also refers here to the exteriorization of the four levels of *tawḥīd* in existence as the manifestation of *ḥusn* ("goodness/

---

182. Ibid., 35. See also Hamadānī, *Insāniyyah*, MS. 4275/4, Malek, Tehran.
183. Ibid., 42.

beauty"), deriving from *ṣuwar-i rūḥānī* ("spiritual forms"), in the *āiyna-yi qālib* ("mirror of molds").[184] In other words, *jamāl* and *ḥusn* ("beauty and goodness"), as two interconnected concepts, represent the most defining characteristics of all *'ukūs* ("images/reflections"), which everlastingly become "manifested" (exteriorized) from the *aḥadiyyah* ("exclusive unity") by the *wisāṭah* ("intercession") of the *āyina-yi wāḥidiyyah* ("mirror of the inclusive unity").[185]

Hamadānī views the love for *jamāl-i 'āriyatī* ("borrowed beauty") as an unworthy imagination due to its constant changes. He also refers to the *maḥabbat-i jamīl* ("love for the Beautiful"), as one of the *asbāb-i maḥabbat* ("mediums for love"), and concludes that this type of love, in reality and essence (*fī dhātih*), is for the Only *Maḥbūb* ("Beloved"). Therefore, although he often decries the love for *jamāl-i ṣūrī* ("formal beauty") by such allegories as *parda-yi nijāsat* ("polluted veils"), at the same time he believes that "lover-beloved ties are the [necessary] medium for the essence of Love."[186]

In Hamadānī's approach, the *asha'a-yi shumūs-i jamāl-i ḥaqīqī* ("rays of the Suns of Real Beauty") manifested from the *awj-i 'izz-i maḥbūbī* ('Zenith of the Beloved's Majesty") do not reach the *ḥaziẓ-i ḍull-i muḥibbī* ("lover's abyss of humility").[187] Hamadānī apparently sees reciprocations between the concepts of *jamāl* ("beauty") and love, and points to the signs of Beauty in existence as the *sarayān* ("penetration of all things") by the signs of love.[188]

By employing the plural forms of the "Sun" (i.e, *shumūs*/Suns), and "ray/sunshine" (i.e., *asha'ah*/rays), in the above description of the manifestation of Love, Hamadānī perhaps refers to the both multiple and unifying aspects of the lover-Beloved ties, i.e., the endless faces of *jamāl-i ḥaqīqī* or the One *Beauty* or One *Reality*. Hamadānī mentions that the *ahl-i kashf* ("people of unveiling") refer to the *nisbat-i muḥibbī-maḥbūbī* ("lover-Beloved ties") as *amr-i mubham* ("an ambiguous matter").[189] The lover, Hamadānī explains, enters the path of love only by the *jadhb* (attraction) of the beloved, either *ṣūratan* or *ma'nan* ("in form or in essence"),

---

184. See ibid.
185. See ibid.
186. See ibid.
187. See ibid., 43.
188. See ibid.
189. Ibid.

and "no beloved is able to boast in the glory of love, without the attachment which stems from the love of the lover."[190] Hamadānī then ponders upon the "unity" between the lover and beloved, and writes that "in reality each beloved is the lover and each lover is the beloved."[191] Also by referring to the concept of *waḥdat* again, he states that "when the Sun of Love shines from the Tower of Unity (*burj-i waḥdat*), the shadows of relativity…join the non-existence (*'adam*) and the mystic finds the Lover, Beloved, and Love as One Reality."[192]

190. Ibid.
191. Ibid., 44.
192. Ibid.

Chapter Two

‘Alā ad-Dawlah Simnānī and His Criticism of the Concept of *Waḥdat al-Wujūd*: The Birth of the *Shuhūdī* Triangle

Among major Kubrawī mystics, ‘Alā ad-Dawlah Simnānī is renowned for opposing the concept of *waḥdat al-wujūd.* Simnānī’s disproval of this concept is clearly projected in his seminal work, *al-‘Urwah li ahl al-Khalwah wa’l-Jalwah*, specifically in the several letters written to one of the famous commentators of the school of Ibn ‘Arabī, ‘Abd al-Razzāq Kāshānī (d.736/1335).[1]

Perhaps one of the main reasons for Simnānī’s criticism is his understanding of *waḥdat al-wujūd* as tantamount to the concepts of *ḥulūl* (“incarnationism”) and *ittiḥād* (“unificationism”).[2] In his handwritten comment on one of Ibn ‘Arabī’s praises of the Absolute in the book of *Futūhat* which states, “Glory be to the One Who brought entities to light and [who at the same time], is the [very entire being of the] entities (*subḥana man aẓhar al-ashyā’ wa huwa ‘aynuhā*),” Simnānī writes:

> O Shaykh if you heard someone saying that the feces of the Shaykh is the very same as the being of the Shaykh, you certainly would not take his word seriously but you would be angry at him. Then how is it possible for a wise man to apply such a meaningless saying to God. Repent....[3]

We will discuss the aspects of Simnānī’s criticism later in this chapter.

---

1. See Simnānī, *al-‘Urwah*, 37-45. See also Landolt, “Simnānī on Waḥdat al-Wujūd,” 99.
2. See Landolt, “Simnānī on Waḥdat al-Wujūd,” 95.
3. Simnānī, *al-‘Urwah*, 43. See also Landolt, “Simnānī on Waḥdat al-Wujūd,” 99.

Ibn 'Arabī and the Absolute Existence (Wujūd al-Muṭlaq)

In the above praise, which resulted in the harsh criticism by Simnānī, Ibn 'Arabī has considered God as *wujūd al-Muṭlaq* ("Absolute Existence"). This might be the main reason why Simnānī identified the idea of *waḥdat al-wujūd* with *ḥulūl* ("incarnationism") and *ittiḥād* ("unificationism").

One of the well-known commentators of Ibn 'Arabī's *Fuṣūṣ al-Hikam*, 'Abd al-Raḥmān Jāmī (d.898/1492), in his celebrated work, *Nafaḥāt al-Uns*,[4] commented on Simnānī's misunderstanding of Ibn 'Arabī's approach towards the concept of the "Absolute Existence" (*wujūd al-Muṭlaq*). He confirms that Simnānī interpreted the Absolute Existence in Ibn 'Arabī's writing as common existence or *wujūd al-'āmm* (i.e., *bi sharṭ-i shay'* or existence which is restricted by the limitation of entities).[5]

The Akbarian Divisions of Existence (wujūd)

As some of the contemporary scholars have stated, "The identification of God with the "Absolute Being" has a definite place in Ibn 'Arabī's worldview."[6] In order to explain the different levels of *wujūd* ("existence"), members of the school of Ibn 'Arabī, such as Ṣadr al-Dīn Qūnawī and 'Abdul Razzāq Kāshānī, in explaining the words of their master regarding *wujūd*, have developed and utilized certain divisions and subdivisions.[7]

Thus, "the four modes of existence are: *lā bi shar-i maqsamī*, "existence" as absolutely non-conditioned...*bi sharṭ-i lā,* "existence" as negatively conditioned...*bi sharṭ-i shay'* "existence" as conditioned by something...[and] *lā bi shart-i qismī*, "existence" as relatively non-conditioned."[8]

As Izutsu describes through affinities with the above modes of *wujūd*, "four basic stages" of *wujūd* have been recognized in the Akbarian approach to this concept:

> *Dhāt al-wujūd*, or *Ghayb al-ghuyūb*, i.e, Existence-only by Himself (Essence of the Existence) in its Absoluteness which

4. See Heravī, introduction to *al-'Urwah*, 36.
5. See ibid.
6. Landolt, "Simnānī on Waḥdat al-Wujūd," 100.
7. See ibid.
8. Izutsu, *The Concept*, 55.

pertains to the mode of *lā bi sharṭ-i maqsamī*.

Aḥadīyyah, or exclusive unity, in which existence manifests no articulation or outer manifestation, and corresponds to the state of *bi-sharṭ-i lā* or existence as negatively conditioned.

Waḥidīyyah, the inclusive unity; existence with inner articulations, the appearance of immutable entities, *a'yān al-thābitah*, which pertains to the mode of *bi-sharṭ-i shay'* (existence as conditioned by being something, i.e., the appearance of *a'yān al-thābitah,* or the manifestations of their knowledge as being [or as it is] fixed in the Absolute's knowledge).

Nāsūt or phenomenal existence: the domain of the phenomenal appearances (*lā bi sharṭ-i qismī*, existence as partially non-conditioned).[9]

As noted before, major figures among Simnānī's critics, such as Jāmī, believed that Simnānī failed to recongnize the fact that Ibn 'Arabī considered the *Wujūd al-Muṭlaq* ("Absolute Existence") as *lā bi sharṭ-i shay'* ("absolutely unconditioned"). One might be able to see a proof of Jāmī's criticism in the above quote from Simnānī, in which he sees an "identical" understanding of the "Absolute" and the "Absolute's manifestations" in Ibn 'Arabī's words (i.e., *man aẓhar al-ashyā' wa huwa 'aynuhā).*

The followers of Mullā Ṣadrā's Transcendental Theosophy, *Ḥikmat al-Muta'āliya,* which is influenced by the teachings of Ibn 'Arabī's school, have propounded five meanings for the concept of *waḥdat*.[10] One of the creative types of these categories of *wujūd* is called *waḥdat-i tajallī*.[11] This particular interpretation of *waḥdat* seems to be similar to the concept of "unity" in the above praise of the Absolute by Ibn 'Arabī. This approach to the concept of "unity" (i.e, *waḥdat-i tajallī*; the unity of manifestation) conveys a combined meaning of *waḥdat al-wujūd* and multiplicity of manifestation (*kathrat-i ẓuhūr*).[12] This particular meaning of unity is also very close to another approach to the concept of *waḥdat* ("unity") in the school of Mullā Ṣadra, i.e., *waḥdat-i sa'iy* ("unity of all-

9. See ibid., with modification, and added explanations.

10. See Qāsim Kākā'ī, *Waḥdat-i Wujūd bi Ravāyat-i Ibn 'Arabī wa Meister Eckhart* (Tehran: Initishārāt-ī Hermes, 1382/2003), 73.

11. See ibid.

12. See ibid.

embracing").[13] Although in this understanding of "unity," the attribute of *wujūd* exclusively belongs to the Absolute, but because of its infinite *wus'at* (all-embracing nature) and all-surrounding characteristic, the "unity" encompasses everything else in the cosmos. This interpretation of unity is also called *waḥdat dar 'ayn-i kathrat wa kathrat dar 'ayn-i waḥdat*[14] ("unity in multiplicity and multiplicity in unity"). The above praise by Ibn 'Arabī seems to be a proximate indication of this understanding of *waḥdat*.

Considering the crucial place of the concept of Absolute's *tajallī* ("manifestation") in Ibn 'Arabī's worldview, we might be able to refer to Simnānī's lack of attention to the meaning of the term *aẓhara* (-in "*Subḥāna man aẓhara…*" or "the act of making something present or appear") as the missing element in Simnānī's criticism of Ibn 'Arabī. By employing this term (*aẓhara*), Ibn 'Arabī seems to affirm that the *tajallī* ("manifestation") of the *ashyā'* [or their very mere appearance or presence in the cosmos] exclusively originates from the Absolute (similar to the concept of *waḥdat-i tajallī* in the Ṣadrian school). Therefore, in Ibn 'Arabī's worldview, the only Real and non-fictitious existence is the Existence of the Absolute.

This Only Source of Existence is the very being of the entire entities (*wa huwa 'aynuhā*, in Ibn 'Arabī's praise). However, their appearance has absolutely no effect on the Existence of the Absolute (i.e, *waḥdat dar kathrat*); the entities' mere existence absolutely depends upon Him.

Laṭā'if ("subtle mystical receptacles"), ḥulūl ("incarnationism"), ittiḥād ("unificationism") and Simnani's Approach to Nūr al-Muṭlaq ("Absolute Light")

Some of the contemporary scholars suggest that Simnānī's misunderstanding of Ibn 'Arabī's expression of *wujūd al-Muṭlaq* ("Absolute Existence"), which he seems to identify with any "manifestation of existence," has its roots in his objection to some Christian and Buddhist beliefs.[15] Simnānī may have discerned a similarity between some of the Buddhist teachings and the concept of *waḥdat*

13. Ibid.

14. Ibid.

15. See Landolt, "Simnānī on Waḥdat al-Wujūd," 95. To see an example of an Islamic philosopher's approach to the concept of "unity" in the texts of Hinduism, see Mīr Ab'al-Qāsim Findiriskī, *Muntakhabāt-i Jug-Basasht: Selections from the*

al-wujūd, along with some Christian influence on this concept, through its ties with the concepts of *ḥulūl* ("incarnationism") and *ittiḥād* ("unificationism").[16]

The place of "visionary experiences" in the mystical experiences of the Kubrawī tradition[17] may be considered another possible reason for Simnānī's hasty judgement of the concept of *Wujūd al-Muṭlaq.* In such visionary experiences the mystic attains his own *ḥiṣṣa* ("portion") of reality in each "single visionary experience." These experiences have usually been described and distinguished from one another by certain colors.[18] One would be able to see the numerous systematic examples of such color-specific visionary experiences by looking at Najm al-Dīn Kubrā's *Fawāi'h*, Najm al-Dīn Rāzī's *Mirṣād al-'Ibād* as well as Simnānī's *Risāla-yi Nūriyya.* Simnānī describes different visionary experiences with their color-specific resemblances such as red, white, blue, yellow, black and green.[19]

Therefore, in his understanding of Ibn 'Arabī's aforementioned praise, Simnānī disagrees with Ibn 'Arabī's assumption that "limitations"[20] of the Absolute result from the "manifestations of His creation." In other words, "recognizing the Absolute in the presence of things" (as Simnānī's understanding of Ibn 'Arabī's praise) is to accept "the limitations of the Absolute through the limits of visible and material entities." In Simnānī's view, this belief confines mystical experiences "only" to the realm of the outside world, by which the concealed and personal domain of the "authentic mystical experiences" in the way which the Kubrawīs have described, is not considered.[21]

Majd al-Dīn Baghdādī (d.615/1219), one of the masters of the Kubrawī order, whose spiritual teachings Simnānī followed wholeheartedly, seems to describe "the repudiation of incarnation (*ḥulūl*)" as one of the characteristics of the "mystical venture of the

---

Yoga-vasishta, ed. Fatḥullāḥ Mujtabā'ī (Tehran: Iranian Institute of Philosophy, 1384 /2006).

16. See ibid.
17. See ibid., 96-97, and also Elias, *The Throne Carrier of God*, 135-141.
18. See Elias, *The Throne Carrier of God*, 135-141.
19. For more information, see ibid.
20. See Landolt, "Simnānī on Waḥdat al-Wujūd," 100-101.
21. See Ibid.

elite of the elites (*safar-i khāṣṣ al-khawāṣṣ*)."[22] The reason for this description is that he sees *ḥulūl* as "the affirmation of existence of a physical place or entity (*dar ḥulūl ithbāt-i maḥall ast*)."[23]

Simnānī also seems to recognize "a physical characteristic" of this kind (or as we have mentioned, a "limitation" or *qayd*[24]) in Ibn 'Arabī's approach. In other words, between the two dimensions of *tashbīh* and *tanzīh* ("similarity and peerlessness of the Absolute"), Simnānī seems to put a much heavier stress on *tanzīh*.[25] Many examples of Simnani's preference for *tanzīh* over *tashbīh* appear in his writings. At the beginning of his most important doctrinal work, *al-'Urwah*, Simnānī outlines the content of the first chapter of his book. In this chapter, he tries to prove the existence of God as the only *wājib al-wujūd* ("Necessary Existence") and *qā'im bi-dhāt* ("Self-Subsisting Existence").[26] In his description of the contents, Simnānī employs his preferred term for referring to God, "first chapter: *dar ithbāt-i wujūb-i wujūd-i Ḥaqq*"[27] ("in affirmation of the necessary existence of the Real")." We shall return to the doctrinal connotations of the usage of this term (*Ḥaqq*) in Simnānī's criticism of Ibn 'Arabī's worldview later.

In his *'Urwah*, where he sounds more like a theologian (*mutakallim*) than a mystic (*'ārif*), Simnānī, without mentioning anything substantial regarding the concept of *tashbīh* or its place in his worldview, dedicates most of his analytical efforts to the concept of *tanzīh*.

In the first chapter of this book, he states that "know [believe in] three things if you do not belong to [the darkness of] misguidance (*tīh*): *hastī* ("Existence"), *yagānagī* ("Oneness") and *tanzīh* ("God's peerlessness")." He also calls the one who does not recognize God's peerlesness as the *ẓālim-i ḥaqīqī* ("real oppressor").[28]

In the Fourth chapter of *al-'Urwah*, Simnānī embarks upon his arguments on the annulment of *ittiḥād* ("unificationism"),

22. See Majd al-Dīn Baqdādī, "Risāla-yi dar Safar," ed. Kirāmat Ra'nā Ḥussainī, in *Collected Papers in Islamic Philosophy and Mysticism*, ed. Mehdī Muḥaqqīq and Herman Landolt (Tehran: The Institute of Islamic Studies McGill University, Tehran Branch, 1971), 189.

23. Ibid.

24. See Landolt, "Simnānī on Waḥdat al-Wujūd," 100-101.

25. See ibid., 105.

26. See Simnānī, *al-'Urwah*, 64.

27. Ibid.

28. See ibid.

ḥulūl ("incarnationism") and *tanāsukh* ("transmigration"). Here again the aspect of *tanzīh* serves as the very cornerstone of his discussions: "[this chapter] is [dedicated to prove] the exaltation (*tanzīh*) of the Absolute Necessary Existence...and the annulment of *ittiḥād, ḥulūl* and *tanāsukh*."[29]

The preference for *tanzīh* over *tashbīh* is also clearly visible in Simnānī's *Risāla-yi Nūriyya* ("Treatise of Light") in which he states: "manifestation of the Light of the "Real" (*nūr-i Ḥaqq*) is exalted above all causes, *nothing resembles It* and It resembles everything."[30] [Emphasis added]

Simnānī's comments above sheds light on his vigorous criticism of Ibn 'Arabī's praise of the Absolute. In Simnānī's worldview, the impossibility of the resemblance of the manifestation to the Absolute is all-inclusive. He believes that no entity should be named or referred to as the real example of such manifestation. Simnānī's utilization and description of this particular Light (*nūr-i Ḥaqq*), among other lights, seems to serve more than one purpose. "The Absolute's Light" is not only part of the systematic understanding of Simnānī's cosmology of lights, but it is also the basis of Simnānī's objection to concepts such as *waḥdat al-wujūd.*

As we have mentioned before, one of the main reasons for Simnānī's opposition to the concept of "unity of existence," is the fact that he identified it with *ḥulūl* and *ittiḥād.* Simnānī's particular understanding of this concept seems to be the crucial reason that led him to expound upon the unique characteristics of the *nūr-i Ḥaqq* ("Absolute's Light"). As quoted above, Simnānī mentions that nothing resembles this Light. He then provides us with another characteristic of the Absolute Light:

> This is a particular attribute of God exalted above dwelling (*ḥulūl*) and union with (*ittiḥād*) any other [being], sanctified beyond association and disassociation...The manifestation of the "absolute light" is not possible except in paradise.[31]

Simnānī then embarks upon the internal modes in the experiences of mystics in the manifestation of this Light:

---

29. Ibid., 264.

30. Jamal Elias, "A Kubrawī Treatise on Mystical Vision: The Risāla-yi Nuriyya of 'Alā ad-Dawlah Simnānī," *Muslim World* LXXXIII, no. 1 (1993):74.

31. Ibid.

> The effects that appear in it, that is in this manifestation, are firstly, the annihilation of mystic, then standing on the boundary, splitting of the sky, transformation of the earth, the flying of the mountains, the dispersal of fixed stars, the changed rising of the sun, the dimming of the planets, the assemblage in open spaces, judgement of the accounts on the balance, traversing the path, being thrown into the abyss, and being lifted up in levels.[32]

After describing a series of profound experiences, Simnānī again focuses on the internal aspect of experiencing this Light:

> When the mystic sees these signs, he should know himself to be in the eternal garden. Then he should pay complete attention to the beauty of His presence in accordance with the command "Neither did sight falter nor exceed the bounds" (53:17). He should not incline to anything so that the "holy essence" (*dhāt-i muqaddas*) may be manifested. Witnessing this instantaneously and miraculously returns light to his ailing eyes.[33]

In Simnānī's description and in his account of encountering the "Absolute Light" there is no room (or importance) for the external visualizations of such manifestation (light). For him, the *authentic* mystical experiences happen through the *laṭā'if* of the mystics, the subtle receptacles for mystical perceptions and experiences.[34]

Similar to his use of the term *nūr-i Ḥaqq* ("the Absolute's Light"), in his *Risāla-yi Nūrīyya* ("Treatise of Light"), Simnānī also employs another term in his seminal work, *al-'Urwah li Ahl al-Khalwah wa'l-Jalwah,* to refer to the ultimate and most inaccessible level of the Divine Self-disclosure, namely *wujūd al-Ḥaqq* ("the existence of the Real"). Perhaps Simnānī uses this term to delineate his differences with Ibn 'Arabī, who, as mentioned earlier, employs the term *wujūd al-Muṭlaq* ("Absolute Existence") instead.

As some of the contemporary scholars, such as Hermann Landolt have stated, Simnānī's worldview is based on the idea of "theophany" (Divine manifestation).[35] This act of manifestation occurs in a systematic manner which Simnānī explains in terms of four

32. Ibid.
33. Ibid.
34. On the concept of *laṭā'if* see Elias, *The Throne Carrier of God*, 157-60.
35. See Landolt, "Simnānī on Waḥdat al-Wujūd," 106.

categories of existence, i.e., *dhāt* ("Essence"), *ṣifāt* ("attributes"), *af'āl* ("acts") and *āthār* ("traces") respectively.[36]

Through reciprocation within these catagories, and affinities among the four categories, the Absolute emanates His Will in the process of *khalq* ("creation") and human beings will return to the kernel of their origination, thus constitualizing a process of emanation and return.[37] The experience of return takes place through the *laṭā'if,* the subtle receptacles of mystical experiences.[38] On the pathway of return there are several types of *laṭā'if*, which correspond to different levels of cosmic creation. In Simnānī's worldview, the categories of *laṭā'if* begin with *laṭifa al-qalbīyyah* ("the subtle receptacle related to/of the heart") and end with *laṭifa ḥaqīqīyya* ("the subtle receptacle of reality").[39]

For Simnānī, the act of emanation or creation (as a necessary act for the Absolute), which represent the function of *kathrat*, does not originate from the Essence, i.e, NOT from *Aḥadiyyah* ("exclusive unity"), but from *ṣifāt al-fi'l* ("Absolute's attribute of act") or from *wāḥidiyyah* (i.e., unity at the level of external manifestations).[40]

In his *al-'Urwah*, Simnānī mentions *Dhāt* ("Essence") as the closest of the four categories to the Oneness of God.[41] Simnānī also demonstrates his creativity by referring to *Mūjid* [42]("Creator") as the first attribute of God and *nūr* ("Light") as the last. Thus, he adds two attributes to the traditionally known eight *thubūtiyya* ("affirmative") attributes of God [i.e., *sam'* ("Hearing"), *ḥayāt* ("Life") *baṣar* ("Vision"), *kalām* ("Speech"), *'ilm* ("Knowledge"), *irāda* ("Will"), *qudrat* ("Power") and *ḥikmat* ("Wisdom").][43]

By considering the concept of *wujūd* ("existence") in the first of these attributes (*Mūjid*), Simnānī distinguishes this attribute from the attribute of Life (*ḥayāt*). By making this meaningful distinction and adding "Light" as the very last Essential attribute of God, Simnānī elucidates his approach to the concepts of *waḥdat* ("uni-

36. See Ibid. See also Elias, *The Throne Carrier of God*, 61.

37. See Elias, *The Throne Carrier of God*, 61.

38. See ibid.

39. See Elias, *The Throne Carrier of God*, 157-160. See also Andreas D'Souza, "Simnānī's Cosmology and Mystical Implications," *The Bulletin of the Henry Martyn Institute of Islamic Studies* VIII, no. 4 (1985): 102, 109-111.

40. See Landolt, "Simnānī on Waḥdat al-Wujūd," 108.

41. See Simnānī, *al-'Urwah*, 75.

42. See ibid. See also Landolt, "Simnānī on Waḥdat al-Wujūd," 108.

43. See ibid., 393.

ty") and *kathrat* ("multiplicity"). This point seems to be clear in Simnānī's words regarding these two added attributes:

> Among these…ten attributes, [the attribute] of *wujūd* (Existence) and *nūr* (Light) have no other names. Because, Light is the ultimate/perfect appearance (*kamāl-i ẓuhūr*) and Existence is the source [and principle] of appearance (*mabda'-i ẓuhūr*).[44]

Then Simnānī explains the impossibility of naming these two attributes (i.e., *wujūd* and *nūr*) by any other names.

> Because of its [unique] characteristic [which is] its proximity to the Essence, there is no name for *wujūd* other than the name of the Essence (*ism al-Dhāt*) and [also] there is no [other] name for *nūr* except itself (*illā nafsih*).[45]

Simnānī and Ibn 'Arabī on the Absolute's Similarity and Peerlessness (tashbīh and tanzīh)

One might be able to identify Simnānī's creativity (i.e., adding these two essential attributes) as another method through which he emphasizes his preferred aspect, *tanzīh*. Simnānī not only considers *wujūd* as the closest attribute to the Essence, but he also believes that "there is no name for *wujūd* other than the name of the Essence." Therefore, in his view, there is *no* resemblance for *wujūd* from which any similarity (*tashbīh*) to the Essence of God can be conveyed. Thus, *wujūd* as the most proximate attribute of God to the "Essence" does not contain the aspect of *tashbīh* and accessibility of the only "Real" (*al-Ḥaqq*, Simnānī's preferred Name for God).

In Simnānī's worldview, it is absolutely impossible for the Essence to be a source of *kathrat* ("multiplicity'). Perhaps, for this reason, Simnānī considers *nūr* as the last of the ten attributes. Being the closest to the concept of *kahtrat*, "light" enters at the very end of Simnānī's list of God's attributes.

The same preference for *tanzīh* over *tashbīh* appears in his usage of the term, *wujūd al-Ḥaqq* ("the Real Existence"), which shows Simnānī's terminological divergence from Ibn 'Arabī. In Simnānī's view, *Wujūd al-Muṭlaq* ("Absolute Existence," Ibn 'Arabī's favorite term for the Existence of God), becomes *muqa-*

44. Ibid.
45. Ibid.

yyad ("limited") if used in its *munāsibah* ("relation") to creatures through the aspect of *tashbīh*. In other words, the Absolute will lose its *iṭlāq* ("Absoluteness") and becomes limited. Simnānī' believes that the Real *Wujūd* (*wujūd al-Ḥaqq,* Simnānī's favourite term to refer to the absolute peerlesness of God), due to His inaccessibility and *tanzīh* ("peerlessness"), even in His relation and ties with the unreal existence (creatures), will always stand out as the Only Real in His Absoluteness.

By referring to Simnānī's criticism of Ibn 'Arabī, Herman Landolt addresses Simnānī's approach to the "Absolute Existence."

> Absolute Existence, according to Simnānī is not a substantially existing entity at all, since it is the act of existentiation itself, the "missing link" as it were, between the Subject of theophany and its Object. On the level of the Trace, there is neither necessary nor absolute existence, that is to say limited by its ontological status of causedness and contingency (*muqayyad bi'l-imkān*).[46]

In the chapter four of his *al-'Urwah,* specifically written to prove the aspect of *tanzīh* ("God's peerlessness"), Simnānī, without mentioning Ibn 'Arabī's name, seems to comment on his praise of the Absolute (*subḥāna man aẓhara*…):

> And you know that the written material (*maktūb*) can't be the same as the essence of the writer (*dhāt-i kātib*) and they do not become one...therefore, know that the confession to the fact that no possible being (*mumkin*) [can] become one with the Necessary Being, [is] a religiously incumbent act (*wājib*). I seek refuge in God from this belief of union with God (*ittiḥād*).[47]

Contrary to what Simnānī seems to perceive from Ibn 'Arabī's worldview regarding the aspect of *tashbīh* as the "identification of the Necessary Being with possible beings," Shaykh al-Akbar, in numerous occasions, clearly referred to the incomparability/peerlessness (*tanzīh*) of the Absolute. For example, in his introduction to *Shajarat al-Kawn*, Ibn 'Arabī states:

> All praise to Allāh, who is One and Only in His Essence and unique in His attributes. Sanctified is He whose regard encompasses everything while transcending all directions. His purity

46. Landolt, "Simnānī on Waḥdat al-Wujūd," 108.
47. Simnānī, *al-'Urwah*, 265.

is free and clear of the things seen and imagined. He goes to places unrestricted by the six directions. He does what he does without acting or doing. He sees every thing without looking. He is far above the meaning of all these things. *His uniqueness does not permit any other to be like Him, nor can anything own or attach itself to Him. His power always reaches its goal and is never spent. His all-dominating will bears no resemblance to the lowly desires of humankind, nor His will change with the wishes of His creation; neither will it be in opposition to their solicitation.* His Divine attributes, which He manifests upon His creation, neither increase nor decrease when shared with them, for all of His many attributes, are but one. He is the cause of all and everything. And when He willed the creation to be, all that He had to do was to say *kun* (Be!), and all that exists came to be. All that exists was born from the hidden depths of the secret meaning of this word *KUN*. Even all that is hidden from the eye and the mind is but the result of this mysterious sound. As Allāh most high says: For to anything We have willed, We but say *kun* (Be!) and it becomes (*Surah Nahl*-40). *His word is in itself the deed.*[48] [Emphasis added]

In defining the Absolute Existence, Ibn 'Arabī also denies any *qayd* as partiality or limitation attached to Him: "*al-wujūd al-Muṭlaq al-ladhī lā yataqayyad*: the Absolute Existence which is not limited."[49]

As some of the contemporary scholars have pointed out, Simnānī "was opposed to any doctrine which compromised divine unity and transcendence"[50]and his "basic conviction" was the fact that "divine transcendence must be saved at any price."[51]

Here, we are facing an evident question. How can we justify what Ibn 'Arabī states in passages such as his controversial praise of the Absolute? If the Absolute is the same as the entities which He has created (*wa huwa 'aynuhā*), would it be possible to still believe in His transcendence?

Is it possible to put the above criticism with its vivid *tanzīhī*

48. Ibn 'Arabī, *The Tree of Being: Shajart al-Kawn an Ode to the Perfect Man*, interpreted by Shaykh Tousan Bayrak al-Jerrāhī al-Halvetī (Cambridge: Archetype, 2005), 89-90.

49. Cited in Landolt, "Simnānī on Waḥdat al-Wujūd," 103.

50. Elias, *The Throne Carrier of God*, 57.

51. Landolt, "Simnānī on Waḥdat al-Wujūd," 105.

aspect, which denies any resemblance of the Absolute to any other entity, and Ibn 'Arabī's controversial praise with its *tashbīhī* nature, which conveys the comparability of the Absolute to His creation, in one container of dialectical inquiry? Contemporary scholars have tried to answer this question by pointing out Ibn 'Arabī's particular understanding of the "double notion of the Absolute's manifestation."

> Although the act of theophany is essentially one, Ibn 'Arabī distinguishes it in two levels. The "visible" theophany, *tajallī shuhūdī*, which is divine manifestation in the present world (*shahāda*) and in the mystical experience, presupposes in the first place the event of an un-visible or hidden manifestation (*tajallī ghaybī*), that is to say a manifestation taking place in the Unseen (*ghayb*), which Ibn 'Arabī also calls "theophany of the Essence" (*tajallī dhātī*). This distinction between two level of theophany corresponds to the classical Sufi neo-platonic distinction between the spiritual and the material world, *'ālam al-ghayb* and *'ālam al-shahāda*, which terminology is taken from the Quranic designation of God as the One who knows both the Unseen and Visible (*'ālam al-ghayb wa l-shahāda*). But for Ibn 'Arabī the important point is here that the two levels of theophany which he distinguishes from a logical point of view are not different in terms of reality, because there cannot be more than One Reality, and this is why, incidentally, *waḥdat al-wujūd*, in Ibn 'Arabī's sense is something other than pure and simple neo-Platonism. In reality, according to Ibn 'Arabī, theophany in visible form *is* essential or hidden theophany; for the divine Essence, just because it is essentially hidden and absolute, has no other means to show itself than in the very form of the one to whom it shows itself (*al-mutajallā lahū*). In other words: because the divine Essence has no forms in its absolute oneness (*aḥadīya*) and therefore can never appear as such, its form is identical with the forms of the things. All this amounts to the perhaps shocking paradox, that, and I am quoting Ibn 'Arabī, "the Really divine Being (*al-Ḥaqq*) is limited through all limits," because "to isolate the absolute from the Limited means precisely to limit the Absolute." There can be little doubt that this paradoxical "Absolute which is limited by all limits" is not in the same way absolute as the first metaphysical category

> since Ibn 'Arabī defines the latter, as the "absolute Existence which is not limited" (*al-wujūd alladhī la yataqayyadu*). Rather its absoluteness is the same as the third category of the *ḥaqīqa*... which is all-inclusive.[52]

Other scholars have attempted to explain the ties that Ibn 'Arabī considers in balancing *tashbīh* ("similarity") and *tanzīh* ("peerlessness") by explaining God's attributes of Mercy and Wrath. In this regard, they have also considered the difference between his approach and that of the theologians. Simnānī's approach to the concept of *tanzīh* and *tashbīh*, particularly in his *al-'Urwah*, as we have mentioned, is similar to the view of the *mutakallimin*.

> In theological language, Ibn 'Arabī describes the vision achieved through human perfection as the balanced combination of the declaration of God's incomparability (*tanzīh*) and that of His similarity (*tashbīh*). The *mutakallimin* considered *tanzīh* the correct position and condemned *tashbīh*. Ibn 'Arabī embraces *tashbīh* so long as it is kept in balance with *tanzīh*. Neither term can be employed to refer to God in any particular sense. It is important to grasp how Ibn 'Arabī correlates *tanzīh* and *tashbīh* with the two broad categories of Divine Attributes that are often discussed by Muslim thinkers. They are called the Attribute of Mercy (*Raḥmah*) and Wrath (*Ghaḍab*), or Bounty (*faḍl*) and Justice (*'Adl*), or Beauty (*Jamāl*) and Majesty (*Jalāl*), or Gentleness (*Luṭf*) and Severity (*Qah*r)...Generally speaking, Ibn 'Arabī maintains that God is understood in terms of *tanzīh* in as much as He is accessible, but He is grasped in terms of *tashbīh* in as much as He is "closer to the human being than the jugular vein" (Quran 50:16). When the Quran says that God created human being with His own two Hands (Quran 38:75), Ibn 'Arabī understands this to mean that He employed Attributes of both *tashbīh* and *tanzīh* to bring His own image into existence. Hence God is both present with His creatures and absent from them.[53]

The difference between the balancing view of Ibn 'Arabī and that of theologians, manifests its defining elements in the methods through which they have viewed *tawḥīd* ("God's Unity"), *ṣifāt*

52. Ibid., 103.
53. William C. Chittick, "Ibn 'Arabī," 501.

("God's attributes") and the concept of *waḥdat*.

> Ibn 'Arabī's position on the intimate connection between *tanzīh* and *tashbīh* has a direct bearing upon epistemology... In Ibn 'Arabī's view the rational thinkers – whether *mutakallimun* or philosophers – dissect reality such that they lose sight of the underlying unity of all things, and they do this because of the inherent nature of the rational mode of understanding. In other words, rational perspicuity keeps God at a distance by affirming *tanzīh* and denying *tashbīh*. As a result, both *falsafah* and *kalām* focus on God's Majesty, Severity, and Wrath and tend to lose sight of His Beauty, Gentleness and Mercy. In contrast, those who undergo unveiling (*ahl al-kashf, al-mukāshifūn*) perceive God's presence in all things, and they do so through the fact that unveiling is rooted primarily in imagination (*khayāl*), which bridges gaps, establishes relationships and understands by means of concrete images. As a result, unveiled Sufis see God in all things and focus on His nearness-His Mercy, Compassion, Gentleness and Love.[54]

These differences also define the ways in which the nature of the ties between God and cosmos is perceived in both worldviews.

> Through affirming *tanzīh*, people recognize the otherness (*ghayriyyah*) of all things; through affirming *tashbīh*, they acknowledge God's withness (*ma'iyyah*)...To focus upon either *tanzīh* or *tashbīh* and to de-emphasize the other perspective is to distort the actual relationship between God and the world. True knowledge depends upon seeing all things with both the eye of imagination and the eye of reason.[55]

But – as mentioned earlier – a more comprehensive approach might better reveal the domination and preference of God's "withness" (as *tashbīh*) over His "otherness," (as *tanzīh*) in Ibn 'Arabī's worldview. As Chittick states:

> The harmony that needs to be established between reason and imagination does not mean that *tanzīh* and *tashbīh* have equal rights in all situations. In the last analysis, *tashbīh* predominates, even if *tanzīh* has a certain priority in the present world....

---

54. Ibid., 502.
55. Ibid.

The theological principle here is set down in the famous *ḥadīth*, "My [God's] Mercy takes precedence over My Wrath." In other words, nearness to the Real (*al-Ḥaqq*), which is Sheer Being (*al-Wujūd al-Maḥḍ*) and Absolute Good (*al-Khayr al-Muṭlaq*) is more basic to existence than distance from Him, because nearness provides existent things with everything they have. Their distance, though necessary in order for creation to take place, marks their connection with non-existence (*'adam*), also known as the unreal (*bāṭil*).[56]

For Ibn 'Arabī, Mercy of God (*Raḥmah* – which stands for *tashbīh* and also projects the Absolute's Beauty – or *jamāl*), is the real substance of existence, and Wrath (*Qahr*, which represents the aspect of *tanzīh* and defines the Absolute's Majesty or *jalāl*) is inessential to existence, compared to the Mercy of the Absolute. Ibn 'Arabī dedicates one of the longest chapters (558) of his magnum opus, *Futūḥāt al-Makkiyah*, to the concept of the "Breath of the Merciful." In his introduction to this chapter, Ibn 'Arabī seems to approach the concept of "unity of existence (*waḥdat al-wujūd)*," by referring to the "Divine Presence" (*ḥaḍra*).

> This is the Presence that comprehends (*jāmi'*) all presences. Hence no worshipper of God worships anything but this Presence. God judges (*ḥukm*) this in His words "thy Lord has decreed that you shall not worship any but Him (Quran 17:23), and His words, "you are the poor toward Allāh." To God belongs what is hidden, to God belongs what appears. How excellent is that which is God, that which is none other than Him.[57]

"Divine Presence," for Ibn 'Arabī, appears to have a direct coorrelation with the concept of *tashbīh*. Comparability, predicates Divine Mercy, and manifests proximity, closeness, friendship and love between the Absolute and existence in general and between Him and *insān* in particular. As mentioned above, Ibn 'Arabī, makes a connection between worshiping the Absolute (as the *only* form of worship) and His Divine Presence. Therefore, the act of worship or servanthood (as the ultimate representation of the ties between God and man, and God and existence in general) happens within the *ḥaḍra* ("Divine Presence"). On the other hand, *tanzīh* refers to the

56. Ibid.

57. Ibn al-'Arabī, *The Meccan Revelations,* ed. Michel Chodkiewicz, vol. 1, 59.

inaccessibility. As Chittick rightly puts it:

> God's never-ceasing presence with the creatures must show its effects. Absence has no roots in Being, no foundation in the Real. Hence God's presence – Mercy – predominates in this world and the next. Wrath and Chastisement pertains to situations that are accidental to the universal economy of the Good and the Real...Ibn 'Arabī constantly comes back to the theme of mercy as the underlying, all embracing, fundamental reality that must show itself in the end (*bi'l-ma'āl*).[58]

It appears that, in Ibn 'Arabi's approach, the concepts of *Raḥmah* ("Divine Mercy"), and *wujūd* are intertwined in every aspect. The all-comprehending realm of *ḥaḍrah* ("Divine Presence") which reveals *Raḥmah* (Mercy), and brings everything into existence, encompasses and unifies the whole existence.

Although Ibn 'Arabī, on several occasions, emphasizes *tashbīh* in order to reveal its predominance over that of *tanzīh*, in a more comprehensive view of his ideas, the core doctrinal, more prevalent and underlying understanding of Ibn 'Arabī appears to be the one which harmonizes these two aspects (*tashbīh* and *tanzīh*) in a single balanced view. This combined approach is named by him as *huwa-lā-huwa* ("He/not He").[59]

In this creative approach to the Absolute's *tashbīh* and *tanzīh*, every single *tajallī* ("manifestation") of the Absolute in existence carries both aspects of similarity and peerlessness. Every entity manifests the Existence of the Absolute (*tashbīh*) but *it* is not (or comparable with) the Absolute. In this view, both aspects are applicable to the One Reality in every single approach, and therefore, they are not in conflict, but rather complement each other. In the chapter 73 (question 115) of his *Futūḥāt,* Ibn 'Arabī directly deals with the aspects of *tashbīh* and *tanzīh* as two cardinal types of the Absolute's Names, related to His similarity and peerlessness. One of the contemporary scholars refers to this expression (*Huwa/lā-huwa*) as follows:

> The contrast between these two types of Names, or kinds of relationship which God possesses with creation, is one of the key topics in Ibn 'Arabī's writings. It might best be summed up in

58. Chittick, "Ibn 'Arabī," 502.

59. See Chittick, *The Sufi Path of Knowledge,* 110 and 113.

> the expression He/not He...or simply "yes and no," which is the basic answer to most questions asked about the world's status in relation to God. In other terms, the world always remains in an ambiguous situation halfway between Being and nothingness.[60]

In Ibn 'Arabi's understanding, *huwa* is the Name that reveals the entire attributes of God. He explains the essential importance of this Name in his *Futūḥāt*:

> Do you not see that all attributes come back to *Allāh* and *Allāh* to *Huwa*? *Huwa* thus encompasses all Names and Attributes. The name that Allāh has given to Himself is also the name through which He created. He is the Supreme Light, the Unraisable Veil, the Extra, Mystery, Possibility (*imkān*), the "Mother of the Book" and Principle (*aṣl*). He contains all that has been and all that will be. He is the knowledge that God reserves for Himself in His Mystery...He is where decisions are made regarding all things (*al-maqādir*) in an undifferentiated and non-distinct manner. In uttering the word *kun*, He detaches them from His mystery. Their separation takes place via the spoken word (*qawl*) or via an action (*fi'l*).[61]

Huwa, for Ibn 'Arabī, appears to be the representation of the Supreme Unity of the Absolute in both His *tanzīh* and His *tashbīh*. He considers this Name to be the reservoir of both aspects. Therefore, for Ibn 'Arabi, in each approach to the Absolute, both these aspects must be considered together at once. One might be able to claim that this term (*huwa*), which characterizes the *huwiyyah* (ipseity) of *wujūd* – in its sheer ties to and absolute dependence upon the Absolute *Wujūd* – manifests the same function as that of the term *waḥdat al-wujūd*. This, however, as mentioned earlier, is a term which Ibn 'Arabī never employed in his works.

Simnānī's Approach to the Concept of tajallī

As one of the contemporary scholars states, "in an effort to balance the ideas of divine manifestation and creation of the world... [Simnānī] developed the existing notion of *tajallī* (theophany) in terms of varying degrees of divine self manifestation occurring through intermediaries, as opposed to the concept *that all of cre-*

60. Ibn 'Arabī, *The Meccan Revelations*, ed. Michel Chodkiewicz, vol. 1, 42.
61. Ibid., vol. 2, 138.

ation shares in divinity. This facet of his thought placed him in opposition to the school of Ibn 'Arabī" [62] [Emphasis added]

In order to describe his distinctive approach to the idea of *tajallī*, Simnānī considers four substantial sub-divisions for the concept of *tajallī*. These four categories result in a "fourfold structure of existence…[that] occurs all over his writings"[63]

Simnānī did not categorize the theophanies at the level of "self-manifestation of the Divine Being." He considers this type of theophany as "the process of creation or existentiation (*ījād*)."[64] He seems to leave this particular type of manifestation *without* any mystical interpretation. The reason for this absence of interpretation, perhaps, is that Simnānī found it necessary to protect the sanctity of the realm of Divinity from any experiential incursion and to make a clear distinction between the theophany in the Original form (cosmic creation) *and* what mystics perceive as their own mystical experience or Divine manifestations in the *nāsūt* ("finite realm").[65] We might be able to consider this distinction made by Simnānī as another sign of his preference for the eminence of *Ḥaqq* ("the Real") or the aspect of *tanzīh* ("God's peerlessness"). Therefore, Simnānī considers only a "grammatical"[66] four-fold structures for the theophanies of the Divine Being on the level of cosmic creation, "namely the Essence (*dhāt*), Attributes (*ṣifāt*), Acts (*af'āl*), and Effects (*āthār*)"[67] respectively.

As for the theophanies on the level of "mystical experiences,"[68] Simnānī indicates a four-fold structure based on the degree of their agreement with "forms" or "images." "The theophany in visible forms (*tajallī ṣūrī*)"[69] stands at the lowest category among these theophanies, because of its total involvement with images.[70]

Tajallī nūrī ("theophany of light"), *tajallī ma'nawī* ("theophany of idea"), and finally the *tajallī dhawqī* ("theophany of taste"), constitute the second to fourth categories in ascending order.[71]

62. Elias, *The Throne Carrier of God*, 2.
63. Landolt, "Simnānī on Waḥdat al-Wujūd," 106.
64. Ibid.
65. See ibid.
66. Ibid.
67. Ibid.
68. See ibid.
69. Ibid.
70. See ibid.
71. See ibid.

The highest category (*tajallī dhawqī*), Simnānī believes, is the purest type among these four, i.e., it has no association with forms or images.[72]

By focusing on the concept of *tajallī* ("theophany") as the cornerstone of his cosmology, and in an evident effort to find a solution for saving God's transcendence, Simnānī changes his focus from *wujūd* (as it is presented by the *Akbarian* school) to theophany (*tajallī)*. As one of the contemporary scholars has stated, Simnānī aims his focus on the concept of *af'āl* ("God's Acts") and not Existence, in order to pursue a "dynamic entity rather than an static one."[73]

In order to protect God's transcendence, Simnānī made a systematic endeavor. As mentioned above, in his two sets of four-based structures, Simnani considers *āthār* ("traces") and *tajallī ṣūrī* ("theophany of forms") to be at the lowest and farthermost levels from the Essence and *tajallī dhawqī* ("theophany of taste"). Both of these levels (i.e., *athār* and *tajallī sūrī*) are defined in their connections with "forms" and and therefore, in Simnani's view, cannot in any way interfere with the Sanctity of *Ḥaqq* ("the Real"). For Simnānī, these two closest levels to the "forms" (which represent *tashbīh*) have no affinities with the Real and therefore, must be considered un-real. On the other hand, the Essence and theophany of taste (which represent *tanzīh*) reveal their correlation with the Real.[74]

Shaykh Aḥmad Sirhindī, Simnānī and the Shuhūdī School

The specific approach to the concept of *tajallī* – as the "mere reflections" of God's Existence by Simnānī – has encouraged one of the celebrated Sufi figures, Aḥmad Sirhindī (d.1033/1624) known as *Mujaddid-i Alf-Thānī* ("reviver of the second millennium"), to de-

72. See ibid.

73. Ibid., 109.

74. In his *Diwān*, Simnānī perhaps refers to the same type of *tajallī dhawqī* when he explains the characteristics of the lovers (*āshiqīn*) on the Path. He recites "when the secret of the Real's light become manifest to their souls...[and their] uncertainty (*shakk*) becomes certainty (*yaqīn*). Every moment they go through a new [spiritual] ascension (*urūjī dīgar*) in experiencing the Real. Explanation and description fall short in recounting the perfection of their [spiritual] state." See 'Alā addwalah Simnānī, *Diwān-i Kāmil-i Ash'ār-i Fārsī wa 'Arabī*, ed. 'Abd al-Rafī' Ḥaqīqat (Shirkat-i Mu'allifīn wa Mutarjimīn-i Irān, 1364/1985), 195.

velop the idea of *waḥdat al-shuhūd* ("unity of witnessing") – as an alternative to the idea of "unity of existence" ("*waḥdat al-wujūd*").

Sirhindī was one of the most influential figures in *Naqshbandiyya* order (*ṭarīqah*) of Sufism, and he played a major role in propagating this order in India.[75] Some contemporary scholars believe that Sirhindī's idea of unity of witnessing was "derived from" Simnānī's worldview of *tajallī*.[76] But there are also others who go further and regard Simnānī as the "founder" of a school which has been referred to as *shuhūdīyyah* (i.e., unity of witnessing),[77] that favors criticism of Ibn 'Arabī's school of *wujūdiyyah* (i.e., unity of existence). Both schools (of *waḥdat al-shuhūd* and *waḥdat al-wujūd*) share the belief that the real Existence (Being) is only One, but the ways in which, they describe the bonds between God and the world in general, and God and *insān* in particular, are different. In order to define these ties, in the school of *waḥdat al-shuhūd* ("unity of witnessing"), a set of opposite parallels between *wujūd* ("existence") and *'adam* ("nonexistence") have been employed. The summary of this approach is explained in Sirhindī's principal work, *Maktūbāt*:

> God is the Perfect Being comprehending all attributes of perfection in His Essence. Before the existence of the world there was this Perfect Being alone with all His perfect attributes and names. Now opposed to God's existence or *wujūd* there is pure nothing or *'adam-i maḥaḍ* and opposed to His Life is a form of '*adam*' called death and opposed to His knowledge is a form of '*adam*' called ignorance and so on. Thus there are two things: 'perfections' which are beings or *wujūdat* and 'imperfections' which are non-being or *'adamāt*. When God decided to create

75. For more information see Hamid Algar, "The Naqshbandī Order: A Preliminary Survey of its History and Significance," *Studia Islamica* 44 (1976): 123-152. See also Yohanan Friedman, *Shaykh Aḥmad Sirhindī: An Outline of His Thought and His Image in the Eyes of Posterity* (Montreal: McGill University Press, 1971), Annemarie Schimmel, "The Sufi ideas of Shaykh Aḥmad Sirhindī," *Die Welt des Islams*, NewSer., 14 (1973): 199-203. J. G. J. Ter Haar, *Follower and Heir of the Prophet: Shaykh Aḥmad Sirhindī (1564-1624) as Mystics* (Leiden: Het Ooster Institute, 1992), Burhān Aḥmad Fārūqī, *Mujaddid's Conception of Tawḥīd: Study of Shaykh Aḥmad Sirhindī's Doctrine of Unity* (Lahore: Institute of Islamic Culture, 1989), and Shaykh Muḥammad Hishām Kabbānī, *Classical Islam and the Naqshbandī Sufi Tradition* (Washington D.C.: Islamic Supreme Council of America, 2004.

76. See Elias, *The Throne Carrier of God*, 2.

77. See Mīr Valiuddīn, "Reconciliation between Ibn 'Arabī's Waḥdat-i Wujūd and the Mujaddid's Waḥdat-i Shuhūd," *Islamic Culture* XXV (1951), 48.

> the world He cast a reflection or shadow (*in'ikās* or *ẓill*) of His pure *wujūd* or existence into its *'adam-i mutaqābila'* or 'opposed nothing,' i.e. pure *'adam* or nothing and there came to be finite existence. He cast a reflection or shadow of His life into its 'opposed nothing,' death and came to be finite life. In the same manner finite knowledge and power came to existence by the reflection of God's knowledge and power into the opposed nothing of ignorance and powerlessness. Thus by the reflection or *in'ikās* of the attributes of God into its opposite non-beings there appeared realities whose 'matter' is non-being and whose 'form' is the reflection.[78][Emphasis added]

As we see, after explaining his belief in Oneness of the Perfect Being, Sirhindī makes an immediate distinction between *wujūd* ("existence") and *'adam* ("non-existence"). By employing the concept of *'adam*, Sirhindī makes a distinction between the sheer Existence (i.e. the Perfect Existence) and the rest of existence. What the "rest of existence" carries from the notion of "existence" is only a "form" which is a "reflection" of the Perfect Existence's attributes, and in reality, remains "non-existence" forever. In other words, each of God's attributes (as the Only Perfect set of Attributes), has a *in'ikās* ("reflection") in its *'adam-i mutaqābila* ("opposed sheer imperfection of non-existence"). This reflection contains the only borrowed reality of the so-called "existence."

Sirhindī's creative examination of the ties between God and the world, and using the term, "Perfect Existence" (instead of Ibn 'Arabī's "Absolute Existence") remind us of Simnānī's expression, *Wujūd al-Ḥaqq* ("Real Existence/or Existence of the Real"). Both expressions (Real Existence and Perfect Existence) seem to serve one crucial purpose, which is to protect the transcendence of God. From the perspectives of Simnānī and Sirhindī, this transcendence is the missing link in Ibn 'Arabī's approach to God as *Wujūd al-Muṭlaq* ("Absolute Existence"). Sirhindī's theory of *in'ikās* ("refelections of God's attributes"), which was influenced and inspired by Simnānī's worldview, and designed as both a criticism of and an alternative approach to Ibn 'Arabī's school, was not an abruptly conceived and haphazard worldview, but rather one that was shaped gradually and systematically.

Sirhindī experienced a "mystical development" before reach-

78. Ibid.

ing his preferred theory. He explains different processes of this development on several occasions. On one of these occasions, he provides us with a summary of this gradual transition, from what he calls *tawḥīd-i wujūdi* [*waḥdat al-wujūd* (unity of existence)], to the mystical station which he regards as his ultimate mystical experience.

> I believed in the *tawḥīd-i wujūdi* [i.e. *waḥdat al-wujūd*] from the time I was a boy. My father apparently believed in the doctrine, and used to carry on spiritual exercises on *wujūdi* lines....I knew the doctrine very well, appreciated and enjoyed it. Later on, when God brought me to Shaykh Bāqībillāh, and he taught me the Naqshbandī *ṭarīqah* and attended closely to my development, the Unity of Being (*tawḥīd-i wujūdi*) was revealed to me in a short period in virtue of following the Naqshbandī *ṭarīqah*. I was completely absorbed in that experience, and the ideas associated with it began to pour in on me. There was hardly a truth that was not revealed to me. I was informed of the profoundest ideas of Shaykh Muhyi'l-Dīn Ibn 'Arabī 's philosophy and was blessed with the experience of Divine Self-illumination (*tajallī-i dhātī*) which the author of the *Fuṣūṣ* had said to be the culmination of spiritual ascent, and beyond which there was nothing, according to him, except pure non-being. I also came to know in detail the truths of that *tajallī* which the Shaykh had claimed to be a privilege of the 'Seal of Saints.' I was so much engrossed in the *tawḥīd* and intoxicated with it that in one of my letters to the Khwājah I wrote the following two couplets which were the product of sheer intoxication (*sukr*).
>
> This Shari'ah is, alas, the way of the blind.
> Our way is the way of infidels and fire-worshipers.
> Infidelity and faith are the lock and the face of that beauty
> In our way infidelity and faith are one.
> This condition prolonged to months and years.[79]

Simnānī's principal work, *al-'Urwah*, which seems to describe the ideas of a theologian rather than a mystic, contains a harsh criticism of *waḥdat al-wujūd.* On the other hand, in his *Diwān*, he reveals a similar experience to that of Sirhindī. Simnānī even employs

79. M. 'Abdul Ḥaq Ansārī, "The Life and Mission of Shaykh Aḥmad Sirhindī," *Islamic Culture* LLX, no.2 (1985): 97-98.

similar expressions used by Ibn 'Arabī's followers, in expressing the unity of existence, such as *jām-i waḥdat* ("cup of unity"). He also employs expressions to refer to the state of *sukr* (mystical intoxication).

Time has come in which we become drunkards in the garden of soul...
We drink the wine of His remembrance (*bāda-yi dhikrash*) from the cup-bearer's hand (*kaf-i sāqī*)
We become free from the lowly world and the passing of time
We break the head of repentance with the stone of jealousy (*sang-i ghayrat*)
We drink from the cup of unity (*jām-i waḥdat*) and become the head of libertines (*sarwar-i rindān*)...
Take one step in the realm of Oneness (*'ālam-i tawḥīd*) bravely
Until when do we have to wander, like a caliper with two heads?[80]

Simnānī also utilizes expressions such as "*daryā-yi waḥdat*" (sea of unity) and *baḥr-i tawḥīd* (sea of Oneness).

If you are not lost in the sea of unity
That is because there is no pearl of "meaning" (*durr-i ma'nā*) in your belly
If you become annihilated (*fānī shawī*) in the sea of Oneness
You will see clearly that there are no "why" and "how" there.[81]

Sirhindī further explains his gradual move from the stage of *waḥdat-i wujūdi* (*waḥdat al-wujūd*) to the next stage, which he calls the stage of *ẓillīyāt* ("reflections").

After a period, I had a new vision of things which dominated my consciousness. But I hesitated at first to revise my attitude towards *tawḥīd* (*wujūdi*) in deference to, rather than in disregard for, that doctrine. I remained in a stage of indecision for a long time. At last, I was induced to renounce that doctrine. I was shown that *tawḥīd* (*wujūdi*) was a lower stage, and was asked to move to the stage of *zillīyāt* [i.e. the vision that things are the shadows of God and different from Him]. But I did not like to move from that stage since many Ṣūfīs were stationed there. But I had no choice. I was brought to the stage of *zillīyāt* where

80. Simnānī, *Dīwān*, 24.
81. Simnānī, *Chihil Majlis*, 88.

I realized that I and the world were shadows.[82]

The vision of "sheer difference" between the world and God which serve to save God's transcendence, might be also regarded as Sirhindī's preference of the aspect of *tanzīh* ("God's peerlessness") over *tashbīh* ("God's similarity"); the preference which was also shown in Simnānī's writings.

In Simnānī's view, as it was partially mentioned above, in order to reach his particular vision of God's *tanzīh*, one needs to develop the mystical medium of *laṭīfah* ("the subtle mystical receptacle"). The concept of *laṭīfah*, with its different types and categories, is perhaps one of the most dominant concepts throughout Simnānī's works more than any other *Kubrawī* mystic.

As Elias explains: "The term *laṭifa* (plural *laṭā'if*) has been variously translated as "spiritual substance," "mystical subtleties," "subtle centers of perception," "centers subtils," "organs subtils."[83] He also suggests that: "In the context of Simnānī's thought, the most accurate translation is "subtle substance," identical with the

---

82. Anṣārī, "The Life of Sirhindī," 98. See also Fazlur Raḥmān, "Islamic Thought in the Indo-pakistan Subcontinent and the Middle East, *Journal of Near Eastern Studies* 32, no. ½ (Jan.-Apr. 1973):194-200. In this article, Fazlur Raḥmān defines the *'adamī* side of Sirhindī's parallel methodology as "evil or *sharr*," and in order to distinguish between the views of Ibn 'Arabī and Sirhindī, states as follows: "According to Ibn 'Arabī, God, in his absolute unity, transcends all categories of thought and being. This absolute, however, undergoes certain stages of descent (*tanzzulāt*)...According to Sirhindī who accepts the framework of this theory of descent, when the absolute becomes self-conscious and the contents of divine consciousness become multiple, a very basic development takes place. Parallel and in opposition to these contents-the attributes of God-non-beings arise. The attributes represent pure being and goodness; these non-beings represent pure negation of being and negation of goodness. When the attributes of God, cast their reflections, or rather, their shadows (*ẓilāl*), they cast them not on the being of God, but on these non-being (*'adam*). This constitutes the generation of the world. Also, parallel to the undifferentiated consciousness of God arises the undifferentiated non-being (*'adam maḥḍ*) or evil or (*sharr*), and parallel to the differentiated or particular attributes arise particular evils or non-beings. The attributes of God are not, therefore, the "essences of contingents" (*māhīyatāt-i mumkināt*) as Ibn 'Arabī believes, these latter are rather the non-beings on which the attributes of God cast their shadows. The world is, therefore, originally rooted in non-being. But the reflections or shadows of God that have been cast on it create a struggle between good and evil."

83. Elias, *The Throne Carrier of God*, 157.

German "Feinstoff."[84]

The founder of the Kubrawī order, Najm al-Dīn Kubrā refers to the *qalb* ("heart") as *laṭīfah* because, as he elaborates, "...it is [constantly] transformed (*tataqallabu*) from one state to another [and it is] like water which its color changes with the [change of the color of its] container."[85] He also refers to the seminal place of this *laṭīfah* (i.e., heart) as the transforming medium of "existence and [its] meaning" (*...annahu qalbu'l-wujūd wa'l-ma'ānī*).[86] Kubrā seems to allude to the function of the heart as the *laṭīfah* into which the entities of existence are reflected in the same way that forms are reflected in the mirror and lucid water.[87] Due to this function he refers to the [Perfect Man's] heart as "the light in the heart...of existence" (*nūrun fī qalb... al-wujūd*).[88] As seen above, Kubrā makes a correlation between *laṭīfah*, *lawn* ("color"), and *nūr* ("light"). Generally speaking, it seems that in Kubrawī understanding, *laṭīfah* is considered as the central subtle receptacle of mystical experiences, in which these experiences are constantly reflected, examined, and then visualized and interpreted by the mystic in varieties of colors and lights. The reciprocation between *laṭīfah*, colors and lights was later developed in a systematic manner by his cardinal followers such as Simnānī.

Simnānī refers to this concept in detail, in almost all of his Persian writings. Each of these subtle substances (*laṭā'if*) has an affinity with one of the categorical types of "lights."[89]

Through the reciprocation between a particular *laṭīfah* and its specific and designated light (*nūr*), the mystic is provided with a particular "vision."[90] In Simnānī's view, even some of the spiritual acts (such as *wuḍū'* "ablution" and *dhikr* "recollection of God's Names") correspond to their specific *anwār* ("lights").[91] Mystical visions provided by these lights, serve as "mediums," through

---

84. Ibid.

85. *Fawā'ih*, 132.

86. See ibid.

87. See ibid., 133.

88. Ibid.

89. See Elias, "A Kubrawī Treatise on Mystical Visions." See also his *Throne Carrier of God*, 157-160.

90. See ibid. Also see Marcia K. Hermansen, "Shāh Walī Allāh's Theory of Subtle Spiritual Centers (*Laṭā'if*): A Sufi Model of Personhood and Self-Transformation," *Journal of Near Eastern Studies* 47, no. 1 (1998):1-25.

91. See ibid., 69.

which the reality of fondness and ties between God and man as well as God and the world, and also the reality of *ashyā'* ("entities"), are unveiled to the mystics. Simnānī refers to these lights as *anwār al-qudsiyya* ("sacred lights"), and explains their characteristics as follows:

> Know O friend, that God has illuminated your heart with "sacred lights" (*anwār al-qudsiyya*), which is what the light of things is called in actuality so that it may know itself and know them. It can see and know all things with it. This absolute light (*nūr-i Muṭlaq*) is a particular attribute of God.[92]

In another occasion, Najm al-Dīn Kubrā also emphasized the concept of *laṭīfah* and its relationship with light. He refers to this subtle mystical receptacle as the essential element in his approach to the mystical path (*ṭarīqah*):

> Our path (*tariquna*) is the path of alchemy, so the only way is to bring out (*istikhrāj*) the subtle substance of light (*al-laṭīfah al-nūrāniyya*).[93]

Among well-known mystics of Islam who have discussed the concept of *laṭīfah*, is Abū Ḥāmid Ghazālī (d. 505/1111) who refers to it as "the essential reality of the human being and…the possessor of divine knowledge."[94] For Ḥallāj (309/992), "the *laṭā'if* are substances which are distinct entities attached in some manner to the physical body…Upon death *laṭā'if* survive in individual human beings and transform them into their resurrection bodies."[95] This receptacle of mystical experience was also noted and explained by some of the members of Ibn 'Arabī's school.[96] 'Abd al-Razzāq Kāshānī describes *laṭīfah* as "a subtle allusion which its meaning cannot be expressed adequately in writing."[97] He also explains the meaning of *al-laṭīfah al-insāniyyah* ("subtle human substance"[98]).

> …it is the rational soul, called [by mystics] the heart, and in fact it causes the spirit to descend to a rank close to that of the soul.

92. Ibid., 71.
93. Kubrā, *Fawā'iḥ*, 5.
94. Elias, *The Throne Carrier of God*, 159.
95. Ibid., 158-9.
96. See ibid.
97. Ibid., 160.
98. See ibid.

> It is related to soul in one form and to spirit in another. The first form is called breast and the second heart.[99]

In Simnānī's understanding, the *laṭīfah* is "a subtle substance, non-corporeal in form and imperceptible to the natural causes. As such, one variety of these subtle substances belongs to the spiritual realm and constitutes an integral part of the mystical body."[100] This "medium" or spiritual receptacle is the essential faculty through which the mystic experiences existence, or God's theophanies.

Although *laṭīfah* does not seem to appear as an essential term in Ibn 'Arabī's list of favorite expressions, he has used it to elaborate on the Perfect Man's standing in his relation to the two aspects of *tashbīh* ("Absolute's similarity") and *tanzīh* ("Absolute's peerlessness"). Referring to these two aspects, Ibn 'Arabī states as follows:

> The perfect servant stands between these two relationships...In respect of his reality and subtle substance (*laṭīfa*), man stands opposite God through the relationship of incomparability. And through that very face he stands opposite God in respect of the Divine Descent to those attributes which suggest similarity; this is the other relationship.[101]

In other words, Ibn 'Arabī seems to view the concept of *laṭīfah* as the medium through which the Perfect Man comprehends his "reality" as the one who stands between the two intertwined ties with the Absolute; i.e., *tashbīh* and *tanzīh* (He/not He). Therefore, we might mention that from Shaykh al-Akbar's standpoint, the realization of the Absolute's attributes of *jamāl* and *jalāl* becomes attainable through this medium (*laṭīfah*). As mentioned above, Simnānī also sees the vital necessity of an advanced *laṭīfah* for realization of God's *tanzīh*.

Similar to Ibn 'Arabī's above approach to this concept in its relation to both *tashbīh* and *tanzīh*, is also the well-known Kubrawī figure Sayyid 'Alī Hamadānī's view of *laṭīfah*. Hamadānī connects the two concepts of *'ilm* and *laṭīfah* and mentions an elevated type of *laṭīfah* (i.e., *'ilm al-laṭīfah al-khafiyyah* or knowledge of the concealed mystical resceptacle) which "belongs to [or provides] the se-

99. Ibid.
100. Ibid.
101. Chittick, *The Sufi Path of Knowledg*, 277-278.

crets of *al-maḥabbah wa'l-tafrīd*"[102] ("love and singleness"). This type of *laṭīfah*, as he seems to suggest, "seeks assistance from the [realm] of Unseen of all Unseen (*ghayb al-ghuyūb*)."[103] through both attributes of *jamāliyyah* and *jalāliyyah* (related to the Absolute's Beauty and Majesty), which assists the mystic in refraining from *ithnainiyyah* ("duality').[104] In other words, this *laṭīfah* provides the mystic with the realization of both aspects of the Absolute's *tashbīh* and *tanzīh* which grants him the general knowledge (*'ilmun ijmālī*[105]) of *waḥdah* ("Unity").

In Simnānī's view, *laṭīfah* is also the organ or receptacle which provides the mystic with the experience of the fact that the most elevated outcome of the most advanced mystical experiences is to be an attestant to God's attributes and acts, and therefore witnessing (*shuhūd*) God's Oneness "*not* being *part* of that Oneness or being contained in It" (which Simnānī considers to be the meaning and outcome of Ibn 'Arabī's idea of *waḥdat al-wujūd*). In other words, in Simnānī's worldview, a more advanced and unveiled *laṭīfah* with a clearer "vision" (which defines the limit of a mystical experience) leads to a more advanced mystic, a *shāhid* ("witness") to God's attributes and acts (*ṣifāt* and *af'āl*) who comes to the realization of God's Oneness through experiencing *waḥdat al-shuhūd*.

But Aḥmad Sirhindī, in his gradual conversion from *waḥdat al-wujūd* to *ẓillīyāt* (the idea that entities are *shadows* "i.e, *attributes and acts*" of God and different from Him, i.e., *Oneness of witnessing*), goes further and considers another development from this stage (*ẓillīyāt*) to the stage which he calls *'abdiyyāt* ("servanthood"). In describing this development, Sirhindī states as follows:

> I wished I were not moved again from that stage of (*zillīyāt*) because it had an affinity with *waḥdat al-wujūd* which was still a symbol of perfection for me. But it happened that God, by a pure act of grace and love carried me beyond that stage and brought me to the stage of *'abdiyyāt* [i.e., the vision that man is nothing more than a servant of God, that things merely are His creation and that He is absolutely other and different from the

102. Hamadānī, *Asrār al-Nuqṭah*, 81.

103. Ibid.

104. See ibid.

105. See ibid. Hamadanī uses this expression in his description of the above mentioned *laṭīfah* when he states: "*'ilmu'l laṭīfah al-khafiyyah wa huwa 'ilmun ijmālī yata'allaq bi asrār al-maḥabbah wa'l-tafrīd.*"

> world]. At that time I realized the greatness of that stage and scanned its lofty heights. I regretted my earlier experiences, turned to God and begged for His mercy. Had I not been guided in this manner and shown the greatness of one stage after the other, I would have remained at the stage of *tawḥīd* (*wujūdi*) because in my view there was no grace higher than that. God alone establishes the truth and shows the way.[106]

Although Sirhindī mentioned his "affinity" with the idea of *waḥdat al-wujūd,* he clearly criticized the followers of *waḥdat al-wujūd,* almost with the same style and harshness as Simnānī. In his *Maktūbāt*, he expresses his views regarding the followers of this idea.

> Those who subscribed to *waḥdat al-wujūd* cared little for the *Shari'ah*. They believed that the goal of *Shari'ah* was to attain knowledge; hence if any one realized the truth of *waḥdat al-wujūd,* he did not have to perform the duties of the *Shar'*. Some of them disparaged *ṣalāh* because it differentiated between God and the servant; others equated resurrection with the Sufi experience of *fanā'* (annihilation) and denied judgement and punishment. Some even loved to gaze at beautiful faces and hear sweet voices, because they were the manifestation of the Eternal Beauty.[107]

Sirhindī appears to be very persistent in condemning what he declared to be different *bid'ah* or religious innovations of his time. On several occasions in his writings, Sirhindī explains the responsibility which he felt in denouncing those innovations. Besides Sirhindī's personal account of mystical experience, which convinced him to discard the stage of *waḥdat al-wujūd* and encouraged him to move to the next stage, one of the main reasons for his departure might be his personal encounter with what he referred to as *bid'ah*, practiced by the followers of *waḥdat al-wujūd.* In this regard, he openly criticizes the *'ulamā'* ("official religious figures") of his time, particularly those who were stationed in court, because of their support of or lack of attention to these innovations. On one of these occasions, while mentioning an example of these *bid'ah*, by one of the believers in *waḥdat al-wujūd,* Sirhindī condemns the

106. Anṣārī, "The Life of Sirhindī," 98.
107. Ibid., 103.

negligence of the *'ulamā'* of his time in dealing with religious innovations (*bid'ah*).

> The *'ulama'* of our times have become the preachers of *bid'ah* and destroyers of the *Sunnah.* No one has the courage to speak against *bid'ah* and revive the *Sunnah.* Most of the *'ulamā'* lead people to *bid'ah*, and proved that they are commended and desirable. The *'ulama'* did not stop at *bid'ah*, they moved to change the very face of religion. One *'Ālim* for instance, who was the highest authority on religion in the country, issued a *fatwā'* saying that the Hajj was no longer incumbent as the journey to *Makkah* was unsafe. Other *'ulamā'* at Lahore ruled that charging interest was legal; still others came out with the verdict that prostration before the king for honour was quite proper. One "crown of the gnostics" (*tāj al-'arifīn*), using his insight into *waḥdat al-wujūd,* supported this verdict on the ground that "the king was one with God, nothing less." The cousin of another gnostic ruled that shaving one's beard was perfectly in order because the inhabitants of Paradise were said to be beardless youths.[108]

As we see above, similar to Simnānī, Sirhindī was also vigilant about the compatability of every act with *Sharī'ah.* Simnānī and Sirhindī viewed *waḥdat al-wujūd* as an idea, intertwined with religious deviations such as *ḥulūl* and *ittiḥād.* Sirhindī's criticism of one of the followers of *waḥdat al-wujūd*, in the matter of *ittiḥād* or union between God and king, in the above quotation, is an example of this approach. In one of the letters to his deputy Aḥmad Barkī,[109] in his *Maktūbāt*, Sirhindī stresses the duty of religious people of his time to safeguard *Sharī'ah* and stand firm against innovations:

> Try to spread the knowledge of the *Sharī'ah* and the rules of *fiqh* at place where ignorance prevails and *bid'ah* rules, and do it with the same concern and love which, by the grace of God, you have for your friends...Prepare yourself for the task and discharge the duty of enjoining good and forbidding evil which you have towards the people there, and do it only for the

108. Ibid., 105.
109. See ibid., 106.

pleasure of God.[110]

Although written in a different period and under different historical and social circumstances, in defining the concept of *bid'ah* and focusing on the role of *Sharī'ah*, Sirhindī's *Maktūbāt* projects interesting similarities with Simnānī's style of writing, especially in his *al-'Urwah*. For example, as mentioned above, Sirhindī, by pointing to the manifestations of *kufr* (disbelief), *ittiḥād* (unificationism) and *ḥulūl* (incarnationism), states that "the world is drowned in the sea of *bid'ah* and delightes in its black acts."[111] In a similar style, Simnānī, in describing those who believe in *ittiḥād* and *ḥulūl*, considered them among the people of *kufr* and referred to them as those who "claim the Divinity for themselves and their claim [in the level of going astray] goes beyond [i.e., is worse than] what Christians and Jews believe."[112] Simnānī continues by stating "therefore, I consider them the Pharaoh of [my] time...and...they have become bewildered and drowned in the abyss of *kufr* and sea of disbelief/misguidance (*zandaqa*)."[113]

As seen above, Sirhindī, passing through different mystical experiences, did not remain in the stage of *zillīyāt* ("shadowy beings"). He moved to the third (and final) stage (i.e., *'abdiyyāt* or "servanthood"), which he described as the purest and most elevated among the three. These three stages are also referred to as "union" (*jam'*) rather than non-difference (*jam' al-jam'*), separation after union (*farq ba'd al-jam'*), and absolute difference, respectively."[114]

---

110. Ibid. See also Fazlur Raḥmān, *Selected Letters of Sirhindī* (Karāchī: Iqbāl Academy, 1968).

111. Ibid., 105.

112. Simnānī, *al-'Urwah*, 274.

113. Ibid., 274-275.

114. Anṣārī, "The Life of Sirhindī," 99. See also 'Abdul Ḥaq Ansārī, "Shāh Walīy Allāh Attempts to Revise Waḥdat al-Wujūd," *Arabica* 35, no. 2 (1988):197-213. The author elaborates on the differences between the worldviews of Sirhindī and Ibn 'Arabī as follows: "Sirhindī said the mystical experience has three levels: one is the level of pure union (*jam'*) which in modern terminology called unitive experience; next is the experience of separation after union (*farq ba'd al-jam'*) in which mystic is one with God in one sense, and different from him in another. The final stage of experience is that when the feeling of oneness or union completely disappears and God is perceived as transcending the world absolutely. Sirhindī says that some Sufis like Al-Ḥallāj...remained at the first stage till the end of their life; others moved to the second stage, but stayed on there; only few rose up to the third stage. He claims that Ibnul 'Arabī stayed on the second stage, and could not

The "absolute difference," (between God and His *'abd* "worshipper," or the stage of *māwarā'iyyat*) is, perhaps, the most important indication or characteristic of Sirhindī's stage of *'abdiyyāt* or servanthood. This stage reveals the most uncluttered experience of Sirhindī in touching upon the absolute *tanzīh* ("God's peerlessness").

> Sirhindī mentions these stages time and again...He wants first to bring home to the mystics of his day, most of whom were moving at the first stage or stationed at the second, that there is a higher stage of mystic experience at which one stops seeing that man is one with God, or that the world and God are One Being, and realizes instead that God is completely different and absolutely other, that the world has nothing in common with God, and that man is simply a creature and a servant.[115]

Sirhindī's inspirer, Simnānī, also seems to prefer the stage of servanthood as the purest stage of mystical experience. The reason for this preference, besides his possible mystical experience, similar to that of Sirhindī, may have been to underline the crucial importance of the non-delimited and absolute *tanzīh* of God. One of his clarifying approaches in this regard appears in chapter four of *al-'Urwah*, dedicated to the concept of *tanzīh-i wājib al-wujūd* ("incomparability of the Necessary Existence"). In this chapter, Simnānī explains the beliefs and worldviews of different *firāq* ("groups") along with his arguments for their *ibṭāl* ("discrediting").

In Simnānī's approach, this set of beliefs, such as *ittiḥād* ("union with God"), *ḥulūl* ("incarnationism"), *tanāsukh* ("transmigration"), *ibāḥa* ("antinomianism"), besides their differences, have one thing in common. This one common factor among them, Simnānī believes, is the fact that they all stand against the total *tanzīh* (God's peerlessness) in different respects.[116]

While refuting these beliefs, Simnānī explains the ideas of a *jamā'at* ("group of people") who are safeguarded from misguidance and criticism. Simnānī refers to this group as *ṭālibān-i kamāl-i*

---

separate the Divine from non-Divine, though he upheld a kind of transcendence for God (*tanzīh*), he could not affirm his absolute otherness. For himself, Sirhindī claimed the experience of God's absolute transcendence (*māwarā'iyyat*), and on the basis of that experience, developed his theosophy of *waḥdat al-shuhūd*."

115. Ibid.

116. See Simnānī, *al-'Urwah*, 273.

tawḥīd wa tanzīh-i Ḥaqq-i Ḥamīd-i Majīd ("seekers of the perfect [absolute] Oneness and incomparability of the Praiseworthy [and] Exalted Real"), and approves their worldviews. Simnānī unveils his reasons for favoring this group by describing the important aspects of their thought:

> Those who prove the existence by [its] necessity (*wujūb*), and they prove the Unity (*waḥdāniyyat*), purification of His Essence (*Dhāt*) and Attributes by negation of [His] imperfection and flaws, and they do confess to their servanthood (*'ubūdiyyat*), and they believe in [His] Sovereignty/Lordship (*khudāwandī*) and Divinity (*ulūhiyyat*) Who is the Creator of every thing, and His Presence is everyone's Deity, and they [*ṭālibān-i kamāl-i tawḥīd...*] make endeavor for His obedience and are afraid of His punishment, while they love Him more than any one else, and they have hope for His Countenance.[117]

As seen above, Simnānī differentiates between the groups who face his major criticism and the "true seekers" whose crucial outstanding characteristics are their dedication to*'ubūdiyyat* ("God's servanthood") and their elevated understanding of God's *tanzīh*, and therefore His *tawḥīd* ("Oneness").

At the end of the chapter, Simnānī returns to the last group among his list of refuted groups, meaning *ibāḥī* or *mubāḥī*. Before mentioning Simnānī's meaningful approach to this group, we should first observe the way he recounts the characteristics of their beliefs. *Mubāḥī,* Simnānī tells us, is a name for the "one who brings together the ideas of all the other three groups (i.e., those who believe in *ittiḥād, ḥulūl,* and *tanāsukh*)."[118] Based on Simnānī's explanation, the believer in *ibāḥa* (i.e, *mubāḥī* or *ibāḥī*) is the most careless person regarding *Sharī'ah*, and therefore, *ibāhīs* are considered to be the worse among four rejected groups on Simnani's list. He believes that they are "the most abominable and ignorant among creatures, and his [i.e., *mubāḥī*'s] idea is the most abominable among beliefs, because he [i.e., *mubāḥī*] has become the servant of [his] desire and his [evil] soul."[119]

Simnānī's description of *mubāḥī*'s beliefs regarding *Sharī'ah* continues by stating that "he is the enemy of the affairs of *Sharī'ah*,

117. See ibid.
118. Ibid., 275-276.
119. Ibid., 276.

and denies [the existence and/or teachings of] the prophets, peace be upon them, and he desires the removal of religious verdicts (*aḥkām*) among people."[120] Simnānī adds to the *mubāḥī*'s characteristics that "they have no faith in [God's] punishment and they provide meaningless interpretations for [Qur'ānic] verses and *aḥadīth* which are based on their own cravings (*hawā*), and they take all forbidden matters (*ḥarām*) as permitted (*ḥalāl*)....and they have become servants of [their] stomach and desire, and the [Qur'ānic] verse of 'have you seen the one who has taken his desire as his deity' fits their situation...."[121]

Among well-known Sufi masters, Shaykh 'Abd al-Qādir Gīlānī (d. 561/1165), mentions *ibāḥīyya* as one of the eleven groups among Sufis who practiced innovations in *Sharī'ah*, and therefore went astray. Although his description of *ibāḥīyya* is shorter than Simnānī's account, it appears to be very similar. He states that the "*Ibāḥīyya* has no belief in *amr bi'l ma'rūf* ("commanding for good deeds") and they consider the religiously forbidden matters (such as *zinā* "adultery") as permitted acts."[122]

After finishing his account of the *mubāḥīs*, Simnānī ends the chapter of *al-'Urwah* with a short paragraph on the characteristics of "those who believe in the *Wujūd-i Muṭlaq* ("Absolute Existence") and identify the Absolute Existence with the Essence of God."[123] Although Simnānī does not refer to this group (*jamā'ah*) as members of Ibn 'Arabī's school or those who believe in the unity of existence (*waḥdat al-wujūd*), as mentioned earlier, "the identification of God with the Absolute Being has a definite place in Ibn 'Arabī's worldview."[124]

Simnānī states that this group (i.e., believers in the Absolute Existence) is also considered by him as *mubāḥīs*, and it is *wājib* (religoulsy mandatory) [for those who believe in *Sharī'ah*] to shun them (*tabarrā*).[125] He also refers to them as worse than *dahrī wa ṭabi'ī* ("materialists and atheists") and writes, "Although this group does not manifest some of the *mubāḥī* characteristics, it is possible to

120. Ibid.

121. Ibid.

122. 'Abd al-Qādir Gilānī, *Sirr al-Asrār*, trans. into Persian, Muslim Zāmānī and Karīm Zamānī (Tehran: Nashr-i Nay, 1385/2006), 144.

123. Simnānī, *al-'Urwah*, 276.

124. Landolt, "Simnānī on Waḥdat al-Wujūd," 100.

125. See Simnānī, *al-'Urwah*, 276.

guide the atheists and materialists [in the direction of *Sharī'ah*], but this *ṭā'īfah* ("group") has no capability for being guided."[126] This lack of capability, as Simnānī states, is "because the mirror of their capabilities (*qābilīyyat*) [for accepting guidance] is far away from [their] natural predisposition (*isti'dād*)."[127] Then, Simnānī ends his description of their beliefs by stating that "God guides them by His Power or destroys them in the Muslims' land by His Wrath and Glory."[128]

As we have seen above, without mentioning Ibn 'Arabī or his followers, Simnānī seems to identify him and his school with the group of *mubāḥīs.* Here again, Simnānī understands Ibn 'Arabī's expression of *Wujūd al-Muṭlaq* ("Absolute Existence") as God Himself, i.e, considering manifestations of the Absolute as the same as His Existence (or "His Essence" [*Dhāt*] in the above quotation from Simnānī).

Defending Shaykh al-Akbar: Shaykh Makkī on ittiḥād and ḥulūl

One of the commentators of Ibn 'Arabī's works, Abul Fatḥ Muḥammad ibn Muẓaffar al-Dīn Muḥammad ibn Hamīd al-Dīn ibn 'Abdullāh, known as Shaykh al-Makkī (d.926/1519), explains a set of ideas similar to what Simnānī described above. He also explains the differences between the worldviews of Ibn 'Arabī and others.

In the second *faṣl* (section) of his concise, but important commentary, *al-Jānib al-Gharbī fī Ḥall-i Mushkilāt-i Muḥiyaddīn Ibn 'Arabī* ("the Western Side in Solving the Difficulties of Shaykh Muḥyiddīn Ibn 'Arabī's [Worldview]")," Shaykh Makkī explains the ideas of *wujūdiya* (("those whose ideas focus on the concept of existence"). He divides *wujūdiya* into two branches of *mulḥidīn* ("apostates") and *muwaḥḥidīn* ("unitarians/believers in *tawḥīd* or "Oneness of God").[129]

Shaykh Makkī then distinguishes between the ideas of the two branches. First, he mentions the ideas of *mulḥidīn* ("apostates")

126. Ibid.

127. Ibid.

128. Ibid., 276-277.

129. See Shaykh Makkī, *al-Jānib al-Gharbī fī Ḥall-i Mushkilāt-i Shakh Muḥyiddīn Ibn 'Arabī*, ed. Najīb Mayīl Heravī (Tehran: Instishārāt-i Mowlā, 1364/1985), 122-200.

whom he also calls *ṭā'yifa-yi khabītha* ("the wicked group"):[130] "They believe that God Almighty is not an independent being of the world of spirits and bodies (*'ālam-i arwāḥ wa ajsām*), but He is the entire world....therefore the world is Allāh and Allāh is the world. There is nothing besides the world which is to be called Allāh, but all that *is*, is this world and nothing else."[131]

Shaykh Makkī considers the above mentioned belief of *mulḥidīn* to be a "*kufr-i ṣarīḥ* ("clear blasphemy")."[132] He also adds that "there is no such idea in Ibn 'Arabī's *Futūḥāt,* and Shaykh al-Akbar, in his *Risālat al-Ma'rifah* clearly condemns this idea and states that this group (*ṭā'yifah*) has gone astray from the path of verification (*taḥqīq*), therefore they have said that...the world is Allāh."[133]

He then attempts to identify Ibn 'Arabī's concept of the *Wujūd al-Muṭlaq* ("Absolute Existence") with the second branch among the *wujūdiya* (i.e., *muwaḥḥidīn* or unitarians). Shaykh Makkī states that he is concerned that a group of people whom he calls the *mu'taqidān-i nādān* ("ignorant believers") and *munkirān-i bāḥirmān* ("deprived disbelievers"),"[134] might identify Ibn 'Arabī's approach to the Absolute Existence with the first branch of *wujūdiya* (i.e, *mulḥidīn* or apostates). He then quotes from Ibn 'Arabī's *Futūḥāt al-Makkīyyah.* Shaykh Makkī believes that this and other similar words of Shaykh al-Akbar have caused his critics to misunderstand his views on the concept of Absolute Existence. Ibn 'Arabī' states:

> The world in its totality exists because of Him, and He is the Self-Existent, His Existence has no beginning, and His Subsistence has no end, but He is the Absolute Existence.[135]

After listing the criticisms provided by Ibn 'Arabi's critics, Shaykh Makkī defends Shaykh al-Akbar by responding to them in detail. Here, we briefly review a few of his remarks. Shaykh Makkī explains that Ibn 'Arabī's critics understood this expression (i.e., Absolute Existence) to mean that God is one of the "secondary in-

130. See ibid., 122.
131. Ibid., 122-123.
132. Ibid., 123.
133. Ibid.
134. See ibid., 125.
135. Ibid., 126.

telligibles" or *ma'qūlāt-i thānia.*[136] As he explains, this misunderstanding caused his critics to conclude that it is impossible for a secondary intelligible to exist (or to be available) in *khārij* ("the outside world"), unless through or by another *maẓhar* ("manifested existent or a place/locus of manifestation") at all times. Therefore, they have considered Ibn 'Arabī's concept of the Absolute Existence, as a *kullī-yi ṭabi'ī* ("natural universal") and also as *amr-i i'tibārī* ("a fictitious/conceptual matter"), and thus, with no possibility of being self-existent.[137]

In order to defend Ibn 'Arabī against such criticism, Shaykh Makkī quotes from chapter six of the *Futūḥāt* where Ibn 'Arabī

136. See ibid. For futher information on the concept of "intelligibles," see, for example, the following article: Sadra Islamic Philosophy Research Institite, Iran, "Epistemology," "http://www.mullasadra.org/new_site/English/Mullasadra/Epistemology.htm" (1 March 2008), where the concept of intelligibles (*ma 'qūlāt*) and its different types have been explained as follows: "Intellectual perception means the presence of the universal form of any intelligible before the mind (and wisdom). 'Intelligible,' which is what man's mind and soul perceive universally (abstractly and free from any relation) is divided into three groups: 'primary intelligibles,' secondary philosophical intelligibles,' and 'secondary logical intelligibles.' Primary intelligibles consists of those universal principles and known facts which are abstracted and inferred from external objects and phenomena, such as the principles of natural sciences, physics, chemistry, and the like. Aristotelian intelligibles are of this type. Primary intelligibles are those universal forms and issues that man abstracts from particulars, such as individuals and objects. When studying these intelligibles and universal concepts, we sometimes encounter certain common universal issues among them. For example, they are either a cause or an effect; either one or multiple; either potential or actual. Moreover, they might consist of those universal attributes that qualify the objects out of the mind. Such secondary universals are called secondary philosophical intelligibles. There are also some other secondary intelligibles whose receptacles of qualification is the mind, such as universal abstraction and being particular, which are called secondary logical intelligibles. There is a linear relation or connection among these perceptions, including sense and intellectual perceptions, and its degree could be assimilated to the degrees of water temperature. The degrees of this line are different from the fixed degrees on ruler, and, in fact, they represent a kind of fluctuation in mental and philosophical acts that indicates the soul's descent and ascent. Such intelligibles have been explained and demonstrated in a number of philosophical books." See also Michael M. Marmura, "Avicenna's Psychological Proof of Prophecy," *Journal of Near Eastern Studies* 22, no. 1 (1963):49-56, and Zailan Morris, *Revelation, Intellectual Intuition, and Reason in th Philosophy of Mullā Ṣadrā: An Analysis of the al-Ḥikmat al-'Arshiyyah* (AnnArbor: Routledge/Curzon, 2003), 40-42.

137. See ibid.

states that God as the Absolute Existence is neither a *ma'lūl* ("an effect") nor an *'illat* ("cause"), but He is the Self-Existent.[138]

Shaykh Makkī also refers to the second chapter of the *Futūḥāt*, where Shaykh al-Akbar confirms that "God is Self-Existent and not *muqayyad* ("limited") by something else, and He is neither an effect nor a cause for something else, but He is the Creator of the effects and causes, and He is the Eternal Sacred King, and the world exists because of Him, and not due to its [own] essence, and [the world] is limited by His Existence."[139]

Shaykh Makkī then concludes that there is a *farq-i 'aẓīm* ("huge difference") between Ibn 'Arabī's words which refer to God as the Absolute Existence, and the similar words of *mulḥidīn* (apostates) among *wujūdiya*.[140] This "huge difference," as he explains, is the fact that in Ibn 'Arabī's wordview, the Absolute Existence (God) is not an *'illat* but *mulḥidīn* ("apostates") proposed that the Absolute Existence is the *wujūd-i 'āmm* ("common existence") and therefore, a *ma'qul-i thāni* ("secondary intelligible").[141] Shaykh Makkī refers to the first approach (i.e., that of Ibn 'Arabī and his followers), as *imān-i ṣarīḥ* ("clear faith") and calls the second (i.e., the idea of *mulḥidīn), kufr-i ṣarīḥ* ("clear disbelief").[142]

Gisūdirāz: the Last Side of the Shuhūdī Triangle

The major sides of what I have termed as the "*shuhūdī* triangle," consist of Simnānī's approach to *Wujūd al-Ḥaqq* ("the Real Existence") and Sirhindī's understanding of *wujūd-i ẓillī* ("shadowy existence"). Both sought to invalidate Ibn 'Arabī's concept of *Wujūd al-Muṭlaq* ("Absolute Existence") in order to save God's transcendence. Their effort was completed with Gisūdirāz's concept of *warā'al-warā'* ("beyond the beyond") as the last side of the *shuhūdī* triangle.[143]

Sayyid Muḥammad al-Ḥusaynī Gisūdirāz (d.825/1422) of Delhi, one of the well-known critics of Ibn 'Arabī, is another prominent member of the *shuhūdī* school. As some of the contem-

---

138. See ibid., 127.
139. Ibid., 128-129.
140. See ibid., 129.
141. See ibid.
142. See ibid.
143. See Syed Shāh Khusro Ḥussainī, "Shuhūd vs. Wujūd: A Study of Gisūdirāz, "*Islamic Culture* LIX, no. 4 (1985): 325.

porary scholars have also stated, Gisūdirāz "belonged to the same mystical tradition as that of Simnānī."[144] In criticizing Ibn 'Arabī and his school, his words projects almost the same severity found in Simnānī's writings. Similar to Simnānī, Gisūdirāz focused his worldview on the concept of *tajallī* ("theophany").[145] His methodical and uninterrupted effort to underline "God's transcendence," seem to be consistent with the views of both Simnānī and Sirhindī. For example, in his approach to the well-known *ḥadīth-i qudsī* ("Divine tradition") regarding creation (i.e., "I was a hidden treasure, then I liked to be known, so I created the creation to be known"), Gisūdirāz manifests his creativity to stress upon the concept of *tanzīh*.

In his approach to this *ḥadīth* (which was also essential to Simnānī's worldview), Gisūdirāz seems to suggest that the phrase, "I liked to be known" (*faḥbabtu an 'uraf*) is possible to be understood as both passive and active voice.[146] This means that, this (*ḥadīth*) in the active voice indicates that "I created the creation in order to know myself."[147] He explains his understanding of the *ḥadīth* by making an effort to clarify that "God is in everything, with everything (but) everything is from Him and subsists through Him."[148] Then he concludes that; "He [God] Himself sees Himself and plays with Himself, NOT that He engages in something other than Himself."[149] [Emphasis added with some modifications]

The phrase 'I created the creation (*khalq*)' in the above *ḥadīth*, is changed in Gisūdirāz's version of the *ḥadīth* to "I created Muḥammad the seal of the Messengers"[150] (i.e., as the Perfect Human Being *par excellence*). Although Gisūdirāz interprets the *khalq* ("creation") in the above *ḥadīth* as the Prophet Muḥammad (i.e., the kernel of all creation), on the other hand by utilizing the term *warā' al-warā'* ("beyond the beyond") as his key terminology in saving God's transcendence *in its totality*, he re-emphasizes the point that

---

144. Ibid. See also Syed Shāh Khusro Ḥussainī, *Sayyid Muḥammad al-Ḥusaynī-i Gisūdirāz (721/1321-825/1422) on Sufism* (Delhī: Idāra-yi Adabiyāt-i Delhī, 1983).

145. See ibid., 330.

146. See ibid., 332.

147. Ibid.

148. Ibid., 333.

149. Ibid.

150. Ibid., 332.

God is *beyond* any comprehension, even that of the prophets.[151]

Therefore, God, because of His absolute transcendence, is *warā'al-warā'* ("beyond the beyond"), which Gisūdirāz refers to as "looking for pulp (*maghz*) in an onion."[152]

Through his understanding of God's transcendence as "beyond the beyond," Gisūdirāz criticizes Ibn 'Arabī. "He writes that, Ibn 'Arabī pointed out God as being in all the forms and shapes because he was himself not conscious of "beyond the beyond."[153] He considers Ibn 'Arabī's approach as a view which is opposed to God's transcendence by considering a set of limitations for Him.[154] The "shapes and forms" in existence have been regarded by Gisūdirāz as "God's emanation and not God"[155] Himself. Gisūdirāz claims that, because of God's endless and everlasting *Dhāt* ("Essence"), the "stage of "beyond the beyond" can only be described as "he who knows God, becomes dumb."[156]

Therefore, we may conclude that the idea of "beyond the beyond" is the outcome of man's *ḥayrah* ("bewilderment') when faced with God's endless and incomprehensible Essence (*Dhāt*). Although Gīsūdirāz employs this notion to criticize Ibn 'Arabī, this particular stage (dumbness intertwined with *ḥayrah*) is surprisingly similar to Ibn 'Arabī's description of the stage of *ḥayrah* as one of the most eminent characteristics of man's highest stage on the spiritual Path (i.e., perfection).[157] In Ibn 'Arabī's worldview, this spiritual bewilderment is *beyond* any other elevated mystical stage and is only experienced by the very elites of the Path (or Perfect Human Beings). In order to explain this stage (*ḥayrah*), Ibn 'Arabī has referred to the well-know prophetic *ḥadīth* of *Ilāhī zidnī fīka taḥayyurā* (O God increase my bewilderment in [reflecting upon]

---

151. See bid., 334.
152. Ibid., 338.
153. Ibid., 334.
154. See ibid.
155. Ibid.
156. Ibid.
157. See *Futūḥāt* II, cited in Chittick, *The Sufi Path of Knowledge*, 296. Here, Ibn 'Arabī mentions two kinds of human beings: "...and man is divided into two kinds: One kind does not receive perfection...A second kind of man receives perfection. Within him becomes manifest the preparedness for the Divine Presence in Its perfection and for all Its names. God appointed this kind a vicegerent and clothed him in robe of bewilderment (*ḥayra*) toward Him...So man's perfection is through the preparedness for this specific self-disclosure."

Thee) on several occasions.[158] In one of his numerous discussions of the concept of *ḥayrah* and experience of profound wonder in the mystical path, Ibn 'Arabī writes in the chapter 366 of the *Futūḥāt*:

> This spiritual waystation also includes the knowing of what God has placed in the world as (a subject of) wonder – and the "wondrous" (as people ordinarily understand it) is only what breaks with their habitual perception of reality. But for those who comprehend things from the divine perspective, *everything in this habitual course of things is itself a subject of wonder* – whereas the people of habits only marvel at what departs from that habitual course.[159]

He also dedicates chapter 50 of his *Futūḥāt* to the "people of spiritual bewilderment."[160] While describing the characteristics of these wayfarers, Ibn 'Arabī explains the mystical state in which *ḥayrah* increases. In this state of overwhelming spiritual bewilderment, mystics "*witness nothing but (God), and He is the object of their witnessing.*"[161]

In his work, *Khātimah,* Gisūdirāz directs harsh criticism at Ibn 'Arabī by referring to the concept of "beyond the beyond:"

> If he (Ibn 'Arabī) were alive during my times, I would have made him conscious of "beyond-the-beyond" by taking him up (into the spiritual realm), and would have revived his belief (*imān*) and converted him into a Muslim.[162]

Gisūdirāz's harsh criticism seems to be similar to Simnānī's criticism of Ibn 'Arabī in some respects. As we have noted before, Ibn 'Arabī believed that the Absolute (or the Truth "*al-Ḥaqq*") is in reality limited by all limits.[163] He also pointed out that "to isolate the Absolute from the Limited means precisely to limit the Absolute."[164] Such observation of the Absolute which is seemingly conjoined with "limitations" was not an acceptable approach for the mystics

158. For example, see Chittick, *The Sufi Path of Knowledge*, 199 and 381.

159. James Weston Morris, *The Reflective Heart: Discovering Spiritual Intelligence in Ibn 'Arabī's Meccan Revelations* (Louisville: Fons Vitae, 2005), 180.

160. Ibid., 82.

161. Ibid.

162. Ḥussainī, "Shuhūd vs. Wujūd," 325.

163. See Landolt, "Simnānī on Waḥdat al-Wujūd," 103.

164. Ibid.

such as Simnānī, Sirhindī, and Gisūdirāz. The first and foremost attribute of the Truth for these major members of the *shuhūdī* lineage (particularly for its main figure Simnānī, whose opposition to this subject led him to replace Ibn 'Arabī's favorite expression, *Wujūd al-Muṭlaq* or the Absolute Existence, with *Wujūd al-Ḥaqq or* the Real Existence), was His limitless attributes. Therefore, one of the main reasons for these three figures to aim their criticisms at Ibn 'Arabī, was his particular approach to the concept of the Absolute Existence.

For these critics, Ibn 'Arabī's *tashbīhī* approach to the concept of the Absolute Existence, was impossible to reconcile with his other *tanzīhī* interpretations. In order to solve this ambiguity and to explain the relevance and proper place of Ibn 'Arabī's *tanzīhī* approaches (which dismantle any "limitation" of the Absolute), the concept of the Absolute Existence was later on "categorized" by some of the major advocates of his school.

Borrowing a previously utilized philosophical notion, some of the well-known Akbarian figures such as Ṣadr al-Dīn Qūnawī and 'Abdul Razzāq Kāshānī, attempted to address this problem.[165] The 11th century world-renowned Persian philosopher, Ibn Sinā (known as Avicenna in the West) had previously applied the three *i'tibārī* ("conceptual") categories of *lā-bi sharṭ-i shay'* ("absolutely unconditioned"), *bi-sharṭ-i lā* ("negatively conditioned"), and *bi-sharṭ-i shay'* ("positively conditioned") for the concept of *māhiyya* ("quiddity").[166] This conceptual triad was later applied by the Akbarians to the concept of *wujūd* ("existence").[167] Ibn

165. See ibid.

166. See ibid. 103-104.

167. See ibid. 104. For a philosophical distinction between the two concepts of *wujūd* ("existence") and *māhiyyah* ("quiddity"), see, for exmple, Ḥamīdrezā Āyatollāhī, "Principality of Existence and the Problem of Evil," *Journal of Islamic Philosophy* 2 (2006):188. He states, "When we study certain evidence of reality, like the existence of "I," the existence of "earth," the existence of the "tree," the existence of "whiteness" and so on, we realize that we have many conceptions of things like "tree," "earth," "I," "whiteness," and so on, and each of them differs from the others. But in spite of their differences they have one similarity: "all of them exist and have reality outside the mind." So we know that we have two notions of things, one of them is the notion of tree, whiteness, earth, etc., and the other is the notion of existence or reality that is connected to all of those notions. The first one, that is the thing-ness, is called "quiddity," and the second one "existence." Also see Ṣadr al-Dīn al-Shirāzī (Mullā Ṣadrā), *al-Ḥikmat al-Muta'āliyah fi'l Asfār al-'Aqliyyah al-'Arba'ah*, ed. Muḥammad Riḍā Muẓaffar (Beirut: Dār al-Iḥyā' al-

'Arabī's notion of the *Wujūd al-Muṭlaq* ("Absolute Existence") was considered by his followers as equivalent to the second category (i.e., *bi sharṭ-i lā*).[168] Therefore, they concluded that based on Ibn 'Arabī's approach, it is absolutely inconceivable to consider any limitation for the Absolute Existence. The borrowed existence (*anything* other than Him) cannot be any part of Him, but only His manifestations. Thus, He is absolutely Self-Existence and every other type of existence, in its totality, depends upon Him.

On the other hand, the worldly *wujūd* ("existence"), in the Akbarian approach, falls into the third category (*bi sharṭ-i shay'* or positively conditioned).[169] This consideration points to the "limitations of existence," due to the multiplicity of its components and their necessities, compartmentships, companionships and ties with each other.

In his *Isṭilāḥāt al-Ṣūfiyyah*, Ibn Arabi's renowned commentator and follower, Kāshānī, clarifies the relevance between the above-mentioned categories and the absolutely unconditioned Divine Unity as the Unlimited Source.[170]

> According to Kāshānī...not only is the divine Essence identical with Existence...but the absolutely unconditioned Oneness of Existence, which he calls *waḥda*, is also the "origin" (*mansha'*) of both the "negatively conditioned" or "exclusive" aspect of divine Unity (*aḥadiya* as meaning *bi-sharṭ lā*) and the "positively conditioned" or "inclusive" aspect of divine Unity (*wāḥidiya* as meaning *bi-sharṭ shay'*); that is to say of both the "exclusive" Unity of the divine Essence considered in its stage "before creation," as it were (*kāna Allāh wa-lam yakun ma'ahu shay'*) and of the "inclusive" Unity of the Essence considered together with its Names or "after" creation, as it were.[171]

Although the efforts of the prominent members of the Akbarian school such as Kāshānī and Qūnawī produced considerable and systematic clarification of Ibn 'Arabī's notion of the Absolute Exis-

---

Turāth al-'Arabī, 1981) 7:57-90, and Sari Nuseibeh, "al-'Aql al-Qudsī: Avicenna's Subjective Theory of Knowledge," *Studia Islamica* 69 (1989): 44-48.

168. See ibid.

169. See ibid.

170. See ibid.

171. Ibid., 104-105.

tence, theses interpretations seemed unacceptable to his critics such as Simnānī and Gisūdirāz.

In the case of Simnānī, as Landolt points out, his criticism of Ibn 'Arabī has to be understood as "an opposition to any sort of identification of God with any Absolute Existence whether *lā bi sharṭ* or *bi sharṭ-i lā* – a distinction, by the way, which he does not seem to make – out of his basic conviction that divine transcendence must be saved at any price."[172]

In addition to his opposition to identifying God with Absolute Existence which he refers to while introducing his alternative solution of *warā'a al-warā'* ("beyond the beyond"), Gisūdirāz uses the Akbarian usage of the Avicennian triad to criticize Ibn 'Arabī and his school.[173] Because Avicenna utilized the above-mentioned triad in the discussion of *kullī ṭabi'ī* ("natural universals"), Gisūdirāz seems to suggest that considering the Absolute Existenc as *lā-bi sharṭ-i shay'* ("absolutely unconditioned") by the Akbarians, is tantamount to referring to God as a *kullī ṭabi'ī*.[174]

As mentioned earlier, "a natural universal (*kullī ṭabi'ī*) "ex-

172. Ibid., 105.

173. See Ḥussainī, "Shuhūd vs. Wujūd," 329.

174. See ibid. For further elaboration on the concept of natural universals (*kullī ṭabi'ī*) see, for example, Nicholars Heer, "The Sufi Position with Respect to the Problem of Natural Universals," http://faculty.washington. edu/heer/universals.txt. He explains this concept as follows: "Muslim works on logic distinguishes between three kinds of universal: the natural (*al-kullī al-tabi'ī*), the logical universal (*al-kullī al-manṭiqī*), and the mental universal (*al-kullī al-'aqlī*). The difference between each of these is usually explained as follows: If one says for example, that humanity is a universal (*al-insān al-kullī*) three concepts are involved: first, the concept of humanity as it is in itself (*min ḥayth huwa huwa*), without regard to whether it is universal or particular. This is the absolute quiddity or essence (*al-māhiyah al-muṭlaqah*) unconditioned by anything (*lā bi-sharṭ*). It is known as the natural universal; second, the concept of universality, which is predicated of humanity. This is known as the logical universal; and third, the combination of these two concepts, that is humanity plus universality, or humanity insofar as universality is predicated of it. This is called the abstracted quiddity (*al-māhiyah al-mujarradah*), or the quiddity conditioned by nothing (*bi sharṭ lā*) rather than unconditioned by anything (*lā bi-sharṭ*). This is known as the mental universal. It was generally agreed that both the logical universal and the mental universal existed only in mind. What was in question was the external existence of the natural universal." Also see Jeppe Sinding Jensen, "Universlas, General Terms, and the Comparative Study of Religion," *Numen* 48, no. 3 (2001):238-266, Morris Lazerowitz, "The Existence of the Universals," *Mind*, New Series 55, no. 11 (1936): 281-288, and Joyce Engmann, "Aristotelian Universals," *Classical Philology* 73, no. 1 (1978):17-23.

ists as a part of its every particular (*juz'ī*) which exists, and a part of what exists has existence; like animality which is a part of any animal which exists."[175] Gisūdirāz views the correlation of the concept of "natural universals" with the above-mentioned Akbarian triad as a practice of negating the transcendence of God. In his *Asmār al-Asrār,* Gisūdirāz writes:

> Muhyi al-Din Ibn 'Arabī and his followers say that beyond this existence (*wujūd*) there is no other existence, on which account they have called Him "Absolute" (*Muṭlaq*) and "limited" (*muqayyad*), and have made God into something similar to a natural universal.[176]

Mullā Ṣadrā of Shīrāz (d. 1051/1641), whose thought –as mentioned earlier – was influenced by the teachings of Ibn 'Arabī and his school, built his worldview around *aṣālat al-wujūd* ("primacy of existence") instead of *aṣālat al-māhiyyah* ("primacy of quiddity"). He refutes the validity of the concept of "natural universals" in its connection with the "reality of existence." Ṣadra then refers to some of the Qur'anic verses in order to manifest the possibility of grasping some modes of this "reality" through mystical experience.

> ...the reality of existence is neither genus, nor species nor accident, since it is not a natural universal. Instead, its inclusion happens in another mode of inclusion, and no one has gnosis of it except the mystics i.e, those who are firmly grounded in mystical knowledge [3:7]. Sometimes it is interpreted as the spiritual soul [i.e., Holy Spirit], other times as that grace 'which extendeth to all things [7:156]. Sometimes [it is as the] 'reality from which entities have been created' according to the mystics. [Also, it is the] the expansion of the light of existence to the structures of contingent entitites, and the essences which are receptive to it; finally [they speak of] its descent towards the abode of inner nature.[177]

Gīsūdirāz's approach to the concept of *waḥdat al-wujūd*, has been referred to by some of contemporary scholars, as a "link"[178] which connects the ideas of Simnānī and Sirhindī in their criticism of Ibn 'Arabī and his school. Although "Naqsbandī interest in the

175. Ibid., 329-330.
176. Ibid., 330.
177. Kamāl, *Mullā Ṣadrā's Transcendent Philosophy*, 4.
178. See Ḥussainī, "Shuhūd vs. Wujūd," 339.

legacy of Ibn 'Arabi waned more or less everywhere in the post-Sirhindī period,"[179] some efforts have been made to bring about a reconciliation between the two worldviews of Ibn 'Arabī and the Mujaddīd Sirhīndī. One of most prominent efforts in this regard was undertaken by the well-known Naqshbandī Sufi master, Shāh Walī Allāh of Delhī (d. 1176/1762). He suggested that "if we leave simile and metaphor aside, this doctrine of the Mujaddid…is essentially the same as that…manifested by Ibn 'Arabī." [180]

In developing his systematic and creative worldview, Shāh Walī Allāh has utilized some of the notions of Mullā Sadrā's transcendent theosophy. Among the most notable elements, found in both Ṣadra's and Wali Allāh's philosophies, are *aṣālat al-wujūd* ("primacy of existence"), *bidāhat al-wujūd* ("self-evident nature/ un-definability of *wujūd*"), and the function of *wujūd al-munbasiṭ* ("self unfolding reality of existence").[181]

Shāh Walī Allāh's key expression (i.e., *wujūd al-aqṣā*[182] or "Furthest Being") reveals certain similarities with the Akbarian notion of *waḥdat al-wujūd* ("unity of existence') and Shaykh al-Akbar's expression of *wujūd al-Muṭlaq* ("Absolute Existence"). For example, *wujūd al-aqṣā*, as Shāh Walī Allāh states, "encompasses the units of being from above and from below and enfolds them from every side, offering no possibility of escape from Its encompassment."[183] In other words, this type of *wujūd*, unifies the entire existence by surrounding it in every single aspect, which alludes to the reality of *tawḥid*. In terms of its characteristics, the encompassing nature of *wujūd al-aqṣā* which surrounds the entire existence from every dimension, manifests its proximity and thus, accessible similarity or *tashbīh*. On the other hand, the term *aqṣā*, i.e., furthest, refers to its inaccessibility, peerlessness or *tanzīh*.

---

179. Hamid Algar, "Reflections of Ibn 'Arabī in Early Naqshbandī Tradition," *Journal of Muḥyiddin Ibn 'Arabī Society* 10 (1991), 60.

180. Mīr Valiuddīn, "Reconciliation," 50. On Shāh Walī Allāh's worldview see also his following works: *Alṭāf al-Quds (The Sacred Knowledge)*, ed. D. Pendlebury, trans., G. Jalbānī (London: Octagon, 1982), *al-Tafhīmāt al-Ilāhiyyah*, ed. Ghulām Muṣṭafā Qāsimī (Haydarabad: Ākādimiyāt al-Shāh Walī Allāh Dihlawī, 1967), and *Lamaḥāt*, ed. Ghulām Muṣṭafā Qāsimī (Ḥaydarabad: Ākādimiyāt al-Shāh Walī Allāh Dihlawī, 1965).

181. See Morris, *Revelation*, 201-202.

182. See J. M. S Baljon, *Religion and Thought of Shāh Walī Allāh Dihlawī 1703-1762* (Leiden: Brill, 1986), 59.

183. Cited in ibid.

In his *Tafhīmāt al-Ilāhiyah*, Walī Allāh refers to Ibn 'Arabī with reverence, where he declares that "Ibn 'Arabī's range of (spiritual) knowledge (*'ilm*) is more vast than that of any of God's protégés (*walī*)."[184]

Some Notes on the Concepts of tashbīh and tanzīh in waḥdat al-shuhūd

The continuous efforts of the members of *shuhūdī* school, such as Simnānī, Sirhindī, and Gisūdirāz, to save the *tanzīh* of the Absolute appear as the common factor in their works. These mystics identified the idea of God's transcendence as the essential "missing" element in the worldview of Ibn 'Arabī and his school. By looking at the major works in the *wujudī* school, as we hope to have partially shown in the present work, one is able to view consistent efforts undertaken by Ibn 'Arabī and his major cohorts to make the aspect of *tanzīh* (as the creed of God's transcendence/inaccessiblity/incomparability), the foremost embracing realm for the aspect of *tashbīh* (God's accessibility/comparability or similarity). Although some of the contemporary scholars suggest that the "difference between the system of Ibn ul-'Arabī and...Sirhindī is fundamental,"[185] there are also others who do not find them in direct contrast, or have recognized common grounds between their views.[186]

Generally speaking, the "missing" element in approaching the concept of "transcendence," one might claim, is "missing" the methodical and innate correlation between this concept and *tashbīh*. In other words, *no* affirmation or proof of the concept of *tanzīh*, be it *juz'ī* ("particular") or *kullī* ("general/universal"), has the capability of entering the human being's mind, *without* at least one accessible or immediate ground/means for *tashbīh*. In all occasions, any type or level of "transcendence," necessitates the existence of a subject or concept (either mental or external) for *tashbīh* in the first place. The level and degree of accessibility or in-accessibility of a concept, subject, or an existent entity, will be *always* determined, proved, accepted or denied *after* the formation and function of *tashbīh*, and therefore, making a comparison between something *shabīh* ("accessible/similar") and *munazzah* ("inacces-

184. Ibid., 60 (footnotes).
185. Anṣārī, "Shāḥ Waliy Allāh," 198.
186. See Algar, "Reflections." See also Mīr Valiuddīn, "Reconciliation," 50-51.

sible/peerless").

Thus the works of the aforementioned mystics, such as Simnānī, Sirhindī, and Gisūdirāz must not be excluded from this general rule. The previously discussed expressions, such as *Wujud al-Haqq* ("the Real *Wujūd*"), *māwarā'iyyah* ("beyondness"), *wujūd al-ẓillī* ("shadowy existence") and *warā' al-warā'* ("beyond the beyond"), the favorite expressions of the three critics of Ibn 'Arabī, which represent the culmination of *their* understanding of the *Absolute* or clearer *tanzīh* of God, were all the products of their evident moments of experiencing an *organic existential track*, which I refer to here as *tashbīh→tanzīh reciprocation/equilibrium*. In other words, without *tashbīh*, there would be no *tanzīh*, and every level of *tanzīh*, is the outcome of a precedent (or a priori) level of *tashbīh*.

This *badīhī* ("evident"), *fiṭrī* ("innate"), and *asāsī* ("basic") aspect of correlation between the concepts of *tashbīh* and *tanzīh* seems to receive no serious attention in the observations and assessments of Ibn 'Arabī's critics, or in most of the contemporary treatments of these cardinal concepts (i.e., *tashbīh* and *tanzīh*). As an evidence for functionality of this type of correlation (between *tashbīh* and *tanzīh*), which manifests itself in the gradual (and perhaps, subconscious) changes and discrepancies in the understandings of Ibn 'Arabīs'critics regarding *tashbīh* and *tanzīh*, Sirhindī's case might be a proper example.

By utilizing the term "*ẓill*" (shadow) to describe the idea of *waḥdat al-shuhūd*, Sirhindī attempts to differentiate between God Himself (i.e., His Essence) and the rest of existence or *mā-siwā Allāh* "(everything else"), while trying to present their ties/relevance at the same time. But his usage of this term (*ẓill*) has experienced several revisions during reconsiderations of its meanings.

> At the frist glance, the Mujaddid [Sirhindī] looks like using the term *ẓill* very much in the sense of *'aks* or *partaw*, i.e., *reflection;* implying the suggestion that it is, so to say, somehow a part of *aṣl*. While himself at he stage of *ẓilliyāt*, the Mujaddid tends to think of *ẓill* in this sense, though even there *ẓill* indicates for him a lower reality than 'aks or partaw (M. [Sirhindī's *Maktūbāt*] Vol, II, Ep. 1). Later we find that he uses the term *ẓill* to indicate the *Ghayriyyāt* or *otherness* of the multiplicity from the *aṣl* or God (... M., Vol. I, Ep. 160);

> and that the purpose of employing it is to express the *insignificance* of the multiplicity in contrast to the *aṣl* or God, as well as to show that the multiplicity *cannot exist* without the aṣl (…M., Vol. II, Eps. 1, 11). However, in the discussion of *takwīn* or creation the Mujaddid strongly tends to use the term only in the sense of an *effect* (M., Vol. II. Ep. 4). In the end the Mujaddid realizes the inadequacy of the term, discards it, and speaks, in its place, of the *acts of creation* which are incomprehensible to man (M., Vol. III, Ep. 122).[187] [Emphasis added with some modifications]

Based on the foundational and *existential* correlation between the concepts of *tashbīh* and *tanzīh*, in the way explained above, we might be able to trace the very reason for the appearance of these changes in Sirhindī's approaches to the concpet of *ẓill* and therefore, the idea of *waḥdat al-shuhūd* as a whole. As mentioned earlier, the core motive for designing the idea of *waḥdat al-shuhūd*, was to save the transcendence of God; a factor which was thought by Sirhindī and his co-thinkers, to be "missing" from Ibn 'Arabī's idea of *waḥdat al-wujūd.*

The major reason for considering *tanzīh* as the missing element of Ibn 'Arabī's worldview was the extensive presence of the aspect of *tashbīh* in his approach. But as mentioned above, the drive to any level of *tanzīh*, always begins by/from some level of *tashbīh.* This is evidently clearer in the case of proving the "absolute and perfect transcendence" of the Absolute (God), by the imperfect and non-absolute human being. The above-quoted transformation of Sirhindī's approaches to the term *ẓill*, offers an example of a zealous seeker in a relentless yearning and endeavor to find the best possible representative formula for the *absolute* transcendence of God or *tanzīh*.

Because of the absolute in-accessibility of the Absolute on the level of His Essence (*Aḥadiyyah*, in Ibn 'Arabī's term), which is the very source of His *absolute* transcendence, Sirhindī, in an effort to find the best description of this eminent level of *tanzīh*, had to gradually and systematically change and modify the *other* side of this reciprocation (i.e, *tashbīh*). Therefore, he constantly re-examined the meaning of the most accessible *tashbihī* element

187. Fārūqī, *Mujaddid's Conception of Tawḥīd*, 106-107, with some modifications.

of his theory (i.e., the concept or term of *ẓill*), in order to reach a better understanding of the ties between *ẓill* (either as reflection, multiplicity, or otherness, etc.), and the inaccessible Source of *tanzīh* or *aṣl*.

The side of *tashbīh* is *always* the *first* considerable (or re-considerable) side (of *tashbīh→tanzīh* reciprocation), through which one is able to re-examine his understanding of God's transcendence (i.e., *tanzīh*, the *second* side). Sihindī, perhaps subconsciously, followed the same general rule, and defined the accessible side of *tashbīh* (i.e. existence, or *ẓill* in his term), first, as described in the above quotation, as a shadow or reflection, then as absolutely other (than God) or sheer insignificant multiplicity and later as an effect (compare to the Absolute Cause), and finally replaced it with the "incomprehensible acts of creation."

The "*incomprehensible* acts of creation," described by Sirhindī, manifest his description of the Absolute's *tanzīh*. Although Sirhindī expresses this *incomprehensibility* in relation to the [Absolute's] acts of "creation," and not the Absolute Himself, because, as mentioned earlier, the creation is the only existing source available to us (for *tashbīh*), and therefore, Sirhindī, in order to describe the *tanzih* of the Absolute, refers to His act of creation, hence the evident drive/move from *tashbīh* (the acts of creation) towards defining *tanzīh* (the Source of the acts). By employing this concept (i.e., acts of creation, incomprehensible to man), Sirhindī seems to describe *tanzīh* on the level of *tawḥīd-i af'ālī* ("Oneness of God's acts"), intermeshed with the sense of awe or bewilderment (*ḥayrah*/incomprehensibility). The stage of *ḥayrah*, as mentioned earlier, is also considered by Ibn 'Arabī as the highest stage of the Path and as one of the characteristics of the spiritual elites.

This sense of incomprehensibility, expressed by Sirhindī, reminds us of Gisūdirāz's approach to the state of "dumbness" and *ḥayrah* ("bewilderment") in the stage of *warā'al-warā'* ("beyond the beyond"), which represents his understanding of the absolute *tanzīh*. Expressing the "incomprehensibility of the acts of creation" as a drive from the source of *tashbīh* (creation) to the Incomprehensible *Source of the acts* (i.e, *tanzīh*), by Sirhindī, also brings to mind the creative approach of the celebrated Kubrawī master, 'Azīz al-Dīn Nasafī when stating: *Yekī rā yekī kardan muḥāl ast.*[188] (making the One [Who is Essentially One,] One [again] is impossible).

In other words, understanding *Yekī* (i.e., Absolute in the realm of absolute-perfect Oneness/*tanzīh* or *Aḥadiyyah*, or proving Oneness for the One – in the realm of His Oneness) is impossible. Based on Nasafī's observation, the Absolute in His Absolute *tanzīh* (i.e., *Aḥad* or the level of *Aḥadiyyah*) is incomprehensible, and one has to look for Him on the accessible level (of *Waḥid* or *wāḥidiyyah*) in order to arrive at a possible/limited level of comprehension of His attributes/acts. Therefore, the *only* pathway leading towards understanding some imperfect level of *tanzīh* begins with some level of *tashbīh*. As a result, a more elevated (or simply a new) understanding of God's transcendence or *tanzīh*, – compared to one's previous understanding of His *tanzīh* – will be reached *only* by re-considering, changing, and modifying or re-examining one's available *tashbīhī* understanding or means/source. This *tasbhīhī* means or source is evidently nothing but "existence" in general.

This process appears to define the very nature of the enduring *tashbīh→tanzīh reciprocation/equilibrium*, in traversing towards "Reality" in Islamic mysticism. Mystics such as Ibn 'Arabī, Simnānī, Sirhindī, and Gisūdiraẓ all ventured along the path of *tashbīh→tanzīh*, through different methods. For members of the *shuhūdī* triangle, Simnānī, Sirhindī, and Gisūdirāz, this journey, mostly occurred *subconsciously*, and as a result, particularly in the case of Simnānī and Gisūdirāz, the validity of *tashbīh* was undermined/denied, while both these mystics were employing *it*. On the other hand, Ibn 'Arabī, from the beginning of his theoretical presentation, realized the important role of *tashbīh* in experiencing a more unveiled *tanzīh* of the Absolute.

One of the renowned members of the school of Ibn 'Arabī, Shaykh 'Abd al-Karīm Jīlī (d. 824/1421), in his commentary (*sharḥ*) on the *Futūḥāt*, refers to a subtle point of view regarding the concept of *tanzīh*.[189] Under the topic of *sirr al-tanzīh* (secret of [God's] transcendence), Jīlī describes the *Absolute tanzīh* (of the Real Almighty *Ḥaqq ta'ālā*) as considering (or understanding) His transcendence in the way He knows Himself (or His *tanzīh*) through His Essence. Then, Jīlī concludes that, because this kind

188. See Nasafī, *Bayān al-Tanzīl*, 163.

189. See 'Abd al-Karīm Jilī, *Sharḥ-i Mushkīlāt al-Futūḥāt al-Makkiyyah* (Cairo: Maṭba'at al-Dār al-Kutub wa'l Wathā'iq al-Qawmiyyah, 1424/2003), 127-128.

of (Absolute) *tanzīh*, does not bear (any type) of *tashbīh* (*bal huwa munazzahun 'an muqābilat-i tashbīh*), we have no means of knowing or understanding/rationalizing His *tanzīh* [in the *Absolute* sense] (*fa tanzīhuhū lā na'lamahu wa lā na'qaluh*). He then concludes his remarks by referring to Ibn 'Arabī's saying, *al-tanzīh taḥdīd al-munazzah*, i.e., considering/applying transcendence means making limitations for the Transcendent.[190] In other words, due to the impossibility of realizing the *Absolute tanzīh* of the Absolute (i.e., in the realm of His Essence), any other type of *tanzīh* (i.e., at the level of His attributes and acts) requires a precedent level of *tashbīh* (which represents our limited, portional/partial understating of the Absolute, which is, at the same time, the only way of approaching Him).

One of the contemporary commentators of Ibn 'Arabī's *Fuṣūṣ*, Muḥammad Ḥusayn Fāḍil Tūnī (d.1339 /1960), in his concise but remarkable *sharḥ*, *Ta'līqah bar Fuṣūṣ*, refers to the concepts of *tashbīh* and *tanzīh*, in their relation to Ādam's descent from Heaven.[191] He states that "although from the standpoint of [his elevated] spiritual position (*bi-ḥasab-i rūḥānīyat*), Ādam, was in the Heaven of Intellect (*jannat-i 'aqlī*), and [therefore] reached a superior perfection (*kamāl-i atamm*), i.e., (being) the locus of the attributes of incomparability (*maẓhariyyat-i ṣifāt-i tanzīhī)*, but he lacked (the stage of being) the locus of attributes of comparability (*maẓhariyyat-i ṣifāt-i tashbīhī*)." [192] Fāḍil Tūnī further argues that "although the attributes of comparability are considered as imperfection (*naqs*) in relation to the attributes of incomparability, but [they are considered as] perfection, in relation to the stage of all-encompassing comprehensiveness (*jāmi'īyat wa akmalīyat*)."[193]

Attaining this stage of ultimate comprehensiveness, Tūnī affirms, was absolutely necessary for Ādam, to become God's *khalīfah* ("viceregent"). Therefore, as he explains, "the reason for Ādam's descent (*hubūṭ-i Ādam*) was the actualization (*fi'līyat*) of every [potential] perfection [residing] in his predispositional capability (*isti'dād*), and [in order to execute this essential process, he had to] also contain the attributes of comparability (*ṣifāt-i tashbīh*),

---

190. See ibid.

191. See Muḥammad Ḥusayn Fāḍil Tūnī, *Talīqah bar Fuūṣ* (Tehran: Intishārāt-i Mowlā, 1386/2007), 99-100.

192. Ibid., 99.

193. See ibid.

so that he could reach the stage of comprehensivness and the merit of [God's] viceregency (*istīḥqāq-i khalāfat*), because [achieving] the merit of God's viceregency (*istīḥqāq-i khalāfat*) is impossible without [acquiring] the stage of all-comprehensivness [of God's both attributes of *tashbīh* and *tanzīh*]."[194] Faḍil Tūnī, then concludes his remarks by referring to a well-known Qūr'ānic verse (2:30) regarding the creation of Ādam; "Therefore, God responded to the angels who said ['Wilt Thou place therein one who will make mischief therein and shed blood?] whilst we do celebrate Thy praises and glorify Thy holy (name)?,'by saying that 'I know what ye know not.'"[195]

Fāḍil Tūnī's final remarks remind us of the crucial place and significance of the perpetual functionality of both aspects of *tashbīh* and *tanzīh*, in reaching a more comprehensive realization of God's Existence, *and* in the very creation of *insān al-kāmil* ("Perfect Human Being"), in Ibn 'Arabī's worldview.

Therefore, in Ibn 'Arabī's *conscious* and doctrinal use of *tashbīh→tanzīh* reciprocation, which also plays a major role in characterization of the idea of *waḥdat al-wujud*, the side of *lā huwa* (not He/existence or "*tashbīh*") continuously leads to *huwa* (He/the Absolute or "*tanzīh*"). One might speculate that *haḍrat al-khayāl*, the realm, faculty or presence of imagination, was designed by Ibn 'Arabī in his worldview, as a domain for testing the constant functionality of *tashbīh→tanzīh* reciprocation. This reciprocation, in Ibn 'Arabī's view, ensures the constant and new currents of unveiling mystical experiences.

194. Ibid., 100.

195. Ibid. For translation of the Qur'ānic verse (2:30), I have used its English translation by 'Abdullāh Yusuf 'Alī.

Chapter Three

Waḥdat al-Wujūd and its Affinities with the Concept of *al-Insān al-Kāmil* (the Perfect Human Being): A Kubrawī/Akbarian Approach

As discussed earlier, in the *Shuhūdī* school, both Simnānī and Gisūdirāz seem to have focused their worldviews on the concept of *tajallī* ("God's theophany"). For both masters, this important concept played a significant role in emphasizing the "transcendence of God." Simnānī, as mentioned before, referred to four levels of God's theophany: manifestations of His *Dhāt* ("Essence"), *ṣifāt* (attributes), *af'āl* ("acts"), and *āthār* ("traces").[1] Gisūdirāz speaks of five different levels of theophany, which are in fact "the same as those of Simnānī,"[2] but with two subdivisions at the level of Essence (*Dhāt*).[3] These two subdivisions are the *veiled* Essence (which he refers to as the stage of *warā'al-warā'*, or "beyond the beyond" as the absolutely untouched, unlimited and inaccessible transcendence of God)[4], and the *veiling* Essence, "which veils the former."[5] Similar to one of the major Kubrawī figures, Najm al-Dīn Rāzī (d.654/1256),[6] Gisūdirāz considers five corresponding stages on the Path, namely "*Sharī'ah* ("Divine Law"), *ṭarīqah* ("Spiritual Path"), *Haqīqah* ("Reality"), *Ḥaqq al-Haqīqah* ("Truth of Reality"), and *Haqīqat al-Ḥaqq* ("Reality of Truth")."[7]

1. See Ḥussainī, "Shuhūd vs. Wujūd," 335.
2. See ibid.
3. See ibid.
4. See Ibid.
5. See Ibid.
6. Ibid.
7. Ibid., 337, with some modification.

As we see above, similar to Simnānī (in his use of *wujūd al-Ḥaqq* or "Existence of the Real"), Gisūdirāz employs the term *Ḥaqq* (in *ḥaqīqat al-Ḥaqq*) as an alternative to Ibn 'Arabī's notion of the *Muṭlaq* ("Absolute"). But different from Simnānī, he replaces Ibn 'Arabī's notion of *wujūd* ("Existence') with *ḥaqīqah* ("Reality"). In order to avoid the Akbarian usage of *wujūd* (which Gisūdirāz disregards because of its absolute identification with God in his understanding of this notion), he refers to *wujūd* as *shu'ūr* ("consciousness")[8] and thus does not employ it as one of his key terms. Gisūdirāz made a correlation between the aforementioned five stages *and* stage of *al-insān al-kāmil*[9] (a term apparently rooted in the worldview of Ibn 'Arabī). The Law, the Path, the Reality, the Truth of Reality and the Reality of Truth, in Gisūdirāz's corresponding stages, are referred to by him as the *speech* of the Perfect Man, *action* of the Perfect Man, *sight* of the Perfect Man, *being* of the Perfect Man, and the *being of non-being* of the Perfect Man, respectively.[10]

The systematic reciprocation between Gisūdirāz's five designated stages *and* different characteristics of *al-insān al-kāmil* remind us of a similar view of the well-known Kubrawī master, 'Azīz al-Dīn Nasafī. In his book, *Insān al-Kāmil*, he states that "the Perfect Man is the one who is fully accomplished/perfect (*kāmil*) in [understanding and experiencing] the Divine Law (*Sharī'ah*), the Path (*ṭarīqah*), and the Reality (*ḥaqīqah*)."[11] Nasafī then explains the characteristics of *al-insān al-kāmil*. In his view, *al-insān al-kāmil* has to be fully adorned with four characteristics of "good sayings (*aqwāl-i nīk*), good actions (*af'āl-i nīk*), good morals (*akhlāq-i nīk*), and knowledge [of the Divine Existence] (*ma'ārif*)."[12] He then provides us with his creative approach which appears to be similar to the Akbarian view of *al-insān al-kāmil*. According to Nasafī, "the Perfect Man (*al-insān al-kāmil*) is always present in the world, and is *not* more than *one*."[13] The reason for this singularity – as Nasafī declares – is "because all *mawjūdāt* ("existent beings") are like "one" person, and the Perfect Man is the heart of that person.

8. See ibid., 338, and Ḥussainī, *On Sufism*, 86.
9. See ibid., 337.
10. See ibid.
11. Nasafī, *Insān al-Kāmil*, 74.
12. Ibid.
13. Ibid., 75.

The existent beings are unable to exist without "heart," therefore the Perfect Man has to be always present in the world."[14] Nasafī concludes that "because the heart (of a person) cannot be more than one, thus the Perfect Man can only be one."[15]

We might be able to interpret Nasafī's above words regarding the "singularity" of the Perfect Man as *al-insān al-kāmil*'s characteristic of *jāmi'iyyah* ("comprehensive collectedness"), in possessing the most perfect all-inclusive consciousness of all God's *asmā' al-ḥusnā* ("beautiful Names"). Because of the eminent function of his "comprehensiveness," the Perfect Man manifests a "single" most perfect faculty which carries the entire consciousness of existence within the limitless *ḥaḍarāt* ("presences") of the Absolute through His Names. As "Allāh" is *jāmi'* ("the most perfect and comprehensive") of God's Names which – in Its Singularity – represents all of His Names (i.e, presences)[16], the Perfect Man – in his singularity – represents all God's Names (or presences) in the entire existence.

Ibn 'Arabī, in his *Naqsh al-Fuṣūṣ*, a concise commentary on his celebrated *Fuṣūṣ al-Ḥikam*, refers to the term *al-ḥikmat al-fardīyya*, – Wisdom of Singularity – in describing the unique place of the Prophet Muḥammad as the Perfect Man *par excellence*. The reason for choosing this term, as Ibn 'Arabī explains, is that "he [i.e., the Prophet Muḥammad] is single [or unique] in the station of God's comprehensiveness (*jam'*)"[17] In his *Futūḥāt,* while referring to the Qur'ānic event in which God taught Ādam the Names (2:31), Ibn 'Arabī, in order to refer to the eminent place of the Perfect Man in existence, elaborates upon the correlation between the concepts of *asmā'* ("God's Names"), the *ḥaḍra* ("Divine Presence"), and His *tajallīyāt* ("manifestations").

> God taught Ādam all the names from his own essence through tasting, for He disclosed Himself to him through a universal self-disclosure. Hence, no name remained in the Divine Presence that did not become manifest to Ādam from Himself. From his own essence he came to know all the names

14. Ibid.
15. Ibid.
16. See Chittick, *The Sufi Path of Knowledge*, 64-68.
17. Shaykh al-Akbar Muḥyiddīn Ibn 'Arabī, *Naqsh al-Fuṣūṣ*, trans., Najīb Mayīl Heravī (Tehran: Intishārāt-i Mowlā, 1382/2003), 50.

of his Creator.[18]

In order to expand the above reciprocation between the concepts of God's Names and the Perfect Man, Ibn 'Arabī uses this affinity to emphasize the concept of *tanzīh* ("God's peerlessness). True '*ubūdīyya* ("servanthood") is the outcome of divulging the Names to the Perfect Man, through which he come to know the Path of perfection, as well as his place as the *'abd* ("servant") of the Absolute. This perfection is possible only through fulfilling the claims of servanthood. As mentioned earlier, Simnānī tried to criticize Ibn 'Arabī and his followers by describing the characteristics of a group of perfect prodigies of the Path whom he called *ṭālibān-i kamāl-i tawḥīd wa tanzīh-i Ḥaqq-i Hamīd-i Majīd*[19] ("seekers of the perfect [absolute] Oneness and incomparability of the Praiseworthy [and] Exalted Real"). One of the prominent characteristics of this group, as Simnānī stated, was their *practical* confession to God's '*ubūdīyya* ("servanthood"). This characteristic (i.e., *'ubūdīyya*) made this group (i.e., *ṭālibān-i kamāl-i*) also unique in their full confession of God's *tanzīh*.

Ibn 'Arabī's view regarding man's attainment of perfection through perfecting his sincere servanthood makes a clear distinction between the servant and his Lord (as the outcome of *tanzīh*), and it seems to bring together what both these figures (i.e., Ibn 'Arabī and Simnānī) delineate as the meaning of "perfection." Ibn 'Arabī not only stresses upon God's *tanzīh* by referring to His unique Lordship, he also emphasizes the "animal" aspect of the Perfect Man to delve more into the distinction between the Lord and His servant. He states in his *Futūḥāt*:

> Creation has many levels, and the most perfect level is occupied by man. Each kind in the cosmos is a part with regard to man's perfection. Even animal man is a part of Perfect Man... He created Perfect Man in His form, and through the form He gave him the ability to have all of His names ascribed to him, one by one, or in groups, though all the names together are not ascribed to him in a single word-thereby the Lord is distinguished from the Perfect Servant. Hence there is none of the most beautiful names-and all of God's names are most beautiful-by which the Perfect Servant is not called, just as he

18. Ibn 'Arabī, *Futūḥāt*, II, cited in Chittick, *Heir to the Prophets*, 63.
19. See Simnānī, *al-'Urwah*, 273.

calls his Master by them.[20]

Gisūdirāz's son, Sayyid Akbar Ḥusaynī, in his comments on Gisūdirāz's writings,[21]while describing the fourth stage (i.e., *ḥaqq al-Ḥaqīqah* or truth of Reality) of his father's designated stages of theophanies (*tajllīyāt*), mentions the "Perfect Man's being," and describes this stage as "the reality of being Muḥammad (*haqīqat-i Muḥammadiyyat*),"[22] an expression that has been employed in different variations-by Ibn 'Arabī and his major cohorts in their approach to the concept of the Perfect Man.[23] "On this stage, all the attributes and Names of God are manifested to the Sufi traveler. By virtue of this manifestation of Divine emanation, all the 99 Names of God become the attribute of the ones who experience it."[24]

At the very beginning of the *Fuṣūṣ al-Ḥikam*, Shaykh al-Akbar, elaborating upon the "Wisdom of Divinity in the Word of Ādam"[25] (*faṣṣu ḥikmatin ilāhiyya fī kalimatin Ādamiyyah*), clearly affirms the correlation between the Reality, His Names (*asmā'*), and the Perfect Man.

> The Reality wanted to see the essences of His Most Beautiful Names, or, to put in another way, to see His own Essence, in an all-inclusive object encompassing the whole [divine] Command, which, qualified by existence, would reveal to Him His own mystery [so, He created Ādam].[26]

For both Simnānī and Gisūdirāz, the Perfect Man is the most Perfect Manifestation of the Truth (*al-Ḥaqq*), and for Ibn 'Arabī, the most perfect *tajallī* ('manifestation") of *Wujūd al-Muṭlaq* ("Absolute Existence"). In Ibn 'Arabī's worldview a Perfect Man has the most perfect faculty to "combine the two basic perspectives of incomparability and similarity."[27]

In other words, one of the most distinguished characteristics of being a Perfect Man, in Ibn 'Arabī's view, is an eminent level of perfection through which he can comprehend and experience the

---

20. Ibn 'Arabī, *Futūḥāt*, III, cited in Chittick, *Heir to the Prophets*, 64.
21. See Ḥussainī, "Shuhūd vs. Wujūd," 337.
22. See ibid.
23. See ibid.
24. Ibid., with some modification.
25. Austin, *Fuṣūṣ*, 50.
26. Ibid.
27. Ibn 'Arabī, *Futūḥāt*, cited in Chittick, *The Sufi Path of Knowledge,* 29.

truth of *huwa-lā-huwa* ("He/not He").[28] The Perfect Man might also be described as the human being who is able to experience the concept of *waḥdat al-wujūd* in the state of perfection, through perfecting his ties with the Only Absolute (Unity), and by fully observing His ties with *mā siw-Allāh* ("anything else or existence").

"Perfection" occurs in different levels, with its different envoys such as the prophets through their diverse scopes of elevations in what Ibn 'Arabī refers to as the power or faculty of *khayāl* ("imagination")."[29] This faculty seems to function as a medium for experiencing a particular one or all *ḥaḍarāt* ("presences") of the Absolute. The most perfect example of the Perfect Man, for Ibn 'Arabī – as also indicated in the *Fuṣūṣ al-Hikam* – is the Prophet Muḥammad, "for which reason the whole affair [of creation] begins and ends with him."[30] Using a *ḥadīth*, regarding the creation of the Prophet Muḥammad, Ibn 'Arabī states:

> He was a prophet when Ādam was still between the water and the clay and he is, by elemental make up, the Seal of the Prophets (*khātam al-nabiyyīn*), the first of the three singular ones, since all other singulars derive from it.[31]

Ibn 'Arabī's creative elucidations upon another well-known prophetic *hadīth*, form his approach to what he refers to as the "three singulars." In this *ḥadīth,* the Prophet states that "three things have been made beloved to me in this world of yours, women, perfume, and prayer. And my solace was made to be in prayer,"[32] Ibn 'Arabī employs these three throughout his metaphorical elaborations. He wrote an entire chapter on the Prophet Muḥammad, which is the last chapter of his *Fuṣūṣ*. As Ibn 'Arabī explains, the Prophet "begins by mentioning women and leaves prayer until last, because in the manifestation of her essence, woman is a part of man."[33] Shaykh al-Akbar further explains, while referring to the same *ḥadīth*: "women [were] made beloved to him and he had great affection for them because the whole always is drawn toward its part. This he explains as coming from the Reality, in His saying regarding the elemental

28. See Chittick, *The Sufi Path of Knowledge*, 113-115.
29. See ibid., 115-118. See also Chittick, *Imaginal Words*, 70-95.
30. Austin, *Fuṣūṣ*, 272.
31. Ibid.
32. Ibid., 272 and 282.
33. Ibid., 272.

human makeup, *And I breathed into him of My spirit*."[34] As Austin explains regarding Ibn 'Arabī's approach to this *ḥadīth*:

> The feminine symbolizes microcosmically and therefore in a very succinct way, the very principle of the projected and multifaceted mirror of the cosmic image that reflects to the divine subjects the panoramic beauty of His own infinite possibility to become which is nothing than His own Essential Self which He cannot but love…and into which He pours and "blows" the Breath of His Mercy and Spirit.[35]

Regarding the second singular which is the perfume (*al-ṭīb*), Ibn 'Arabī states as follows, "As for the wisdom of perfume and his putting it after "women," it is because of the aromas of generation in women, the most delightful of perfumes being [experienced] within the embrace of the beloved."[36] Then, Ibn 'Arabī makes an immediate correlation between perfume, personality of the Prophet, and the Breath of the Merciful:

> When Muḥammad was created a pure servant, he had no ambition for leadership, but continued prostrating and standing [before his Lord], a passive creation, until God effected [His purpose] in him, when He conferred on him an active role in the realm of Breaths, which are the excellent perfumes [of existence]. Thus he made perfume beloved to him, placing it after women.[37]

In relation to the third singular in which the Prophet found solace, Ibn 'Arabī confirms the unique characteristics of *aṣ-ṣalāt* ("prayer") by referring to the Qur'ānic verses:

> In the prayer the most effective element is the remembrance of God, by virtue of the words and actions it comprises…God has said, *Surely, the prayer prevents much evil and sin*, seeing that the one praying is forbidden to occupy himself with anything else while he is engaged in it. *But the remembrance of God is greater*, that is to say that, within the context of prayer, God's remembering of His servant when He responds to his request

34. Ibid., 273, with some modification.
35. Ibid., 270.
36. Ibid., 278.
37. Ibid.

> is greater. Furthermore, in the prayer, the servant's praising of God is greater than his remembering Him, since all majesty belongs to God. Thus, He says, *And God knows what you fashion*, and, *or who listens and watches*. The listening derives from God's remembering of His servant in prayer.[38]

Ibn 'Arabī then concludes, "Thus, of the intelligible movement by which the cosmos is transformed from nonexistence into existence, the prayer has all three phases, the vertical movement in which the praying one bows and downwards movement, which is the prostration."[39] Ibn 'Arabī also explains the meaning of the Prophet's words on solace in prayer

> In his saying, "and my solace was made to be in prayer," he does not attribute this to himself, since the Self-revelation of God to one praying comes from God and not the one who is praying. Indeed, had he not mentioned this by himself, God would have ordered him to pray without the [solace of] His Self-revelation to him. Since that came to him as a favor, the contemplative vision is also a favor. He said, "and my solace was made to be in prayer," which means seeing the Beloved, which brings solace to the eye of the lover. This is because the word *qurrah* [solace] comes from the word *istiqrār* [fixing], so that the lover's eye might be fixed [on the Beloved] to the exclusion of all else.[40]

One might be able to see the progression of multiplicity (which is represented in the above metaphorical framework of triplicitiy) towards unity (in the third singular which also happens to be the kernel of solace). In Ibn 'Arabī's view, "the solace found in prayer" proclaimed by the Prophet (as the Perfect Man *par excellence*) is not just a manifestation of spiritual comfort and consolation, but is the perpetual stage in which the Perfect Man finds his real place in creation through "fixing" his eye of certainty on the Unity of the Beloved Real (as conveyed in the above Prophetic saying: "*…wa ju'ilat qurratu 'aynī fiṣ-ṣalāt*"[41]).

As a result, in the everlasting movement towards unity, the

38. Ibid., 281.

39. Ibid.

40. Ibid., 282.

41. See Ibn 'Arabī, *Fuṣūṣ al-Ḥikam*, commentary Al-Shaykh 'Abd al-Razzāq Kāshānī (Beirut: The Arabic History Publishing and Distributing, 1427/2006), 452-453.

Most Beautiful Names as the Absolute's manifestations (symbolized by *al-nisā'* or "women" as the first singular) encompass the entire existence by their *al-ṭīb* or their "perfume" of Mercy, and place the Perfect Man (as the most perfect representation of the entire cosmos) in the most eminent stage of solace through constant praise and remembrance of Unity in *aṣ-ṣalāt* "prayer." Therefore, Ibn 'Arabī sees the Prophet (i.e., the most elevated example of the Perfect Man) as the one who represents and defines the progression of multiplicity (represented in the above triplicity) towards unity. This progression also conveys the everlasting return of the entire existence (as heralded by the Perfect Man) to the Source of Unity.

The Prophet possesses a unique characteristic of *jāmi'iyyah* ("comprehensiveness"), based on which he contains all of the *asmā'* ("Names"), and as Ibn 'Arabī utters, this *ḥadīth* regarding the three singulars is the expression of *maḥabbah* ("love") "which is the origin of all existent beings"[42] ("*qāla fī bāb-il maḥabbat al-latī hiya aṣl al-mawjūdāt*"[43]). Because of this essential comprehensiveness, Ibn 'Arabī in a seemingly paradoxical rendition, called the Prophet first of the three singulars and their source. In other words, because the Prophet contains the very essence and meaning of existence and is the *dalīl*[44] ("reason") for its creation, he carries the entirety of existence (symbolized in the above triplicity) towards Unity. Referring to the Prophet Muḥammad's peerless status, Ibn 'Arabī states, "He was the clearest of evidence for his Lord, having been given the totality of the divine words, which are those things named by Ādam, so that he was the closest of clues to his own triplicity, he being himself a clue to himself. Since, then, his reality was marked by primal singularity and his makeup by triplicity."[45]

The Kubrawī master, Mir Sayyid 'Alī Hamadānī, in his commentary on *Fuṣūṣ al-Ḥikam*, explains the concept of *fardīyya* ("singularity"). In his comments on the first part of the chapter dedicated to the Prophet Muḥammad in the *Fuṣūṣ* which contains the phrase of *awwal al-afrād al-thalāthat-i* ("first of the three singulars"), Hamadānī writes:

The singularity in the existence (*wujūd*) is the outcome of the

42. Austin, *Fuṣūṣ*, 272.
43. Ibn 'Arabī, *Fuṣūṣ*, 435.
44. Ibid., 434.
45. Austin, *Fuṣūṣ*, 272.

three things: one is the Essence of Oneness (*dhāt-i aḥadiyyat*), and the second is the stage of Divinity (*martaba-yi ilāhiyyat*), and the [last] one, the immutable entity belongs to Muḥammad (*'ayn-i thābita-yi Muḥammadiyyah*).[46]

Hamadānī's approach to the concept of "singularity," in considering the Prophet Muḥammad as the first creation (the first immutable entity), or the first *tajallī* of the stage of *ilāhiyyat* or *wāḥidiyyah* ("inclusive unity"), is akin to Nasafī's approach to the concept of the Perfect Man. As mentioned earlier, Nasafī stated that the Perfect Man is no more than "one" person." He also rendered the notion that "all existent beings" are like "one" person with a "singular heart" as the Perfect Man. By considering the Prophet Muḥammad as the first creation, first kernel, and summation of all *wujūd* ("existence/immutable entities"), Hamadānī seems to be alluding to the well-known prophetic saying of *awwal-u mā-khalaq Allāh Nūrī* (My light was the first of God's creation). The last part of this *ḥadīth* has been reported in different variations, such as *Awwal-u mā-khalaq Allāh al-Aql* ("the Intellect"),...*al-Qalam* ("the Pen"),... *al-Jawhar* ("the Substance"), and...*Rūḥi* ("my spirit").[47]

Similar to Nasafī, Hamadānī has referred to *dil-i [insān-i] kāmil* ("the Perfect Man's heart") as the kernel of creation.[48] In his comments on Ibn 'Arabī's phrase in the *Fuṣūṣ*, "*wa faṣṣ-u kull-i ḥikmatin al-kalimat allatī nusibat bihā*"[49] (the seal of each Wisdom is the Word assigned to it[50]), Hamadānī considers the term *kalimah* (Word) as the heart of the Perfect Man.[51]

In a similar approach to that of Ibn 'Arabī, Hamadānī, in his introduction to his *Sharḥ* on the *Fuṣūṣ*, refers to the Perfect Man and particularly the Prophet Muḥammad as "the manifestation of the Essential Ipseity (*maẓhar-i huwiyyat-i dhātiyya*) and all [God's] Names and Attributes."[52] Through a creative approach, Hamadānī continues his words by mentioning some Qur'ānic verses and well-known *aḥadīth*. For example, he makes a direct correlation be-

46. Parsa, *Sharḥ-i Fuṣūs,* 505. As mentioned earlier, this commentary was originally written by Ḥamadānī.

47. See Misgar Nījād, introduction to *Sharḥ-i Fuṣūṣ al-Ḥikam* by Pārsā, 37 and 39.

48. Parsā, *Sharh-i Fuṣūṣ*, 17.

49. Ibn 'Arabī, *Fuṣūṣ*, 42.

50. Austin, *Fuṣūṣ*, 58.

51. See Parsā, *Sharḥ-i Fuṣūṣ*, 17.

52. Ibid., 10.

tween the concept of the Perfect Man and the Prophet Muḥammad, when he writes "[the Divine] announcement of that state [i.e. the state of the Perfect Man] has come evidently as "*mā ramayta iḍ ramayt wa lākinn Allāh-a ramā.*" (thou (Muḥammad) threwest not when thou didst throw, but Allāh threw…"[Qur'ān 8:17]).[53]

Hamadānī then concludes that Qur'ānic verses such as the above verse are considered to be proofs for the Perfect Man, by which he comes to know that "everything (*hama*) is from Him [i.e., the Absolute] and returns towards Him, and even further that, everything is He."[54] Hamadānī seems to directly connect the concept of the "Perfect Man" with the concept of "unity of existence."

Ibn 'Arabī, in his approach to the above mentioned Qur'ānic verse (8:17), provides us with an interesting interpretation of the concept of *ḥayrah* ("mystical bewilderment"), in its association with both negation and affirmation of the Perfect Man (i.e., the Prophet Muḥammad in the verse). He concludes that the Being of the Absolute is the only Real Being who encompasses the past, present and future. In the following passage, Ibn 'Arabī, with a method close to *shaṭḥ* ("theopathic locutions"), elucidates his understanding of the concept of *waḥdah* ("unity"). In this depiction of "unity," the Perfect Man, is the "affirmed middle between two negations."[55] He states as follows:

> He affirmed you, negated you, misguided you and guided you. He made you bewildered in what He made certain to you. Thus, you have ascertained but bewilderment. You knew, therefore, that the affair is all bewilderment, and that deviation (*ḍalāl*) is the same as guidance (*hudā*). He said "You and not-you" and "You did not throw when you threw but God threw," affirming both that Muḥammad is the only thrower and that Allah is the only thrower. But, then, what has become of Muḥammad? He negated him and affirmed him. Then He negated him [for the second time]. Muḥammad is affirmed in His saying: "When you threw" between two negations: an eternal negation in His saying: "You did not throw" and an ever-lasting negation in His

53. Ibid. For the English translation of the above Qur'ānic verse (8:17), I have used Pickthall's translation.

54. Ibid.

55. See *Futūḥāt*, II, cited in Salmān H. Bashier, *Ibn 'Arabī's Barzakh: The Concept of the Limit and the Relationship between God and the World* (New York: State University of New York Press, 2004), 126-127.

> saying: "But Allah threw." Thus, the affirmation of Muḥammad in this verse is like the instant of time (*al-ān*), which is the eternal Being (*wujūd*) between the two times, between the past time, which is realized (*muḥaqqaq*) Nonbeing, and the future time which is absolute (*maḥḍ*) Nonbeing...He rendered him an affirmed Middle between two negations, so he resembled the instant of time (*al-ān*) that is Being. Being (*wujūd*) belongs to Allah not to Muḥammad, since He isWho possesses permanent Being in the past, in the present state (*ḥāl*), and in the future time. Conjectured (*mutawahham*) delimitation (*taqyīd*) is removed from Him.[56]

Ibn 'Arabī, in making correlation between the above mentioned *'adam muḥaqqaq* ("relative non-existence") and *'adam maḥḍ* ("absolute non-existence") as the "two negations," prefers the function of the *'adam maḥḍ* which as he suggests, signifies the position of the Absolute in His absoluteness more clearly than any other concept. In other words, we might say that when the Perfect Man, in the eminent stage of *yaqīn* ("certainty"), comes to "know himself" as the *'adam maḥḍ* ("absolute-non-existence"), in his ties to the *Wujūd maḥḍ* (Absolute Existence), then he is able to experience a vivid Presence and knowledge of the Absolute Unity.

> Absolute (*maḥḍ*) nonexistence is more eminent than relative nonexistence in a certain respect, since in its magnification of God and in the strength of its signifying Him, it does not receive being. It remains as it is in its root and entity, out of jealousy lest it become an associate of the Divine Side in relation to the attribute of being, and lest the Names that are ascribed to God be ascribed to it...After all, absolute nonexistence is better at making known what is worthy of God than relative nonexistence, because it has the attribute of eternity without beginning in His being. This is the description of the Real by the negation of Firstness, which is the description of nonexistence, in that being is negated from it through its own essence. Hence nothing other than God makes God known with greater knowledge than does absolute nonexistence.[57]

The founder of the Kubrawī order, Shaykh Najm al-Din Kubrā, in

---

56. Ibid.
57. *Futūḥāt*, II, cited in ibid, 127-128.

his approach to the concept of *dhikr* ("invocation of God's Names"), has also benefited from description of the concepts of "affirmation and negation."[58] He refers to ten *qawā'id* ("principles") that pave the way of the seekers towards the states of perfection, or as he states, bring *athār-i sa'ādat* ("the signs of felicity") to *sāyirān-i haḍrat-i ṣamadiyyat* ("seekers of the Presence of the Eternal Absolute"). In the sixth principle, Kubrā describes the characteristics of "invocation of God's Names" (*dhikr*).[59]

By utilizing a set of purposefully designated terms, the great shaykh of the Kubrawīs manifests a correlation between the concepts of God's Name/Presence, man's perfection, and *aḥadiyyat* ("exclusive unity"). Kubrā, refers to *dil* ("heart') of the seeker (in the state of perfection), as the *maḥall-i bārgāh-i kibriyā wa maṭla'-i aftāb-i fardāniyyat* ("locus of the threshold of [God's] Splendor and dawning abode of the Sun of Unity"). Najm al-Dīn views *dhikr* as the medium that removes *ghubār-i hudūth wa kathrat-i ẓulamāt* ("dust of impurities and multiplicity of darkness"). This cleansing effect, for Kubrā, represents the content of *nafy* ('negation'), which stems from the encompassing presence of the first segment of *shahādah* formulae (*lā ilāha ill-Allāh*: there is no god but God*)*. "There is no god" (*lā ilāha*) prepares the loci (of the heart) by removing from it any sign of *kathrat* ("multiplicity") which exemplifies darkness and impurities. On the other hand, the second segment (*illa Allāh* "But God"), is the absolute *ithbāt* ("affirmation") of the Absolute which defines the very being of the seeker's heart, and testifies to its wellbeing or *ṣiḥḥat-i dil*.[60]

This dual function of *dhikr* or *shahādah* ("confession to the unity of God"), which Kubrā calls *ma'jūn-i ma'nawī-yi murakkab az nafy wa ithbāt* ("spiritual mixture of negation and affirmation"), leads to the Perfect Man's recognition of the Absolute as the only Affirmed Being.[61] In other words, the unifying *haḍrat-i ṣamadiyyat* ("Presence of the Splendor/Richness"), in Kubrā's terminology,

58. See Kubrā, *Aqrab al-Turq*, 90-95. For a fuller elaboration on the concepts of affirmation and negation in Kubrawī approach, see Seyyed Shahabeddin Mesbahi, *Muqaddama-yī Pirāmūn-i Ravish Shināsī dar 'Irfān: An Introduction to Methodology in Islamic Mysticism* (Shiraz: International Navīd Publishers, 1385/2006), 65-86.

59. See ibid.

60. Ibid.

61. See ibid.

transforms the heart of the Perfect Man, through combined and perpetual progressions of both *nafy wa ithbāt* ("negation and affirmation"), into the perfect locus of the manifestation of God's *fardāniyyat* ("unity/uniqueness").

As seen above, Kubrā utilized the term *fardāniyyat* in his description of God's unity in the Perfect Man's venture towards the abode of affirmation and attaining the reality of *tawḥīd*. It might be interesting to gaze upon the concept of *tafarrud* ("singularity/uniquness") of the Absolute, in the view of Ibn 'Arabī, who utilizes the term *fardiyya* ("oddness").[62]

> Hence oddness (*fardiyya*) becomes manifest through the concept of interconnecting factor, since "three" is the first of the odd numbers..., and these go on to infinity. And evenness, which is called "two," is the first of the pairs (*zawj*) among the numbers, and these also go on to infinity. There is no even number which is not made odd by "one," and thus is found the oddness of that even number. And there is no odd number which is not made even by "one," and thus is found the evenness of that odd number. The factor which makes the odd even and the even odd is the Independent, which determines properties, but which is not determined by any properties. It has no need or poverty, and everything is poor toward It and in need of It. The two feet consist of contrariety of the divine names, such as the First and the Last, the Manifest and Nonmanifest...In the same way, through "one," every object of knowledge possesses a unity through which it is distinguished from everything else. Likewise, oddness, which is the number "three," brings about the manifestation of the property of the two sides and the middle, which is the *barzakh*, the thing between the two, like the hot, the cold, and the lukewarm. From oddness the odd numbers become manifest and from "two," the even numbers. Each number must be either even or odd, and so on ad infinitum. Through the power of the one the properties of the numbers become manifest, and the property belongs to "God, the One, All-subjugating."[63]

In Ibn 'Arabī's view, both evenness and oddness surrender to the encompassing embrace of the Oneness. Utilizing the number

62. See Chittick, *The Sufi Path of Knowledge*, 360.
63. *Futūḥāt*, III, cited in Chittick, *The Sufi Path of Knowledge,* 360-361.

"three," as the first of the odd numbers, he finds the best position for the Perfect Man, between the Non-manifest and Manifest, between *aḥadiyyah* and *wāhidiyyah*, or between the Essence (*dhāt*) and Attributes (*ṣifāt*). The *barzakh*-isthmus (or the Perfect Man) experiences both the coldness of *tanzīh* and warmness of *tashbīh*, as the state of being lukewarm. This way these "three" become One in the unique (*fard*) oddness (*fardiyya*).

Sayyid 'Alī Hamadānī, in a similar approach to that of Ibn 'Arabī's *fardiyya*, prefers the term *tafrīd* ("singleness"). In his *Risālah Dhikriyyah*, Hamadānī attempts to classify the concepts of *tawḥīd*, *tafrīd* and *waḥdat*. He recites the following poem:

> You [must] become lost in Him (*to dar ū gom shaw*); this is [the description] of *tawhid.*[But you have to go further and] Lose [the state of] being lost [in Him]; this is [the description] of *tafrīd.* It would be very difficult [impossible] to reach this abode (i.e., abode of Unity); if there still remains a hair [i.e., slightest part] of your existence. Whoever does not become lost in the sea of Unity (*daryā-yi waḥdat*), is unable to attain the merit [of reaching the abode of Unity even] if he is the envoy of all men.[64]

Hamadānī seems to indicate that *tafrīd* is the practical realization of *tawḥīd.* If *tawḥīd* is the realm in which the very spiritual consciousness of the Perfect Man confesses to or becomes absorbed in the Unity of the Absolute, then *tafrīd* is the station of *fanā' al-fanā'* ("annihilation of annihilation"). In other words, the experience of *tafrīd* occurs when the Perfect Man renews his previous realization of *tawḥīd* at each new experience. He becomes annihilated from the previous realization of *tawḥīd,* tastes the sweetness of *wahdat*, subsides (i.e., experiences *baqā*) for a moment in the in the sea of God's *tajallīyāt* or Mercy, and then again becomes annihilated from his previous realization. Through *tafrīd*, the Perfect Man is able to experience *tawḥīd* in a constant renewal and freshness.

One might be able to interpret Hamadānī's approach to the three concepts of *tawḥīd, tafrīd* and *waḥdat* based on Kubra's aforementioned approach to *nafy and ithbāt* ("affirmation and negation"). The negation of previous realization of *tawḥīd* (or annihilation [*fanā'*] of the previous realization) meets with the affirmation of

64. Mīr Sayyid 'Alī Hamadānī, *Risālah Dhikriyyah* (Tehran: Cultural Studies and Research Institute, 1370/1992), 18.

the newer awareness (in the *baqā* or subsistence of a new realization of *tawḥīd*), and then again experiences the *fanā'al-fanā'* ("annihilation of annihilation") of the previous realization (which was "subsistent" and now is "annihilated"). One might claim that these constant forthcoming realizations of negation and affirmation safeguard the originality and newness of the Perfect Man's awareness of *tawḥīd*.

Hamadānī confirms that this reciprocal pathway between *tawḥīd* and *tafrīd* is eternal, and the Perfect Man must renew his realization of *tawḥīd* constantly; a practice which is the very essence of perfection. This pathway of annihilation continues everlastingly.

> If you pass through the entire Path [of perfection] in each moment
> When you look [with the eye of certainty you realize that] you have taken only one step; not a single seeker (*hīch sālik*) sees [or believes in] the end of the Path (*īn rāh rā pāyān nadīd*)
> [Only] Lovers know…,
> what they went through in the annihilation of love (*fanā-yi'ishq*).[65]

Like Hamadānī, Ibn 'Arabī also confirms the perpetual essence of the path of perfection, through annihilation and subsistence of the awarness of *tawḥīd*. Ibn 'Arabī believes that this everlasting renewal embraces not only the Perfect Man, but also the entire existence:

> A "state" for you to be subsistent or annihilated…It was concerning the states that God commanded His prophet to say, "My Lord, increase my knowledge" (20:114), so that through the new knowledge he might climb to a waystation with God that he did not possess. These states do not pertain exclusively to human beings, nor to this world. Rather they are perpetual forever in this world and the next, and they belong to every created thing. God says, "He is with you wherever you are" (57:4)…that is, in your states. No existent thing ceases to be in a state. Or rather there is no entity, existent or nonexistent, which does not have a state, whether ontological or non-ontological.[66]

Utilizing the above Qur'ānic verses regarding *'ilm* ("knowledge") and *ma'iyyah* ("withness"), and their correlation with the

65. Ibid.
66. *Futḥāt*, II, cited in Chittick, *The Sufi Path of Knowledge*, 264.

concept of *ḥāl* ("state")[67], Ibn 'Arabī seems to refer to the notion of Names, and their *withness* with us, which contain or produce our *knowledge* in every *state* of the spiritual path. Every renewal of our realization of *tawḥīd* occurs through a new manifestation of the Absolute which is the manifestation of His Name. On another occasion, in his *Futūḥāt*, Ibn 'Arabī reminds us of the function of the Names in increasing knowledge:

> There is no divine name that does not wish to attach you to itself and delimit you, so through you its authority may become manifest. At the same time, you know that felicity lies in increase. But you will not have increase without passing to the property of another name. Thereby you may gain a knowledge which you did not have, though which you possess will not leave you. This establishes "flight." But you are warned that the name which is with you must not continue to determine your property. So you flee to the place of increase. Thus "flight" is a property that accompanies the servant in this world and the next.[68]

The path of perfection continues with the endurance of "increasing flight" from one Name to another. This way, the Perfect Man becomes the locus of each Name in this world and the next. As Ibn 'Arabī mentions, the Name Allāh, is the *al-ism al-jāmi'* ("all-comprehensive Name")[69] that contains all Names. This Essential Name represents the locus of the Divine Perfection:

> In actuality the Divine Perfection is found in the penetration of power into the objects of power, desires into the objects of desire, and in the manifestation of the properties of the divine Names. The Essential perfection possessed by the Essence is absolute independence from all this.[70]

The entirety of existence finds its perfection in ascertaining the levels of its absolute *faqr* ("poverty")[71] towards the source of Perfection. The Perfect Man carries an eminent awareness for realiza-

---

67. On Ibn 'Arabī's approach to the "spiritual states," see Chittick, *The Sufi Path of Knowledge*, 264-270.

68. Ibid., 157.

69. See ibid., 30.

70. Ibid., 64.

71. See ibid.

tion of this essential poverty. The realization of the *faqr-i dhātī* ("essential poverty") towards the Source of *kamāl-i dhātī* ("Essential Perfection") determines the levels of perfection among Perfect Human Beings. Utilizing a well-known Qur'ānic verse, Ibn 'Arabī reminds us that the Perfect Man is the one who attains a practical certainty in his realization of this essential poverty. The Name Allāh which represents the Essential Reservoir of Perfection, is the Name towards which this essential poverty is mostly oriented:

> God says, "O people, you are the poor toward Allah, and Allah – He is the Independent, the Praiseworthy" (Koran 35:15). In other words, He is Independent through His names, just as we are poor toward His names. That is why He mentioned [in this verse] the name Allah which brings together all the divine names.[72]

In his *Sharḥ* on Ibn 'Arabī's *Fuṣūṣ*, after referring to the Perfect Man as the locus of the manifestation of the Name Allāh, Hamadānī states that in "the same way that all the Names are sustained by this Name [i.e, Allāh], all bounties which are received by angels are through the Perfect Man."[73] Following Ibn 'Arabī, Hamadānī also calls the Prophet, as the *'ayn-i awwal* or the first entity.[74] As shown in the above example, Hamadānī in his *Sharḥ*, by using his own method, has preferred to look at the concept of human perfection and *al-insān al-kāmil* in their direct kinship and reciprocation with the concept of *waḥdat* ("unity'). Ibn 'Arabī states the following at the beginning of his introduction to the *Fuṣūṣ*:

> Praise be to God Who has sent down the [revelations] of Wisdom upon the hearts of the logoi in a unique and direct way from the Station of Eternity, even though the sects and communities may vary because of the variety of the nations.[75]

In his comments on the phrase of "*bi aḥadiyyat al-tarīq al-umam*,"[76] in the *Fuṣūṣ,* Hamadānī writes:

> *'bā'* in [its affinity with the word] *aḥadiyyat* is for the causality (*sababiyyat*), which means because of the unification (*ittiḥād*)

72. Ibid.
73. Misgar Nijād, introduction to *Sharḥ-i Fuṣūṣ*, 37.
74. See ibid.
75. Austin, *Fuṣūṣ*, 45.
76. Pārsā, *Sharḥ-i Fuṣūṣ*, 14.

> of the straight path (*tariq-i rāst*) and that [straight path] is the call towards Allāh...straight [path] means the elite path (*ṭarīq-i khāṣṣ*), and that is the [unification of the] multiplicity (*kathrat*) of the path of mystics in the unity of the Muḥammadan Path (*waḥdat-i ṭarīq-i Muḥammadī*).[77]

He also mentions that Ibn ʻArabī's views in his *Fuṣūṣ* are all based on the *ḥaḍarāt wa tanazzulāt* ("presences and descending stages").[78] These descending stages in the school of Ibn ʻArabī are described as different *ḥaḍarāt* ("presences") of the Absolute's manifestations.[79] These descending stages act as "mediums" through which the concept of *kathrat* ("multiplicity") defines itself. In other words, each stage of multiplicity as a descending stage is a domain for the Presence of the Absolute with His particular Name or attribute. These descending stages in the form of *qaws-i nuzūl* ("arc of descent"), which represents *kathrat*, are the manifestations of the only *Wujūd al-Muṭlaq* ("Absolute Existence") Who represents the *Waḥdat al-Muṭlaq* ("Absolute Unity"). Therefore, all descending stages constantly return towards Him through *qaws-i ṣuʻūd* ("arc of ascent").[80] Thus, the presences (i.e., both descending and ascending stages of *wujūd*) are the domains in which *waḥdat al-wujūd* ("unity of existence") functions everlastingly. The Perfect Man stands at the defining point (or the isthmus) of this unifying harmony. Recognizing the significant importance of the concept of *tanzzulāt* and *ḥaḍarāt* ("descending stages and presences") in Ibn ʻArabī's view, and particularly in his *Fuṣūṣ*, Hamadānī begins the introduction to his commentary on *Fuṣūṣ* with precisely this concept. He skillfully utilizes the favorite Akbarian expressions, such as *wujūd* ("existence"), *ḥaḍrah* ("Presence"), *ẓuhūr* ("appearance") and *ʻālam* ("world"), in their particular and overlapping occurrences. He usually prefers the term *ahl-i kashf wa taḥqīq* ("people of unveiling and verification") to refer to the school of Ibn ʻArabī over Nasafī's favorite expression *ahl-i waḥdat* ("people of unity"). As Hamadānī states:

> For the people of unveiling and verification (*ahl-i kashf wa taḥqīq*), the Absolute Existence (*Wujūd-i Muṭlaq*) is not more

---

77. Ibid.
78. See ibid., 11.
79. See, for example, Chittick, *The Sufi Path of Knowledge*, 43, 72, 180 and 185.
80. See ibid., 181 and 342.

than One, and that is the Existence of the Truth (*Wujūd-i Ḥaqq*) and the existence of all creatures returns to that Presence (*ḥaḍrat*), and that Presence is the returning abode (*muntahā*) for all (*hama*) [creatures], and this Existence (*Wujūd*) appears (*ẓuhūr*) in each world (*'ālam*) among different worlds.[81]

Hamadānī then points to another important concept in the school of Ibn 'Arabī, namely *ḥaḍarāt-i khams* ("five Divine presences"). He explains the generally accepted categories of these five presences in this school by referring to them in order. He refers to the first Presence as *Ghayb-i Muṭlaq* ("Presence of the Absolute inaccessibility/invisibility"), which is the stage of *Aḥadiyyah* or exclusive Unity. The second presence is the world of *Jabarūt* ("the Presence of invincibility"), in which the *tanazzul* ("descent") from *aḥadiyyah* to *wāḥidiyyah* ("inclusive unity") or *ilāhiyyah* ("Divinity") occurs. This presence, as Hamadānī states, is the *mabda'* ("origin") of all multiplicities and *ḥaḍarāt-i asmā'* ("presences of the Names").[82] The first Divine Attribute that emerges from seclusion into appearance in this realm, as Hamadānī explains, is the Attribute of *'ilm* ("Knowledge"). Thus, in this presence the Name *'Alīm* ("the Absolute Knower") finds its locus of manifestation, and all *a'yān* ("entities") come into appearance. The third presence, which is the presence of *Malakūt* ("Dominion") or spiritual world, correlates to the world of *'amr* ("Command") or *mithāl* ("Image"), which leads to the fourth presence or the realm of *Mulk* (Kingdom), in which the Absolute's *Huwiyyah* (He-ness) manifests in different realms from *'arsh* ("Divine Throne") down to the animal level, which leads to the fifth presence or the realm of *insān* ("the human being") as the last descending stage.[83]

Hamadānī creatively calls these five presences the *ḥaḍarāt-i kulliyah* ("universal presences") and *ḥaḍarāt-i aṣliyyah* ("essential presences").[84] As Hamadānī also mentions, every one of these presences is referred to as a "world" (*'ālam*). Contemporary scholars have pointed out the importance of the concept of *ḥaḍarāt* after the two concepts of *waḥdat al-wujūd* and *al-insān al-kāmil*.[85]

---

81. Pārsā, *Sharḥ-i Fuṣūṣ*, 6.
82. See ibid.
83. See ibid., 6-9.
84. See ibid., 6 and 10.
85. See, for example, William C. Chittick, "Five Divine Presences From al-Qūnaw to al-Qaṣarī," *The Muslim World* LXXII, no. 2 (1982): 107.

Although these two concepts (i.e., unity of existence and the Perfect Man) are two of the most important concepts in the school of Ibn 'Arabī, the concept of *ḥaḍarāt*, seems to indicate "the presences" in which these two major concepts have been constantly discussed by the members of this school. The Perfect Man is the most perfect "manifestation" of the Divine who is also referred to as the most perfect "presence."[86] Viewing the functionality of the concept of *waḥdat al-wujūd* becomes possible through the *kathrat* or multiplicity which becomes *mutajallī* ("manifested") from the Source of *waḥdat* ("Unity"). The Divine presences (*ḥaḍarāt*), perhaps are the loci in which the "manyness" appears in its totality. One might be able to claim that the concept of Divine presences which is systematically summed up in the concept of "five Divine presences[87]," is the realm in which both concepts, the unity of existence and the Perfect Man, are presented with their particular affinities.

Therefore, the concept of "presences" which seems to contextually overlap with such Akbarian concepts as *tajallī* ("Absolute's manifestation"), and *marātib* ("levels"),[88] might be the central realm, without which the crucial concepts of *waḥdat al-wujūd*, and the Perfect Man find no fundamental ground for their constant function. Although Ibn 'Arabī has utilized expressions, such as *ḥaḍrat*, *'ālam*, *ḥaḍrat al-Raḥmān*[89] ("the Presence of the All-Merciful") and *'ālam al-khayāl* or *ḥaḍart al-khayāl*[90] ("the Presence or World of Imagination") in numerous occasions throughout his works, he "does not seem to discuss the "Five Divine Presences" as a separate doctrine."[91]

Ibn 'Arabī discusses the function of the Divine Presence on several occasions, without naming a particular number such as five. On one of these occasions, he provides us with a major dual function of the concept of Divine Presence. He states, "the Divine Presence comprehends the property of the Real in creation and creation in the Real."[92]

86. See ibd., 119, in Farghānī's approach to the "Divine Presences." See also Chittick, *The Sufi Path of Knowledge*, 178, in Ibn 'Arabī's discussion of *ḥaḍrat al-insān*.

87. For a fuller discussion of this concept, see ibid.

88. See ibid., 109.

89. See ibid., 108.

90. See Chittick, *The Sufi Path of Knowledge*, 5.

91. Chittick, "Five Divine Presences," 109.

92. *Futūḥāt*, IV, cited in Chittick, *The Sufi Path of Knowledge*, 124.

As Ibn 'Arabī seems to declare above, the Divine Presence defines the reciprocal ties between the Real and existence. In other words, without considering the fundamental function of *ḥaḍarāt*, the vital ties which represent the functionality of the Real (i.e., the Absolute Source of Unity) through His manifestation (i.e., existence) and thus define the "unity of existence," become dismantled. Chittick explains the affinity and ties between *wujūd*, Divine Presence and the Names as follows:

> For Ibn 'Arabī and his followers, *haḍra* is roughly synonymous with English 'domain' and is almost always used along with some attribute or quality. Ibn 'Arabī himself uses the term in conjunction with various divine names. For example, Chapter 558 of the *Futūḥāt*, one of the longest chapters in the work, is dedicated to explicating the meaning of the divine names, and each name is dealt with in a subsection that is headed by the title, 'the presence of.' Thus we have, *ḥaḍrat al-khalq*, 'the presence of creation,' and the topic is the divine name Creator. So also we have the presence of mercifulness, the presence of peace…In Ibn al-'Arabi's terms, 'the divine presence' is the domain in which the name God exercises its influence, and that domain is *wujūd* and all its concomitants, or, in other terms, God and the whole universe.[93]

The Perfect Man also has a focal standing in the domain of the presences. Ṣadr al-Dīn Qūnawī, the most prominent figure among Ibn 'Arabī's commentators and followers, who introduced the concept of five Divine presences,[94] lists three general domains or presences for *wujūd* ("existence"). These three presences are the worlds or presences of *ghayb* ("unseen"), *shahādah* ("seen"), and the *insān al-kāmil* ("Perfect Man").[95]

In other words, we might be able to say that each of the "presences" presents a partial knowledge of the Absolute at the level of *tajallī* ("Absolute's manifestation"). Knowledge of the Absolute in every unrepeatable manifestation is recognized by the mystic through the Names (*asmā'*).[96] In other words, each Name is a par-

---

93. William C. Chittick, "Presence with God," *Journal of Muḥyiddīn Ibn 'Arabī Society* 20, (1996): 17.

94. See Chittick, "Five Divine Presences," 109.

95. See ibid., 112 and 114-115.

96. See Chittick, *The Sufi Path of Knowledge*, 5.

tially known presence of the Absolute, and each *ḥaḍra* (Presence) is characterized by a Name which manifests or presents a particular attribute of the Absolute, such as *jamāl* ("Beauty") or *jalāl* ("Majesty"). For the Perfect Man, a Name is tailored for each Presence of the Absolute like a unique garment. In each Presence, the Perfect Man meets with a Name in the abode of *waḥdat*. Although the Names convey the boundless presence of *kathrat* ("multiplicity"), the Perfect Man who lives, intuits and experiences, as *barzakh al-jāmi'* ("the comprehensive isthmus") or *barzakh al-barāzikh al-azaliyyah* [97] ("Pre-Eternal isthmus of all isthmuses") between the two realms of *aḥadiyyah* ("exclusive unity") and *wāhidiyyah* ("inclusive unity") or *ghayb* ("unseen") and *shahādah* ("seen"),[98] realizes the Presence of the *Names* as the Presence of the *Named* Who is not but One.[99]

The Names and the Perfect Man in the Abode of Unity

In the first chapter (*faṣṣ*) of the *Fuṣūṣ al-Ḥikam*, Ibn 'Arabī refers to one of the cardinal and favorite terms in his vast array of expressions, i.e., *tajallī* on the two levels of *fayḍ muqaddas* ("sacred") and *fayḍ aqdas* ("the most sacred").[100] The most sacred manifestation is seen as the envoy of the Absolute's *Dhāt* ("Essence') and the sacred manifestation signifies the plurality of His attributes and Names.[101] Here, Shaykh al-Akbar refers to a systematic affinity between the Unity of the Essence and multiplicity of the Names through the Absolute's constant *tajalliyāt* ("manifestations").

God's Names, in every single theophany, also represent His particular *ṣifat* ("attribute") regarding a *ḥaḍra* ("Presence") which reciprocates with that Name.[102] Each Name is a unique key that opens a door to a unique and vast scene of *wujūd*. The Perfect

---

97. See Dawūd ibn Maḥmūd Qayṣarī, *Rasā'il-i Qayṣarī*, ed. Sayyid Jalāl al-Dīn Āshtiyānī (Tehran: Mu'assisa-yi Pajūhishī-yi Ḥikmat wa Falsafa-yi Irān, 1381/2002), 143.

98. See ibid., 121, and 116-117.

99. See ibid.,: "*wa kull mā-fī'l 'awālim al-kulliyyah al-khamsah... aẓlāl-i asmā'-i ilāhiyya-and...* All within the Five Universal Worlds...are the shadows of the Divine Names."

100. See Parsā, *Sharḥ-i Fuṣūṣ*, 24.

101. See ibid.

102. See Chittick, *The Sufi Path of Knowledge*, 33-34.

Man's attained partial knowledge of each Name becomes *renewed* upon the arrival of each new theophany. The vast arrays of *forms* in the corporeal scene, which contain both the content and the level of knowing the Names, function as the indication of Reality or Sheer Existence. These forms perform as the harmonious intercessors in knowing the secrets of the Names. Ibn 'Arabī elaborates upon this essential process at the very beginning of his *Fuṣūṣ*, where he describes "the wisdom of divinity in the word of Ādam."[103]

> The Reality wanted to see the essences of His Most Beautiful Names or, to put it in another way, to see His own Essence, in an all-inclusive object encompassing the whole [divine] Command, which, qualified by existence, would reveal to Him His own mystery. For the seeing of a thing, itself by itself, is not the same as its seeing itself in another, as it were in a mirror; for it appears to itself in a form that is invested by the location of the vision by that which would only appear to it given the existence of the location and its [the location's] self-disclosure to it.[104]

Ibn 'Arabī suggests that the Names (as sacred theophanies or *fayḍ muqaddas*) in their totality become one single *domain/realm* through which *fayḍ aqdas* ("the most sacred manifestation") finds the unifying *ḥaḍra* ("Presence") for its appearance. The multiplicity of the Names mirrored in one realm (of existence) finds its exemplary image in the very being of the Perfect Man. In Ibn 'Arabī's view, the Perfect Man possesses the most perfect faculty to recognize, contemplate, and practice the unity of the Names by pondering upon the Unity of the Source (i.e., by experiencing *ḥaḍrat al-jāmi'* or "the Presence of all-comprehensive"). Ibn 'Arabī refers to the unity of the Names in his *Futūḥāt*:

> All the Divine Names are bound to him [man=Ādam] without one single exception. Thus, Ādam came out in the image of the Name *Allāh*, because this name comprises all the Divine Names.[105]

In his *Fuṣūṣ*, Ibn 'Arabī reiterates the above reciprocation of

---

103. Austin, *Fuṣūṣ*, 47.

104. Ibid., 50.

105. *Futūḥāt*, II, cited in Masataka Takeshita, *Ibn 'Arabī's Theory of the Perfect Man and its Place in the History of Islamic Thought* (Tokyo: Institute for the Study of Language and Cultures of Asia and Africa, 1987), 67.

the Names and their unification in the most essential image of the Absolute (i.e., the Perfect Man).

> For this reason, he [the Prophet] said concerning the creation of Ādam, who is the exemplar (*barnāmaj*) which unites the descriptions (*nu'ūt*) of the Divine Presence (*haḍra ilāhīya*) that is, the Essence (*dhāt*), the attributes (*ṣifāt*), and the Actions (*af'āl*), "God created Ādam in His image." *And His image is nothing but the Divine Presence.*[106] [Emphasis added]

Also in his *Futūḥāt*, Ibn 'Arabī, on several occasions explains different types of Divine Names with different characteristics, such as *tashbīh* and *tanzīh*. In one instance, he elaborates upon the characteristic of *ithbāt* ("affirmation") of the Names. While explaining this characteristic, Ibn 'Arabī refers to the concept of *nisba* ("relation") between the Names. He also clarifies the association of the Absolute's attributes with His Essence:

> There are Names which denote the affirmation of the entities of the Attributes, though the Essence of God does not allow that numbers should subsist (*qiyām al-'adad*). These are the Names that make known (*i'ṭā'*) the entities of the affirmative Attributes of the Essence (*a'yān al-ṣifāt al-thubūtiyyat al-dhātiyya*), such as the Knower, the Powerful, the Willing, the Hearing, the Seeing, the Living, the Responder, and the Thankful; the Names that make known descriptions (*nu'ūt*), so that nothing is understood from their ascription except relations (*nisab*) and correlations (*iḍāfāt*), like the First and the Last, the Merciful and the Nonmanifest; and the Names that make known Acts, such as Creator, Provider, Author, Shaper, etc.[107]

In the case of affirmative Names, Ibn 'Arabī believes that although the Essence negates any type of multiplicity, in order to describe the numerous levels of relations and correlations between the "Essence, attributes, and existence," the attributes are able to convey the manifestations of the Essence to existence. In other words, *takaththur* ("multiplicity") is allowed to manifest the Unity (i.e., the Essence). Ibn 'Arabī, makes this point very clear by stating as follows:

---

106. Ibid., 66.
107. *Futūḥāt*, cited in the *Meccan Revelations*, vol. I, 61.

> All the Divine Names, as many as there may be, can be reduced to one of these kinds, or to more than one; while every one of them must unquestionably denote the Essence.[108]

In order to go through an essential progress from multiplicity to the Unity, Ibn 'Arabī seems to focus on a particular *medium* with an exceptional characteristic. As mentioned above, in Ibn 'Arabī's view, the Name Allāh carries a unique *jāmi'iyyah* ("comprehensiveness"), and is thus discussed in relation to the Perfect Man. Here again, Ibn 'Arabī refers to the unique comprehensiveness of this Name by elucidating Its unique capacity to refer to both concepts of *aḥadiyyah* ("exclusive unity") and *wāḥidiyyah* ("inclusive unity").

> As for the fact that the Name Allah includes the Names of Incomparability, the source for this is near at hand: though every Divine Name is the same in respect of denoting the Essence of God, nevertheless, since every name other than Allah while denoting the Essence of God also denotes – because of its derivation (*ishtiqāq*) [from a specific root having a specific meaning] – a meaning of negation (*salb*) or affirmation (*ithbāt*), it cannot be as strong as this Name in the unity of its denotation (*aḥadiyyat al-dalāla*) of the Essence...God has preserved this proper name (*ism 'alam*) from naming any but the Essence of God. Therefore God says, as an argument against those who had ascribed divinity to something other than this Named One, "[*They ascribe to Allah associates.*] *Say: Name them!*" (Qur'ān 13:33), and those who had held such a view were rendered speechless, for if they had named that thing, they would have named it by other than the Name Allah.[109]

Ibn 'Arabī also elaborates upon the eternal vastness of this Name by referring to the encompassing nature of Its Presence. The Perfect Man, who is related to this Presence, and therefore, experiences the surrounding scenery of Its vastness, has the ability to cross the threshold of *kashf* ("mystical unveiling"). Thus, he comes into an unswerving and unmitigated meeting with the Reality. It is worth mentioning that here, Ibn 'Arabī refers to a clear prerequisite for the authenticity of any promising *kashf*, which is its compatability with the *Sharī'ah*.

---

108. Ibid., 62.
109. Ibid., 60-61.

> So this Presence contains all the Presences. He who knows Allah knows all things. But he does not know Allah who does not know one thing, whatever named possible thing it might be, since the property of the one of these things is the property of them all in denoting knowledge of God, in respect to the specific fact that He is God over the world. Then when you receive unveiling (*kashf*) in respect to works set down in the Law (*al-'amal al-mashrū'*), you will see that you did not know Him except through Him. The denotation (*dalīl*) is identical to what is denoted through that denotation and denoter.[110]

The Perfect Man, in the Presence of the Name Allah, which represents the sacred meeting and the unity of all Names, experiences several eminent mystical states. Ibn 'Arabī's states as follows:

> Though this Presence comprehends all realities, the states which pertain to it most specifically are bewilderment (*ḥayra*), worship (*'ibāda*), and the profession of Incomparability (*tanẓih*). As for Incomparability, which is the fact that He stands above similarity (*tashābuh*) with His creatures, it leads to bewilderment in Him and also to worship.[111]

Ḥayrah ("mystical bewilderment") seems to be an outcome of constant manifestations of the Names upon the *qalb* ("heart") of the Perfect Man in the constant experiences of *fanā'* and *baqā'* ("annihilation and subsistence"). Ibn 'Arabī reminds us of the unique characteristic of the Perfect Man in having both eyes for witnessing the Absolute in the two realms of *tashbīh* and *tanẓīh*. As we have mentioned earlier, these two essential realms pertain to two cardinal types of the Absolute's attributes; i.e., the *ṣifāt* ("attributes") of *jamāl* ("Beauty") and *jālāl* ("Majesty").

Shaykh Najm al-Dīn Rāzī also in his celebrated *Mirṣād al-'Ibād*, refers to the human being as "the mirror of Beauty and Majesty (*jamāl* and *jalāl*) of the Presence of Divinity (*ḥaḍrat-i ulūhiyyat*) and the locus of manifestation (*maẓhar*) of all attributes (*ṣifāt*) [of the Absolute]."[112]

'Azīz al-Dīn Nasafī utilizes the same metaphor of "mirror" in describing the bond between the Absolute and the world. In

110. Ibid., 62.
111. Ibid.
112. See Misgar Nijād, introduction to *Sharḥ-i Fuṣūṣ*, 36.

Nasafī's view, "God's world is a mirror in which He can witness His beautiful Names."[113] The mirror contains *insān-i kabīr* ("Macrocosm/the Great Man") and *insān-i saghīr* ("Microcosm/the Small Man").[114] Nasafī also sees the existent beings as the *maẓhar-ī nūr-ī khudā* ("loci of manifestation for God's light")."[115]

Another well-know Kubrawī master, and one of the cardinal inspirers of 'Alā' ad-Dawlah Simnānī, Shaykh Majd al-Dīn Baghdādī (d.616/1219) refers to the importance of the lineage of the prophets as the source of the light of perfection. Masters of the Path, in his view, are the "mirrors" reflecting the truth of the Path by manifesting this light. Baghdādī states as follows:

> In the transmission of the science of the inward, the more numerous the intermediary transmitters, the better is the nature of transmission, because masters are the reflecting mirrors of the light of the truth from the niche of prophethood. Therefore, the more their inward light is concentrated, the more luminous the path will become for the seeker because of that light, [as the Qur'ān has said]: Light upon light, God guides unto His light whom He wills" (24:35).[116]

We might be able to conclude that in Baghdādī's approach, masters of the Path through their guidance as Perfect Human Beings, become the interpreters of the light of the Truth which emanates from the exemplary images of perfection (i.e., the prophets). In other words, the "broader presence of the masters of the Path" (as mentioned by Baghdādī), due to their reciprocation with the luminous source of prophethood, provides the seekers with a much more purified elucidation of the science of inward. It is worth mentioning that Baghdādī interprets the term *mishkāt* ("niche") in the above Qur'ānic verse (24:35) as the "niche of propethood." One can suggest that the lineage of transmitters, in their perfection, as the lineage of Perfect Human Beings, represent different *shu'ūn* ("tasks/denotations") of the Names in their constant manifestations or transmissions.

---

113. Ridgeon, *'Azīz Nasafī*, 37.

114. Ibid.

115. Ibid.

116. Cited in Shaykh Muḥammad 'Alī Mu'adhdhin Sabzawārī Khurāsānī, *Tuḥfa-yi 'Abbāsī*, trans., Muḥammad H. Faghfoory (Lanham: University Press of America, 2008), 83.

The very "nature of transmission" of the science of the inward which as Baghdādī claims becomes "better" with more "transmitters," reminds us of the well-know Qur'ānic verse, *kulla yawmin huwa fī sha'n* ("each day He is upon some task," 55:29[117]). This verse seems to be central to Ibn 'Arabī's teachings. Both of these aforementioned verses (24:35 & 55:29) convey the concept of *tajallī* ("Absolute's manifestation"). In order to manifest the constant transmission of the Absolute's 'tasks' (*shu'ūn*), Baghdādī prefers a Qur'ānic verse (24:35), which refers to the concept of *tajallī* through the image of undying "lights."

These lights, which based on the mystical interpretation of the verse, open new horizons of the truth to the seekers, become renewed at each *yawm* ("moment") and provide the seeker with the constant and fresh unveiling of the Truth (*nūrun 'alā nūr*/light upon light). Baghdādī, in his utilization of the above Qur'ānic verse, makes a correlation between the concepts of knowledge of *bāṭin*, light, and the Perfect Man. Ibn 'Arabī has also utilized this verse (24:35) on several occasions, particularly in the *Futūḥāt*. Similar to Baghdādī, Ibn 'Arabī refers to God's messengers as the exemplary manifestations of His Name *Nūr* ("Light") through which *bāṭin* or the inner realm of the seeker becomes colored by light.

> According to the tasting of our path, it is not possible to attest to a messenger through rational proofs (*dalāla*), only through a divine self-disclosure in respect of His name "Light." When the person's inward dimensions (*bāṭin*) become colored by that light, then he attests to the messenger. This is the light of faith.[118]

Similar to Baghdādī, Ibn 'Arabī seems to illustrate a systematic reciprocation between the concepts of "knowledge" (as it is perceived by *bāṭin* or *'ilm-i bāṭinī*), *nūr* ("light"), and the Perfect Man (such as the spiritual masters and prophets). In Ibn 'Arabī's explanation, this approach begins from the source of *aḥadiyyah* ("exclusive unity") and proceed towards *wāḥidiyyah* ("inclusive unity"). He affirms, as seen above, that "only through the Absolute's manifestation," would one be able to testify to the authenticity of His messengers. The Light (as God's Name) will bring the color of faith to the hearts of seekers. In other words, *tajallī* of the Light

117. See Chittick, *The Sufi Path of Knowledge*, 434.

118. *Futūḥāt*, II, cited in Chittick, *The Sufi Path of Knowledge*, 196.

(*aḥadiyyah*) is the medium through which the exemplary among Perfect Human Beings become known to the seeker (in the realm of *wāḥidiyyah*). On the other hand, Baghdādī's description of mystical light, as quoted above, begins with the multiple theophanies of lights (i.e., chain of transmitters in the realm of inclusive unity or *wāḥidiyyah*), and ends with the affirmation of His light (on the level of *aḥadiyyah*). Therefore, we might state that these two examples (of Ibn 'Arabī's and Baghdādī's approaches to the concept of light) manifest two patterns of *qaws al-nuzūl* (descending stages of manifestations/Names) and *qaws al-ṣu'ūd* (ascending stages of manifestations/Names), in the function of the Absolute's Names (such as the Light) in existence.

The Perfect Man's Heart, His jāmi'iyyah and the Barzakh

As mentioned earlier, the emphasis upon the role of different colors of lights (*anwār*) in their correlations with *laṭā'if* as subtle mystical receptacles is a distinguishing methodological element in the Kubrawī analysis of the relationship between God, man and existence in general. In describing the role of *laṭā'if*, different Kubawī masters have often reiterated and expressed, either directly or in conjunction with terminological categories of *laṭā'if*, their fascination with the role of "heart" (*qalb*) as the major reservoir/medium of lights.[119] On one of these occasions, the well-known Kubrawī master, Najm al-Dīn (Dāyah) Rāzī, poetically utilizes the concept of light in its reciprocity with "heart" (*qalb*). He makes an effort to envisage, in an organic method, the function of an ascending pattern of the Names, the Perfect Man, and a description of *waḥdah* ("unity") together, as the outcome of these lofty mystical states.

> If the light rises in the Sky of the heart taking the form of one or of several light-giving moons, the two eyes are closed to this world and to the other. If this light rises and, in the utterly pure inner man attains the brightness of the sun or of many suns, the mystic is no longer aware of this world nor of the other, he sees only his own Lord under the veil of the Spirit; then his heart is nothing but light, his subtle body is light, his material covering is light, his hearing, his sight, his hand, his exterior, his interior

119. See, for example, Elias, *The Throne Carrier of God*, 138-140.

are nothing but light, his mouth and his tongue also.[120]

As seen above, Rāzī elaborates upon a state in which the Perfect Man is compared to a unified light. This might be interpreted as a sign for *fanā'* ("annihilation") of the Perfect Man whose entire being, after unveiling of the Real, represents nothing but the Light of the Real. "Veil of the Spirit," which in Rāzī's symbolic language reminds us of a similar function of that of Ibn 'Arabī's *wāḥidiyyah* ("inclusive unity"), seems to mean the encompassing theophany of Absolute's Name, "Light."

Sayyid 'Alī Hamadānī also refers to the Perfect Man's heart as the locus of God's light and the *tawḥīd* of the Absolute. In his *Risālah al-Dhikriyyah*, Hamadānī distinguishes between *ẓāhir* and *bāṭin* or interior and exterior dimensions of *tawḥīd*.

> Know that the Oneness of God (*tawḥīd*) has inward and outward [dimensions], and [also] form (*ṣūrat*) and meaning (*ma'nī*). The heart of [the perfect] man, is the loci of the meaning of inward, and [also represents] interpretive language of the form of the outward. And its (i.e., heart of the Perfect Man 's) inward [embodies] spiritual intuition (*ma'rīfat*) and its outward, [signifies] the invocation of "there is no god but God," allusion (*ishārat*) of the Divine Word (*tanzīl-i rabbānī*), and subtle words of the Prophet…but [we might go further to claim that] sending all [Divine] Books upon the hearts of the most Perfect Human Beings (*qulūb-i kummal*), who were the prophets and messengers, was for describing the difficulties and subtleties of "this meaning" (i.e., the essential reciprocation between the reality of *tawḥīd* and heart of the Perfect Human Beings).[121]

Hamadānī also states an approach of a Sufi master in defining the concept of *tawḥīd*, in a manner close to the point of view of Akbarians. The place of light is also prominent in this approach to the concept of *tawḥīd*.

> Abū Muḥammad Ruwaim said that *tawḥīd* is [the state in which] the Sun of the Essence shines over the desert of [the Perfect Man's] essence, and a drop of the temporal (*ḥudūth*) rain vanishes in the sea of unity (*baḥr-i waḥdat*), in a way that

---

120. Cited in Henry Corbin, *The Man of Light in Iranian Sufism* (Colorado: Shambhala Publication, 1978), 106-107.

121. Ḥamadānī, *Risālah Dhikriyyah*, 19.

it will not find itself [again].[122]

Using a similar terminology to that of Najm al-Dīn Kubrā's aforementioned expression (i.e., *haḍrat-i ṣamadiyyat*) and its correlation with the concept of light, Hamadānī reminds us of the ability of each particle in existence to carry light. This light, in Hamadānī's view has a dual function. Through this light, each entity comes into *ẓuhūr* ("appearance"), and manifests an aspect of the Absolute's *jamāl* ("Beauty"). For Hamadānī, Light is the preferred envoy/ Name, which represents the attribute of Beauty.

> The presence of Lordship's (*rubūbiyyat*) seas of Mercy and zephyr of the Breaths (*nafaḥāt*) of the Presence of Splendor's subtleties (*laṭā'if-i jināb-i ṣamadiyyat*) gave each particle (*dharrih*) of existence a [mode of] light. And that light became the reason of appearance (*ẓuhūr*) of its existence from behind the veiled non-existence, so through that light, it [i.e., each particle] became witness of that Beauty's (*jamāl*) Presence, and it can describe the account of that Beauty, based upon the [attained] degree of its light...because it is not possible to see Him except through Him.[123]

The prominent philosopher, Ṣadr al-Din Muḥāmmad Shirāzī (Mullā Ṣadrā, d. 1050/1641), whose philosophy was influenced by Ibn 'Arabī's worldview, refers to the Perfect Man's eye which carries two lights.[124] These two lights or "*majma' al-nūrayn*" [125] in Sadra's elaboration, seem to represent the comprehensive capability of the Perfect Man to put the aspects of the Absolute's *tashbīh* and *tanzīh* into one unifying realization and perspective (as expressed in Sadrā's words as *'aynun ṣaḥīḥah* or "one truly seeing eye"[126]). The expression *majma' al-nūrayn* (as two conjoined lights) in Ṣadrā's creative terminology by itself manifests the unified essence of these two lights. Seeing *wujūd* through these combined lights leads the Perfect Man to the secret of the *nash'atayn* or "both worlds"[127] (in

122. Ibid., 18.

123. Ibid., 19.

124. See Mullā Ṣadrā, *al-Shawāhid al-Rubūbiyyah*, cited in James Winston Morris, *The Wisdom of the Throne: An Introduction to the Philosophy of Mullā Ṣadrā* (Princeton: Princeton University Press, 1981), 2.

125. See ibid.

126. See ibid.

127. See ibid.

Ṣadrā's term) which is nothing but the eminent realization of *tawḥīd*. Here, Ṣadrā utilizes the expression *al-kāmil al-muḥaqqiq*[128] to refer to the Perfect Man. The term *mūḥaqqīq* ("verifier") perhaps points to the unique quality of the Perfect Man (i.e., *kāmil*) in distinguishing the true Reality from the shadows of erroneous veils. Ṣadrā reminds us that such an eminent goal is not attainable except by having both lights of *tashbīh* and *tanzīh* in one verifying eye:

> The complete and realized man is the one who possesses a truly seeing eye, one in which the two lights [of material and incorporeal being] are conjoined, so that he never keeps his inner vision from perceiving the two states of being: then he will truly know the secret of the two worlds.[129]

Ibn 'Arabī also states that "the Perfect Man possesses light,"[130] and "the Real is sheer light, while the impossible (*muḥāl*) is sheer darkness."[131] He delves into the issue of the Perfect Man's capacity of seeing the Absolute through a creative approach to the Names.

> Hence the Perfect Man is the Real in his poverty, like the names, and the Real in his independence, since he does not see that which is subjected to him, only that which possesses effects. In other words, he sees the divine names, not the entities of the cosmos. Hence he is poor only toward God within the entities of the cosmos, while the cosmos knows nothing of that.[132]

He also explains that:

> Everything manifest in the cosmos is an imaginal engendered form that conforms to a divine form. For He discloses Himself to the cosmos only in accordance with that which corresponds (*munāsaba*)-in the entity of an immutable substance just as man is immutable in respect of his substance. Thus you see the immutable through the immutable and that is "unseen" in respect to you and Him. You see the manifest through the manifest and that is the "witnessed, the witnesser, and the witnessing" in respect to you and Him.[133]

---

128. See ibid.
129. Ibid.
130. *Futūḥāt*, II, cited in Chittick, *Sufi Path of Knowledge*, 366.
131. *Futūḥāt*, III, cited in ibid.
132. Ibid., 369.
133. Ibid., 362.

The comprehensive awareness of the Perfect Man brings all aspects of experiencing the Names in one occurrence. The *ẓāhir* or manifest which represents the Real through the sheer light of His manifestation, resembles the same light, which is attained by the Perfect Man. Thus, he sees Him through the manifested light of His manifestation. Each manifestation corresponds to a Divine Name, and is suited to a state in which experiencing the Name and the Named occur jointly. In this process, the Perfect Man finds himself as the interpreting border between the Named (i.e., the Absolute) and the Name (or manifestation of the Absolute). In other words, he realizes his position as the one who is able the most to differentiate between *aḥadiyyah* ("exclusive unity") and *wāḥidiyyah* ("inclusive unity"), by finding himself as the *barzakh* ("isthmus") between these two realms:

> The Perfect Man is the Son (epitome) of the world. By knowing himself, the Perfect Man comes to know that he is a dividing line between the temporality (*ḥudūth*) of the world and eternity (*qidam*) of the Real, that is between finitude and infinity. The dividing line between finitude and infinity is the moment of creation. Creation is the human being as Ibn 'Arabī says, meaning that the human being is the ultimate purpose or the final cause of creation. The Real created the world because He loved to be known, that is because He loved to realize Himself, and the Perfect Man assists the Real in achieving this realization. The Perfect Man comes to know the Real by differentiating Him from the creation, that is, by differentiating the infinite from the finite. To differentiate the infinite from the finite is to know the Limit that brings them together while at the same time keeping them separate. The Limit that brings the finite and infinite together resembles the instant of time (*al-'ān*), which is the essence of the past time, that is, the time of the manifestation of the Real that has come to be, and future time, that is, the time of the manifestation of the Real that has not come to be. As such, the present state designates the Being of the Real, since the Being of the Real is the Essence of all that has come to be and all that will ever be.[134]

This Limit (or *barzakh,* "the isthmus"), in Ibn 'Arabī's understanding, represents the *jāmi'iyyah* ("comprehensiveness") of the

134. Bashir, *Ibn 'Arabī's Barzakh*, 122.

Perfect Man.[135] This unique characteristic, in its practical realization, is seeing the existence (i.e., Names) through the both eyes of *huwa/ lā huwa* ("He/Not He")[136]. In his realization of the Names, the Perfect Man becomes the interpreter of their multifaceted *wujūh* ("faces").[137] He is also the medium through which, these many-sided *wujūh* meet with their essence of *waḥdat*. This distinctive characteristic of the Perfect Man enables him to earn a constant awareness of both concepts of *waḥdat* and *kathrah* in their essential mutuality. Perhaps, because of this unique characteristic of the Perfect Man, Ibn 'Arabī states that the "circular movement of the celestial spheres follows the movement of the Perfect Man's heart."[138]

'Azīz al-Dīn Nasafī, in his masterpiece *Insān al-Kāmil*, reminds us of the constant reciprocation between unity and multiplicity.

> O Sufi, there is a unity before multiplicity, and [there is] a unity after multiplicity. And this last unity [i.e., unity after multiplicity] is very difficult to reach. If a seeker reaches this last [type of] unity, he will become unitarian/monist (*muwaḥḥid*) and emancipated from polytheism (*shirk*).[139]

Nasafī also reconfirms a vital place for the concept of multiplicity in order to approach the concept of unity. He affirms that "without multiplicity, there is no *tawḥīd*."[140] Nasafī's description of unity and multiplicity seems to be another way of referring to the Perfect Man as the *barzakh* between the Essence (unity) and the Names (multiplicity). As mentioned above, Nasafī divides the concept of *waḥdat* ("unity") into two types. The first type (i.e., the unity before multiplicity) refers to the level of *aḥadiyyah* in which the Absolute manifests no multiplicity and thus unity is exclusive. The second type of unity (i.e., unity after multiplicity) or *waḥdat ba'd az kathrat*,[141] in Nasafī's words, is similar to the level of *wāḥidiyyah*.

135. See Chittick, *The Sufi Path of Knowledge*, 30.

136. See ibid., 4.

137. See ibid., 30.

138. See Mehdī Dahbāshī, *Sharḥ-i Rubā'iyyāt-i Falsafī wa' 'Irfānī-yi 'Allāmah Dawānī* (Tehran: Hermes, 1387/2008), 74. 'Allāmah Dawānī (d.908/1502), one of the prominent spiritual masters and a distinguished advocate of Ibn 'Arabī, in a comment on one of his own *rubā'īyāt* states: "*wa Shaykh [al-Akbar]... dar ba'zī rasā'il farmūdah ka sayr-i dawrī-yi aflāk ṭābi-yi qalb-i insān-i kāmil ast.*"

139. Nasafī, *Insān al-Kāmil*, 214.

140. Ibid.

141. See ibid.

In this realm, the manifestations (i.e., multiplicities, the Names or existence) are accessible, and contemplating *waḥdat,* provides the Perfect Man him with a practical awareness. As a mediating isthmus between unity and multiplicity, the Perfect Man undergoes challenging experience of pondering upon unity within (or after) multiplicities of existence. In the realm of unity after multiplicity, the Perfect Man makes a differentiation between the "Absolute" and "everything else" and then reaches a vision of *waḥdat.*

The well-known Kubrawī master, Sayyid 'Alī Hamadānī, refers to the role of the Perfect Man as the *barzakh* between *shahādah* ("the seen world") and *ghayb* ("the unseen world") in *talāṭum-i daryā-yi irādat* ("clashing waves of the sea of Will").[142] This unique place for the Perfect Man, as Hamadānī states, is the result of the true servant's *maḥabbat* ("love") for God.[143] Hamadānī, in order to describe the foundation of this essential love, utilizes the term *tajallī* ("Absolute's manifestation"), a term crucial to Ibn 'Arabī's school. This love, which is the *tajallī-yi nafaḥāt-i alṭāf-i rabbānī* ("manifestation of the breaths of God's grace"), appears as the outcome of the Perfect Man's function as the *barzakh-i ghayb wa shahādat* ("isthmus between the two worlds").[144] Hamadānī considers this mediating position (*barzakh*) of the Perfect Man as "one of the principles of existence of both worlds."[145]

Ibn 'Arabī's foremost disciple, Ṣadr al-Dīn Qūnawī, in one of his many discussions of the concept of *barzakh,* identifies the position of the Perfect Man as the *barzakh al-i'tidālī* ("moderating isthmus"). This isthmus, as Qūnawī explains, is the reality of man's perfection which resembles a mirror for both realms of unity and multiplicity.[146] Similar to Ḥamadānī, Qūnawī approaches the concept of *maḥabbat-i aṣlī* ("essential love") in defining *barzakh.* In one instance, he regards this love as "the first isthmus between *wāḥidiyyah* and *aḥadiyyah* ("inclusive unity and exclusive unity")."[147] Qūnawī considers the destination and attachment of this essential love as the most beautiful nature and the most just heart of

142. Hamadānī, *Mashārib al-Adhwāq*, 39.

143. Ibid.

144. Ibid.

145. Ibid.

146. Ḥamzah Fanārī, *Miṣbāḥ al-Uns*, trans., Najīb Māyil Heravī (Tehran: Intishārāt-i Mowlā, 1384/2005), 79.

147. Ibid., 64.

the Prophet Muḥammad. These two principal loci (i.e., the nature and the heart of the Prophet) are the places for the *kamāl-i istijlā-yi dhāt-i aḥadī* ("perfect manifestation of the Essence of Unity"), which resembles the light of the Prophet at the beginning of creation.[148]

In defining the essential status of the Perfect Man, Qūnawī employs the allegories of book and mirror in another work.[149] In order to pinpoint the role of the Perfect Man in creation, he compares both the Essence of the Absolute and the Perfect Man to a book. Qūnawī refers to the Essence of the Real as the *mujmal* ("concise") Universal Book that is the comprehensive essence of all books, when they were yet to be opened completely (i.e., before *tafṣīl*). The Absolute's knowledge of His Essence (or Himself) is also the extensive and detailed book which resembles what is sealed and secluded in the Essence. Qūnawī then reminds us of a similarity between this Book and that of the Perfect Man with one difference. The Perfect Man, as he explains, is also a concise book which is the comprehensive principle of all books – after they were opened, i.e., after *tafṣīl*. The Perfect Man's *'ilm* ("knowledge") of himself also resembles a book that explains in detail what is secluded and in concise form within the Perfect Man.[150] Here, Qūnawī approaches the mediating/moderating position *(barzakhiyya)* of the Perfect Man with a different method. The stage of *before tafṣīl* seems to be the same as Ibn 'Arabī's *aḥadīyyah* or the level of *Dhāt* ("Essence") in which the Absolute is yet to manifest the Names (existence). On the other hand, the stage of *after tafṣīl* comes when manifestation of the Names has occurred; i.e., the stage of *wāḥidiyyah* or inclusive unity.

Qūnawī continues delving into the realm of allegories by describing the vital place of the Perfect Man in more detail. He clarifies the knowledge of the Absolute and the Perfect Man by stating that the Perfect Man's knowledge of himself is his mirror in which he is able to manifest himself. The Essence of the Real's knowledge of Himself, as Qūnawī asserts, is also the mirror in which He manifests Himself. Then, Qūnawī concludes that there is a coherence between the "Essence of the Real and the Perfect Man" from

148. Ibid.

149. Ṣadr al-Dīn Qūnawī, *Mirāt al-'Ārifīn*, trans., Najīb Māyil Heravī (Tehran: Intishārāt-i Mowlā, 1387/2008), 8-9.

150. Ibid.

the standpoints of their *kullīyat* ("universality") and the fact that they contain all entities (*ijmāl*). There is also, as he states, a coherence and agreement between the Real's knowledge and the Perfect Man's knowledge from the viewpoint of their *maẓharīyyah* (i.e., "being the loci of manifestation').[151]

Similar to Qūnawī's elucidation regarding knowledge of the Perfect Man, Nasafī also calls the Perfect Man, the locus of manifestation for knowledge (*insān-i kāmil maẓhar-i'ilm ast*).[152] As Qūnawī puts it, the Perfect Man (*al-insān al-kāmil*), because of the above mentioned coherence, is the mirror of the Essence. The Essence from the point of view of *kullīyat wa ijmāl* ("universality and inclusion of the entities within It") is manifested within this mirror (i.e. the Perfect Man).[153] But Qūnawī goes beyond this ending remark and provides us with a more comprehensive conclusion. He believes that these sets of coherences between the Real and the Perfect Man, result in a unanimity between their essence and knowledge. Qūnawī of course, reminds us of the impossibility of *ḥulūl* ("incarnationism") and *ittiḥād* ("unificationism") in his understanding of the unity between the Real and the Perfect Man.[154]

Maqām al-munāzalah: the Completed Circle

In his description of *Wujūd al-Wāḥid* ("Existence of the One"), Shaykh al-Kabīr Qūnawī refers to the three dimensions the of outer, the inner and the mediator (isthmus). The outer dimension is *'ālam* ("the world"), the inner represents the *asmā'* ("Names"), and the *al-barzakh al-jāmi'* ("comprehensive isthmus"), which separates the outer from the inner, is the Perfect Man. Qūnawī concludes that the outer dimension (or the world) is the mirror of the inner dimension (or the Names), in the same way that the outer is the mirror for the inner dimension.[155] Whatever is situated between these two realms (i.e., the inner and the outer) is the mirror of both, *jam'an wa tafṣīlan* (in the way which unites and describes them).[156] In the stage of being a comprehensive isthmus, the Perfect Man, as Qūnawī states,

151. See ibid.

152. See Nasafī, *Insān al-Kāmil*, 272. In Nasafī's words: "*insān-i kāmil maẓhar-i 'ilm ast*."

153. See Qunawī, *Mirāt al-'Ārifīn*, 8-9.

154. Ibid., 9.

155. Ibid., 37.

156. Ibid.

functions in a reciprocal method of *martabah tanazzul* ("descending stage").[157]

This stage consists of two allied levels of mutuality. The first is *tanazzul rabbānī* ("descending the Absolute [through the Names]"). At this level, the Absolute is referred to by *ṣifāt al-'abdānī* ("characteristics similar to that of the servant"). This level also reminds us of the level of *tashbīh*. At the second level, the Perfect Man through his ascending spiritual journey towards the Absolute is referred to by *irtiqā' al-rabbānī* or manifesting the Absolute's attributes.[158] Qūnawī's description of this process, which takes place within the bounties of the Absolute's manifestations (or the Names), is another method of invoking the mediating role ("*barzakhiyyah*") of the Perfect Man. By being the interpreter of the descending Names (in *martabah tanzzul rabbānī*) and also through *iritiqā'* ("journeying towards the Origin of the Names"), the Perfect Man as the par exemplar of the Names, experiences both the descending and ascending stages on the everlasting path towards perfection.

Nasafī also refers to these two stages of "descend and ascend," through which the Perfect Man returns to his Origin:

> The Perfect Man, who in his descent and ascent, will have passed three heavens and three earths and then is firmly established upon the Throne; that is he will have come from and returned to the First Intelligence. Thus the circle, is completed, the First Intelligence is firmly established upon the Throne and the Perfect Man is also firmly established upon the Throne.[159]

Nasafī's "completed circle" pinpoints the combination of the two semi circles of *nuzūl* and *ṣu'ūd* in Ibn 'Arabī's mystical expressions. The *qaws-i nuzūl* (descending stage), stems from the essential and constant *maḥabbah* ("love") of the Absolute for His servants. This love reaches its eminent culmination within the heart of the Perfect Man and will return him, via *qaws-i ṣu'ūd* ("ascending stage") to his Source. Borrowing a Qurānic verse, Ibn 'Arabī', in one of his prayers, refers to the true seekers' yearning for journeying through the complete circle of this fundamental love. As Ibn 'Arabī suggests, the very outcome of the *qaws-i su'ūd* is attaining the realization of unity.

157. Ibid., 45.
158. See ibid.
159. Nasafī, *Insān al-Kāmil*, cited in Ridgeon, *'Azīz Nasafī*, 175.

In this journey towards the One, the moderating position of the Perfect Man as the *barzakh* brings these two semi-circles into "one complete circle" that will be everlastingly renewed. The vivid appearance of the *maḥabbat-i aṣlī* ("essential love") in defining the role of the Perfect Man as the moderating isthmus, which was referred to above, in the words of Qūnawī and Hamadānī, appears in the following invocation of Shaykh al-Akbar. The descent of the Absolute's love upon his servant, marks the beginning of the *qaws-i nuzūl* in the same way that "coming into loving union" resembles the beginning of *qaws-i ṣu'ūd* or ascending stage of the Perfect Man. In his constant standing between *ghayb wa shahādah* ("the unseen and the seen worlds"), the Perfect Man becomes the cardinal interpreter of Absloute Love. In his prayer, Ibn 'Arabī states as follows:

> Burning down upon me, O You who are Eminent in Affection, the Constant in Love, love [extended] from You, so that through it the hearts of Your servants will be guided to me, yielding to me with love, affectionate and unwavering, from the filling with love, the softening of hearts and the coming into loving union in *They love them as if it were love for Allāh, but those who believe are more ardent in love for Allāh.*[160]

One of the prominent Persian advocates of Ibn 'Arabī, Jalāl al-Dīn Mūḥammad ibn Sa'd al-Dīn As'ad Kāzirūnī (d. 908/1502), known as Allāmah Muḥaqqīq Dawānī, in one of his *rubā'iyyāt* concerning the concept of *tanazzul* ("the descending stage") refers to the direct correlation between man's entire being and the Absolute's Being: "Because our we-ness (*mā'ī-yi mā*), is [tantamount to] descending (*tanzzul*) of His He-ness (*oū-īye oū*), that One [i.e., His He-ness] is like the Sea (*baḥr*), and this one [i.e., our we-ness] resembles an stream of water (*jū*)."[161] Dawānī then concludes that the *tanazzul* is the foundation of man's perfection. "Therefore, our perfection is from Him."[162]

Also in his *Futuḥāt al-Makkiyyah*, Shaykh al-Akbar refers to the mutual harmony between the stages of ascent and descent in the

160. Muḥyiddīn Ibn 'Arabī, *A Prayer for Spiritual Elevation and Perfection: al-Dawr al-a'lā (Ḥizb al-Wiqāya)*, trans., Suhā Tajī Faroukī (Oxford: Anqā Publishing, 2006), 86.

161. Dahbāshī, *Sharḥ-i Ruā'iyyāt*, 71.

162. Ibid.

process of envisioning the Real. In this journey of *munāzalah*, the Perfect Man experiences a circle of perfection in returning to the Real.

> When the vision of the Real takes place, it only takes place in a mutual waystation (*munāzala*) between an ascent and a descent. That ascent belongs to us and the descent to Him. To us belong "drawing close" (*tadānī*) and to Him belongs "coming down" (*tadallī*), since coming down must stem from the high. It is ours to climb (*taraqqī*) and His to receive (*talaqqī*) those who come to Him. All of this gives us knowledge of the form in which He discloses Himself to His servants.[163]

Najm al-Dīn Kubrā, in a creative elucidation of what he refers to as *sirr al-sayr* ("secret of the mystical journey"), makes a significant correlation between the descending and ascending lights. This perpetual reciprocation, as Kubrā explains, occurs between the *'arsh* ("Throne") and the Perfect Man's *qalb* ("heart"). In his description, *nūr* ("light") becomes the real substance of both what is *in* Heaven and *in* the Perfect Man's heart. From this light stems the mutual longing between sources of ascent and descent. When this mutuality is nurtured, each particle of the mystic's being finds its counterpart in the Heaven. Najm al-Dīn Kubrā states as follows:

> Each time the heart sighs for the Throne, the Throne sighs for the heart, so that they come to meet...Each precious stone... which is in you brings you a mystical state or vision in the Heaven corresponding to it, whether it be the fire of ardent desire, of delight or of love. Each time a light rises up from you, a light comes down toward you, and each time a flame rises from you, a corresponding flame comes down toward you...If their energies are equal, they meet half-way (between Heaven and Earth)...But when the substance of light has grown in you, then this becomes a Whole in relation to what is of the same nature in Heaven: then it is the substance of light in Heaven which yearns for you and is attracted by your light, and it descends towards you. This is the secret of the mystical approach.[164]

Najm al-Dīn Kubrā also describes how "lights" in the mutual realms of descent and ascent, become one body of lights through

---

163. *Futūḥāt*, I, cited in Chittick, *The Sufi Path of Knowledge*, 342.
164. Kubrā, *Fawā'iḥ*, cited in Corbin, *Man of Light*, 73.

which light appears upon light perpetually. In this description, when the veil of corporeal being is lifted, one might witness a type of *waḥdat* ("unity") that occurs between the lights, as well as the Throne and the heart (or between the Real and the Perfect Man).

> There are lights which ascend and lights which descend. The ascending lights are the lights of the heart; the descending lights are those of the Throne. Creatural being is the veil between the Throne and the heart. When this veil is rent and a door to the Throne opens in the heart, like springs toward like. Light rises toward light and light comes down upon light, *"and it is light upon light"* (Qur'ān 24:35).[165]

Referring to the concept of *tajallī* ("the Absolute's manifestation"), Najm al-Dīn Kubrā, elaborates upon a direct reciprocation between the heart and the Abosolute's attributes:

> The heart participates in every divine Attribute, and therefore in the divine Essence. This participation does not cease to grow, and the mystics differ from each other according to the extent of their participation. Since each Attribute has its seat in one of the places or abodes in question, and since the heart participates in each of the divine Attributes, they are epiphanized in the heart to the extent that the heart participates in these Attributes. The *Attributes revealed to the Attributes, Essence to Essence*...On the one hand, the Attributes (or places) contemplate the heart (cause it to be present to them). On the other hand, the heart contemplates the places of the Attributes (makes itself present to them). Theophany is brought about first by theoretical knowledge, later by visionary apperception, whether the Attributes make themselves witnesses present to the heart, or whether the heart makes itself a witness and present to the *places* of the Attributes.[166] [Emphasis added]

The reciprocation between the heart and the Absolute's attributes constitute a circle in which the *kathrat* of the attributes sees its unifying place within the seeker's heart. Also as seen above, Kubrā speaks of a realm in which "attributes are revealed to the attributes." The well-known member of Ibn ʻArabī's school, ʻAbd al-Karīm Jīlī (d. 812/1410), in his book, *Sharḥ-i Mushkīlāt-i Futūḥāt al-Makki-*

165. Ibid., 72.
166. Ibid.

yyah ("Explaining the Difficulties of the *Futūḥāt al-Makkiyyah*"), refers to an expression utilized by Ibn 'Arabī, which reminds us of Najm al-Din Kubra's above words on "attributes." Jilī mentions that Ibn 'Arabī believed in a constant renewal of what he calls *al-nikāḥ al-qudsī* (sacred marriage) between the Absolute's attributes, which renews and guarantees the very continuation of existence.[167] Perhaps one might claim that this is a method through which the "Absolute's attributes are revealed to the attributes" in the view of Ibn 'Arabī.

As mentioned above, Kubrā also refers to a realm in which the "Essence is revealed to the Essence." 'Abd al-Karīm Jilī refers to an interpretation that is similar to Kubra's words regarding the Essence. He states that the "Absolute loved (*aḥabba*) to become manifested from His Essence (*min dhātihī*) for His Essence (*li-dhātihī*), according to the nature of His Essence (*bi-muqtaḍā dhātihī*)."[168] In order for this process to occur, as Jīlī explains, the Essence is divided (*qussima*) into two *qismayn* ("types"). This division, as Jilī tells us, does not provide any form of manyness in the nature of the Essence (*min ghayr-i ta'addudin fi'l-'ayn*).[169] The first of these two types, in Jilī' s view, is considering the Absolute as *wājib* ("Necessary"), *qadīm* ("Eternal"), *rabb* ("Lord"), and *fā'īl* ("Doer").[170]

The second type consists of *mumkin* ("possible"), *ḥādith* ("temporally originated"), *'abd* ("servant"), and *munfaṣil* ("discontiguous").[171] The first appearance of the second type of the Essence, is called *habā'* ("dust Cloud"), *hayūlā* ("hyle"), or *qudrat* ("power").[172] Then Jīlī refers to both *habā'*and *hayūlā* as *ḥaqq-i makhlūq* ("the created real").[173] This stage is described by *ahl-i taḥqīq* ("people of verification") using expressions such as *aql-i awwal* ("First Intellect"), *rūḥ-i Muḥammadī* ("Muhammadan Spirit"), and *qalam-i a'lā* ("Supreme Pen").[174]

In his *Futūḥāt*, Ibn 'Arabī also utilizes a similar but more lu-

167. See Muḥammad 'Alī Muwaḥḥid, introduction to *Fuṣūṣ al-Ḥikam*, trans., and ed. Muḥammad 'Alī Muwaḥḥid and Ṣamad Muwaḥḥid (Tehran: Nashr-i Kārnāmah, 1385/2006), 70.

168. Ibid., 146.

169. Ibid.

170. Ibid., 147

171. Ibid.

172. Ibid.

173. Ibid.

174. Ibid.

cid expression *al-ḥaqq al-makhlūq bihī* ("the Real through whom creation takes place").[175] As Chittick states, Ibn 'Arabī considers this term to have the same meaning as *habā'* ("Cloud") and *nafas al-Raḥmān* ("Breath of the All-Merciful").[176] Ibn 'Arabī refers to the "Cloud" as "identical with the Breath of the All-merciful"[177] and states that "it is a breathing (*nafkh*) in the Being of the Real, so through it creation takes shape (*tashakkul*) within the Real."[178] Also referring to the term *al-ḥaqq al-makhlūq bihī,* Chittick explains that "The Cloud is the Real through Whom takes place the creation of everything. It is called the "Real" since it is identical with the Breath, and the Breath is hidden within the Breather."[179]

In another place, Ibn 'Arabī, describing the *tajallī* of the Breath of the All-Merciful, seems to pave the way towards defining the concept of *tawḥīd* in the realm of *waḥdat.* We might be able to claim that, in the following passage, he discloses the *secret of the circle* in the *wujūdī* understanding. This circle defines the ties between the Real and the Perfect Man. In this circle, the Perfect Man perpetually goes through both experiences of being manifested from and being returned to the Real. The more he is aware of being encompassed within the circle of the Real's *ḥaḍra* ("Presence"), the more elevated becomes his perfection. Considering his elevated awareness of the Real's encompassing presence, the Perfect Man becomes the perfect witness of the Perfect Real while experiencing an enduring perfection in His encompassing circle (*muḥīṭ*). This circle contains the entire existence which is undelimited in its nature, because of the undelimited Essence of the Real. Ibn 'Arabī states as follows:

> This is the *tawḥīd* of the Real, which is the *tawḥīd* of the Heness...Hence, "There is no God but He" is a description of the Real. That within which the existence of the cosmos has become manifest is the Real; it becomes manifest only within the Breath of the All-merciful, which is the Cloud. So it is the Real, the Lord of the Throne, who gave the Throne its all-encompassing shape, since it encompasses all things. Hence the root within which the forms of the cosmos became manifest

175. See Chittick, *The Sufi Path of Knowledge*, 133.
176. See ibid.
177. See ibid., 134.
178. Ibid.
179. Ibid.

encompasses everything in the world of corporeal bodies. This is nothing other than the Real Through Whom Creation Takes Place (*al-ḥaqq al-makhlūq bihi*). Through this receptivity, It is like a container within which comes out into the open (*burūz*) the existence of everything it includes, layer upon layer, entity after entity, in a wise hierarchy (*al-tartīb al-ḥikamī*). So it brings out into the open that which had been unseen within It in order to witness it.[180]

We might attempt to make a comparsion between Kubrā's description of the function of the Essence mentioned above and Ibn 'Arabī's words. It seems that from the Akbarian standpoint, the fully unique outcome of the reciprocations in which the "Essence is revealed to the Essence," is the appearance of the Perfect Man. One might assert that in the view of the school of Ibn 'Arabī, the constant mutual circle of interaction and wedding between the Absolute's attributes, both governs and ensures the very being of existence, as well as its everlastingness. On the other hand, the Perfect Man is presented to existence as the essential souvenir of the Essence's internal modes. Thus, the Perfect Man, as the summation of the entirety of existence in a nutshell, becomes the perfect outcome of the circle through which "Essence is revealed to the Essence."

Another Kubrawī master, 'Alā ad-Dawlah Simnānī also stresses the definite role of the whole "circle" in the spiritual journey towards the One. In his *Khumkhāna-yi Waḥdat*, which appears to be very different from his much more orthodox and seminal work *al-'Urwah*, Simnānī defines the role of *dāyirah* ("the circle") in the seeker's path of perfection. In Simnānī's worldview, without the very *nūqṭah* ("dot") of the Real's Love, which has to turn into a complete circle (*mustadīr shud*) for its perfection, the shallow line (*khaṭṭ*) of our borrowed being has no share of existence and thus, it falls into the abyss of absolute non-existence (*'adam*).[181] Simnānī affirms:

> This line of our existence (*īn khatt-i wujūd-i mā*) has its surface in non-existence (*'adam*), it has no pen, paper and writing on it. When the circle of existence (*dāyira-yi wujūd*) comes into being, know that the root of the dot (*aṣl-i nūqṭah*) is eternal (*qīdam*). Every moment which is not [i.e., does not belong to]

180. Ibid.

181. Simnānī, *Khumkhāna-yi Waḥdat*, 82.

> Him is a worthless moment, [and] every entity (*har chīz*) which is not [for] Him is certainly non-existence. When that dot becomes a complete circle (*mustadīr shud*), be cheerful (*khush mībāsh*). When the circle is completed (*dāyirah muttaṣil shud*), there remains no place for sorrow.[182]

The dot of the Real's love (i.e., the human being) finds perfection in the everlasting "circle" of perfection, which begins with the Real's manifestation of the Names (*asmā'*), and becomes completed in each return towards Him. The Perfect Man finds his real place in existence within the eternal and encompassing circle of the Real's Existence.

In one of his elucidations of the Perfect Man's characteristics, Ibn 'Arabī identifies the reason for *wujūdun li'l-'ayn* or the appearance of existence, as the Perfect Man's *ḥubbun lil-asmā'* ("love of the Names").[183] This love is the prime reason for the Names to manifest their realities.[184]

The Kubrawī master, Sayyid 'Alī Hamadānī also refers to the Perfect Man's prepared heart for love of the Names, which makes both Names of Beauty (*jamāl*) and Majesty (*jalāl*) to descend upon him.[185] The bounty of the Names, in the Perfect Man's lofty experience, results in his contemplation of *waḥdat* ("unity"). Here the Kubrawī master employs a well-known mystical allegory, *sham' wa parwānah* ("candle and moth"). In the higher realms of his mystical experience, the Perfect Man's "moth of fictitious existence" (*parwāna-yi hastī-yi mawhūm-i khud rā*) embraces the lights of the Unity's majestic candle (*sham'-i jalāl-i aḥadiyyat*).[186] As a result of this closeness, his *wujūd-i fānī* ("fading existence") joins the *ḥaqīqat-i bāqī* ("perpetual Reality").[187]

Hamadānī utilizes the two important Akbarian terms (i.e., *jalāl* and *aḥadiyyat*) in one single combination (i.e., *sham'-i jalāl-i aḥadiyyat*), in order to refer to the *tanzīhī* ("peerless") Names of the Absolute in their relation to the Essence. The candle, which makes the manifestations of the Essence accessible at the level

182. Ibid.

183. See Ibn 'Arabī, *Rasā'il* (Beirut: Dār al-Ṣādir, 1997), *Kitāb al-Manāzil al-Quṭb wa Maqāmuh wa Ḥāluh*, 319.

184. Ibid.

185. See Hamadānī, *Risālah Dhikriyyah*, 11.

186. Ibid.

187. Ibid.

of *wāḥidiyyah* ("inclusive unity"), provides the mystic with the Names which illuminate the Path towards the One. In the eminent levels of mystical experience, as Hamadānī mentions, the Perfect Man goes through constant *fanā'* ("annihilation") and *baqā'* ("subsistence"). This can be taken to mean that in each experience of annihilation, the Perfect Man's awareness become annihilated in one of the Absolute's Names (manifestations) and then will subsist in the next Name.

The Reciprocation of the Names, and the Perfect Man's experience of them through annihilation and subsistence will continue everlastingly. The Perfect Man's mystical experience of annihilation and subsistence in its perpetuality might also confirm his position as the *barzakh* between the two worlds. Each experience of annihilation, in comparison with its immediate pair, is a less genuine realization of the Reality. Each realization of subsistence, in its relation to the next immediate experience of annihilation, is also a less accomplished awareness of Reality. However, in the everlasting and mutual experiences of annihilation (*fanā'*) and subsistence (*baqā'*), the Perfect Man seems to be a *perpetual* isthmus between two *perpetually* renewing forms of awareness of the Absolute (i.e. annihilation and subsistence).

Similar to Hamadānī, 'Alā al-Dawlah Simnānī utilizes the same allegories to elaborate upon the Perfect Man's *'ishq* ("steadfast love") for the Absolute. He makes use of the expressions such as *sham'-i aḥadiyyat*, in his discussion of the Names of *jalāl wa jamāl* ("Majesty and Beauty"). On one occasion, he refers to "Perfect Human Beings" as *'ashiqān-i jānbāz* ("self-sacrificing lovers") who, like butterflies (*parwānah ṣifat*), burn their *ithnīniyyat* ("duality") within the heart of *sham'-i aḥadiyyat* ("Unity's candle").[188] These lovers, as the Kubrawī shaykh states, prepare their *khāna-yi wujūd* ("house of existence") for the *Sulṭān-i tajallīyāt-i ulūhiyyat* ("*Sulṭān* of Divinity's manifestations"), in order to receive the manifestations of His Essence and attributes in both forms of Majesty and Beauty (*jamālī wa jalālī*).[189] Simnānī also elaborates upon the concept of *fanā'* in its relation to these devote lovers. He asserts that these lovers become annihilated in the *asal-i faḍl-i īzadī* ("honey of God's bounty"). Simnānī refers to this experience of annihilation as the *nihāyat-i safar-i awwal* ("end of the first journey"), which

188. Simnānī, *Muṣannafāt-i Fārsī*, 361.
189. Ibid.

is the stage of "*those who... strive in the way of Allah*" (Qur'ān, 2:218)."[190] On the other hand, *bidāyat-i safar-i thānī* ("the beginning of the second journey"), as he suggests, is the stage of "*strive for Allah with the endeavour which is His right. He hath chosen you* (Qur'ān, 22:78)."[191]

Simnānī confirms that there is no end to the Perfect Man's mystical journey and *aqṣ al-amānī* ("furthest destination/end of journey") is not reachable.[192] Although, on this particular occasion, the Kubrawī shaykh does not mention the term *baqā'* ("subsistence"), the phrase *bidāyat-i safar-i thānī* ("beginning of the second journey"), along with its indication *fi-Allah* ("in Allah") in Simnānī's chosen Qur'ānic verse, compared with the Qur'ānic term *fī sabīl-Allāh* ("in the Path of Allah") for the stage of *fanā'*(annihilation), seems to manifest his understanding of *baqā'* ("subsistence"). The Perfect Human Beings, in Simnānī's view, are seekers of the *miyān* ("Middle") who have two wings ("*bāl*") of God's *luṭf* ("gentleness") and His *qahr* ("severity").[193] Through these elucidations, Simnānī seems to confirm the status of the Perfect Man as the *barzakh*, fully enabled to combine both aspects of the Real's Beauty and Majesty (or *tashbīh* and *tanzīh*).

Simnānī indicates that those seekers who attempt to fly only with the wing of *luṭf* ("gentleness") will end up in *bihisht* ("Paradise"), and those who try to fly with the wing of *qahr* ("severity") will join *dūzakh* ("Hell").[194] The most prominent characteristic of Perfect Human Beings that distinguishes them from both groups of *muridān-i ākhirat* ("seekers of the hereafter") and *muridān-i dunyā* ("seekers of the corporeal world"), as Simnānī states, is their *i'tidāl* ("seeking the middle path").[195] As Simnānī asserts, the seekers of the hereafter resemble *magasān* ("flies") who stayed aside (*bar kinār būdand*).[196] By mentioning this characteristic (i.e., staying aside), Simnānī refers to the limitation of these seekers' goal that puts them out of the Middle Path (or aside of it.) Only Perfect Hu-

---

190. Ibid.

191. Ibid. For the two Qur'ānic verses (2:218 & 22:78), I have used their English translation by M. Pickthall.

192. Ibid.

193. See ibid.

194. Ibid.

195. Ibid.

196. Ibid.

man Beings who fly with the *two wings*, i.e., *qahr wa lutf* ("severity and gentleness"), are honored with the title of *muridān-i wajh-Allāh* ("seekers of Allāh's Face").[197]

Considering the resemblance of *wajh* ("Face") to the whole Existence of the Real, Simnānī perhaps chose this allegory to remind us of the Perfect Man's perfection in seeking the the Absolute in His Wholeness (Absoluteness). Through this wayfaring, which Simnānī views as the truest journey towards the Real, the Perfect Man seeks his truest place in existence. Therefore, Simnānī's chosen Qur'ānic verse, for describing the status of the perfect seekers of the *wajh*, portrays them "in a seat of truth [i.e. Paradise], near the Omnipotent King, the Owner of Majesty and Honour"[198] (54:55). Simnānī's ingenuity in choosing this verse matches perfectly his description of the two wings of God's gentleness (as resembled in the Qur'ānic allusion *'inda* "near") and His severity (as manifested in the Qur'ānic term *malīkin muqtadir* "Omnipotent King") regarding the place of "Perfect Human Beings" (i.e., seekers of the *miyān* ("Middle Path") or *muridān-i wajh-Allāh* ("seekers of Allāh's Face").[199]

Simnānī's focal emphasis upon the vital need of the Perfect Man for both *wings* of the Real's Beauty and Majesty (or His Names of gentleness and severity), manifests striking proximity to Ibn 'Arabī's aforementioned realization of the Perfect Man's essential need for both *eyes* in order to witness the Absolute's *tashbīh* and *tanzīh* on the perilous path towatds perfection.

Simnānī's foremost master, Nūr al-Dīn Isfarāyinī, in his *Kāshif al-Asrār*, refers to a group of prodigies whose "two *rak'ats* of prayers are more treasured than the prayers of all pious men until the day of resurrection."[200] In a passage praising these Perfect Human Beings' unique status, Isfarāyinī, similar to Simnānī, affirms that "there is no end to the *kamāl* ("perfection") of their spiritual states."[201] In a brief but lucid statement, Isfarāyinī makes a creative use of both aspects of Absolute's *jalāl* ("Majesty") and *jamāl*

197. Ibid., 362.

198. For English translation of the Qur'ānic verse (54:55), I have used the *Interpretation of the Meaning of the Noble Qur'ān* by Muḥammad Muḥsin Khān and Muḥammad Taqī'ud-Dīn al-Hilālī, with some modification.

199. Simnānī, *Muṣannafāt-i Fārsī*, 362.

200. Isfarāyenī, *Kāshif al-Asrār*, 138.

201. Ibid.

("Beauty"). He refers to the aspect of *jamāl* by taking into account the Absolute's attributes of *raḥmat* ("Mercy"), which is the manifestation of the Absolute's Beauty. In describing the unique status of these Perfect Human Beings, Isfarāyinī portrays their experience of "unity" through experiencing the presence of the Names: "there is no end to the manifestation of [the Absolute's] *jalāl* ("Majesty") upon them, they have become adorned with the attribute of Mercy (*raḥmānī ṣifat*) and [thus] attained the eternal kingdom (*mulk-i jāvdānī*) and even further, they have reached the Beloved."[202]

Sa'd al-Dīn Ḥamūyah on the Concept of waḥdah

One of the well-known Kubrawī masters, Sa'd al-Dīn Ḥamūyah, who referred to Ibn 'Arabī as *daryā-yi mawwāj wa bī-nihāyat* ("endless and fluctuating sea"), and whom Shaykh al-Akbar called in turn *kanzun lā yanfaḍ* ("an unending treasure"),[203] wrote about the attributes of *baḥr-i waḥdat* ("the sea of unity"). He explains that the very source of the sea of unity *dar talāṭum ast* ("perpetually creates new waves"). Each *mawj* ("wave") causes the creation of several *fawj* ("waves"), and every sets of *fawj* bring different contrasting patterns (*ashkāl-i mukhtalifah wa mutabāyinah*).[204] Here, Ḥamūyah speaks of two groups who approach and realize these patterns (or shapes) differently. Among these two, the group of *birūniyān* ("outsiders") becomes *mutaḥayyir* ("bewildered") by experiencing *kathrat-i ashkāl* ("the multiplicity of these shapes").[205] Every one of the "outsiders" is bewildered and entrapped by one of the shapes or patterns produced by the appearance of multiple waves.[206] The Kubrawī master affirms that each of these shapes (*shikl*) functions as a level or stage (*darakah*) of *jaḥīm* ("Hell").[207] On the other hand, the second group, *darūniyān* ("insiders") are those whose *'ayn al-yaqīn* ("eye of certainty") is fixed upon the concept of *waḥdat* ("unity").[208] Ḥamuyah's description of the "insiders" who "do not tremble with every wind (*bād*), and do not look at [i.e., pay no need

202. Ibid.
203. Simnānī, *Chihil Majlis*, cited in Heravī's introduction to *Miṣbāḥ*, 20.
204. Ḥamūyah, *Miṣbāḥ*, 107.
205. Ibid.
206. Ibid.
207. Ibid.
208. Ibid.

to] every dust particle (*khāk*),"[209] manifests the characteristics of the "Perfect Man." (*al-insān al-kāmil*).

The continuation of this description provides us with a more comprehensive understanding of Ḥamūyah's preferred group. As the Kubrawī master states, the *ātash* ("fire") of the insiders is *āb-i ḥayāt* ("the water of life"). This water of life runs through the desert of *fu'ād* ("inner realm of the heart"), the lands of *qulūb* ("hearts") and *nufūs* ("selves").[210] Therefore, Ḥamūyah concludes that these "insiders, [are able to] view the spiritual states in their totality [*ishān dar kull-i aḥwāl nāẓir*]."[211]

In order to pinpoint the essential characteristic of the Perfect Man in his realization of the concept of *waḥdat* ("unity"), Ḥamūyah chooses a set of creative allegorical combinations. As mentioned above, he states that the "outsiders' fire" represents the "water of life." This seemingly contradictory combination of "fire and water" manifests the unique characteristic of these Perfect Human Beings. The qualities distinguished by the "insiders," in Ḥamūyah's words, begin with their "eye of certainty, which is fixed upon the concept of unity." This type of *waḥdat*, with its practical realization, based on spiritual *yaqīn* ("certainty"), provides the Perfect Man with the quality of dissolving paradoxical multiplicities into a vision of unity. For the Perfect Man, the *'ilm al-yaqīn* ("knowledge of certainty") turns into one unifying vision of existence, through the *'ayn al-yaqīn* ("eye of certainty"). In other words, because of the clarity of mystical vision provided through the eye of certainty, as Ḥamūyah explains, *darūniyān* are able to look into *kull-i aḥwāl* ("all states") of the Path at once. This unifying, collective and *kullī* ("universal") vision of existence is the outcome of dissolving multiple and *juz'ī* ("partial") understanding of existence through experiencing the qualities of *waḥdat* ("unity").

Therefore, as seen above, "unity" takes place between paradoxical elements such as *ātash* ("fire") and *āb* ("water"). The Perfect Man's fire becomes *āb-i ḥayāt* ("the water of life"), which runs through the valley of *fu'ād* ("the inner heart").[212] The fire seems to take upon the duty of burning partial multiplicities into a unifying and clarified manifestation of water which is the elixir or source

209. Ibid.
210. Ibid.
211. Ibid.
212. Ibid.

of existence (*āb-i ḥayāt*). The unified drops of water (which have been turned from multiplicities to unity), then wash and renew the very inner heart of existence.

Ḥamūyah utilizes the *singular* form of the term *fu'ād* (instead of its plural, *af'idah*), along with the *plural* terms, *qulūb* ("hearts") and *nufūs* ("souls").[213] It seems that, in Ḥamūyah's description, through the Perfect Man's perpetually renewed *yaqīn* ('certainty"), which circumambulates around *waḥdat* ("unity"), *wādī-yi fu'ād* ("the valley of the inner heart"/the inner heart of existence), becomes renewed, and stays aware and alive. As a result, the rest of existence (represented as "hearts and souls," in Ḥamūyah's words), depends upon this water of life (i.e., Perfect Man's unifying certainty) for its survival. The fixity of the Perfect Man's eye of certainty upon the essence of unity (as mentioned in Ḥamūyah's description of *darūniyān dar'ayn-i yaqīn-i waḥdat thābitand*[214]) enables him to reach a practical realization of the entirety of existence in the abode of *waḥdat* ("unity"). We may then conclude that the Perfect Man's comprehensive consciousness of *wujūd*, enables him to realize the entire existence, in the multiple/*plural* "forms" of *qulūb* and *nufūs* ("hearts and souls"), and also as the only one "reality" manifested in *fu'ād* ("the *single* inner heart of existence"). In other words, the Perfect Man is able to come to the realization of *wujūd* in both aspects of *kathrah* and *waḥdah* at once.

The ability to *naẓar* ("look at") the entire states of the Path (or experiencing the entire existence) in one single experience becomes possible through the *'ayn al-yaqīn* ("eye of certainty"). In Ḥamūyah's view, in order for the Perfect Man to accomplish this unique task, the crucial eye of "certainty" has to be fixed upon "unity." Ibn 'Arabī also explains how this "eye of certainty" provides a clarity through which Perfect Human Beings are able to correct their realization of existence.

In other words, in Ibn 'Arabī's understanding, the eye of certainty seems to nurture the Perfect Man with a more genuine awareness of reality. This awareness, as Ibn 'Arabī seems to suggest, stems from stems from a type of knowledge with unique characteristics:

Imagination follows the authority (*taqlīd*) of that which sense

213. See ibid.
214. See ibid.

perception gives to it. Reflection considers imagination and finds therein individual things (*mufradāt*). Reflection would love to configure a form to be preserved by the rational faculty. Hence it attributes some of the individual things to others. In this attribution it may be mistaken concerning the actual situation, or it may be correct. Reason judges upon this basis, so it also may be mistaken or correct. Hence, reason is the follower of authority, and it may make mistakes. Since the Sufis saw the mistakes of those who employ consideration, they turned to the path in which there is no confusion so that they might take things from the Eye of Certainty (*'ayn al-yaqīn*) and become qualified by certain knowledge.[215]

This type of knowledge, through the "eye of certainty," leads to the One. That is why Ibn 'Arabī tells us that "this is the knowledge of the prophets, the friends, and the possessors of knowledge among the Folk of Allah. They *never transgress their places* with their reflective powers."[216] [Emphasis added]

Therefore, we may conclude that this is the knowledge of Perfect Human Beings which appears in different non-delimited levels and depths.

Through this knowledge, which we may call *'ilm al-waḥdah* ("knowledge of unity'), perfection becomes the substantial, organic and renewing characteristic which provides the Perfect Man with the knowledge of his place in existence as well as perfecting his ties with the One. In other words, this knowledge puts the Perfect Man's whole awareness, within the Absolute's *ḥaḍra* ("Presence"), in a perfect poise and balance. Thus, as Ibn 'Arabī states, "they [i.e., Perfect Human Beings] never transgress their places…"[217] The Perfect Man's spiritual certainty, entwined with a unique realization of "unity," provides him with a collective awareness through which all multiplicities dissolve in the peerless and surrounding Presence of the One.

Ibn 'Arabī's approach to the Perfect Human Beings as those whose unique knowledge enables them to safeguard their perfect place by avoiding any transgression, also reminds us of Simnānī's aforementioned chosen prodigies, *muridān-i wajh-Allāh* ("seekers

215. *Futūḥāt*, II, cited in Chittick, *The Sufi Path of Knowledge*, 166.
216. Ibid., 167.
217. See ibid., with modification.

of Allāh's Face"), whose main characteristic is to stay in the *miyān* ("Middle"). One might suggest that seekers of the "Middle" are those who do not transgress their perfect places (and thus, do not lose their status as Perfect Human Beings) by journeying along the path of *i'tidāl* (i.e., "the Middle Path").

As Ḥamūyah states in his account of the *darūniyān*'s characteristics, "The multiplicity of *ṣuwar* ("forms") does not deprive them of *ma'nā* ("meaning"), and colors and [multiple] realms [of the world] do not become barriers to their *tamkīn* ("stability") [in the Path]."[218] As a result of this assured recognition of "unity" put into constant practice, multiplicities are guided towards a unifying reservoir in the Perfect Man's awareness. In Ḥamūyah's creative elucidation, multiplicities are "swallowed" by the Perfect Man. The Kubrawī master utilizes similes such as "whale" and "ghoul" in order to describe the grave perils of the Path along with the Perfect Man's encounter with multiplicities, which appear as threats to and thieves of his precious awareness of unity.

Perfect Human Beings, or *darūniyān*, to use Ḥamūyah's term, need to safeguard the endurance of this awareness by swallowing all multiplicities of the Path through spiritual perseverance and stability. Ḥamūyah, by utilizing the expression *furū khurdan* ("swallowing") apparently refers to the vast spiritual capacity of Perfect Human Beings in their encounter with the limitless perils of the Path. This unique capacity enables them to move from the unlimited arrays of multiplicity towards unity in every step of the Path, as if they "swallow" all multiplicities at once and thus experience "unity" in each approach to existence: "The whale can't swallow them [i.e., *darūniyān*] and the ghouls of the desert are not able to capture them, on the contrary, they swallow them all and place them into nothingness."[219]

In another section of his masterpiece, *al-Miṣbāḥ fi'l-Taṣawwuf*, Ḥamūyah returns to the concept of *waḥdat* and its reciprocation with characteristics of the Perfect Man. In this instance, the Kubrawī master refers to the concept of "unity" by focusing on one of his favorite symbolisms, the letters of the alphabet. He considers the letter *Alif* (A) the most essential letter, since it represents unity. *Alif*, as Ḥamūyah explains, "exists and is secluded (*muẓmar*) in each let-

218. Ḥamūyah, *al-Miṣbāḥ*, 107.
219. Ibid.

ter both in meaning (*ma'nā*) and form (*lafḍ*)"[220] In Ḥamūyah's view, *Alif* by itself corresponds to the Absolute at the level of *aḥadiyyah* ("exclusive unity") or the level of *Dhāt* ("Essence"). All other letters in Ḥamūyah's understanding characterize the concept of *kathrat* ("multiplicity") or the level of *wāḥidiyyah* ("inclusive unity").

Thus, Ḥamūyah concludes that the Essence (which by Itself is absolutely unknown) is manifested throughout "existence." Thus, multiplicity is represented in Ḥamūyah's symbolism by all the letters of the alphabet except *Alif.* He states clearly that "from [the letter] *bā'* [i.e., the second letter of Arabic alphabet] to the letter *yā'* [or the last letter of the Arabic alphabet] are all the letters [which utilized] in form (*ṣūrat*) [to manifest] the expansion (*basṭ*) of the Essence of *Alif.*"[221] Although these letters (i.e., from *bā'* to *yā'* or from second to the last) are limited in number, he seems to view them as metaphors for boundless and infinite "signs of multiplicity in existence." Each of these characters of multiplicity or existence in general, represents or manifests the *Alif* (Absolute or *Aḥad*), both in its form and meaning.[222] This description of *Alif*, and its substantial reciprocation with the concept of multiplicity reveal a method close to that of Ibn 'Arabī's approach to *waḥdat al-wujūd* ("unity of existence").

This similarity to the views of Ibn 'Arabī becomes more evident where Ḥamūyah delves into the very essential and intermeshed ties between "*Alif* and everything else." He explains that "everything came into existence from *Alif*, and It exists in every thing, and It is *in* everything and *out* of everything, [rather] this whole [existence] is *Alif.*"[223] Other similarities also appear between Ḥamūyah's words on the symbolism of letters and Ibn 'Arabī's depiction of the function of the Absolute's Names. Ibn 'Arabī elaborates on the relationship between the Names and existence, especially human beings, as follows:

> In respect of Itself the Essence has no name, since It is not the locus of effects, nor is It known by anyone. There is no name to denote It without relationships, nor with any assurance (*tamkīn*). For names act to make known and to distinguish, but

220. Ibid., 61.
221. Ibid.
222. See ibid.
223. Ibid.

> this door [to knowledge of the Essence] is forbidden to anyone other than God, since "None knows God but God." *So the names exist through us and for us. They revolve around us and become manifest within us. Their properties are with us, their goals are toward us, their expressions are of us, and their beginnings are from us. If not for them, we would not be. If not for us, they would not be.*[224] [Emphasis added]

In the same way that Names become manifest within us, revolve around us and exist through us as the *tajallīyāt* ("manifestations") of the Absolute (in Ibn 'Arabī words), the letters function as the expansion of the Essence of the *Alif* that exists inside and outside of everything (according to Ḥamūyah). Ibn 'Arabī also reveals the content of one of his dreams, in the year 597/1200[225], in which he weds with all the letters of the alphabet.

> One night (in a vision) I saw myself conjoined with all the stars of the heaven, being united to each one with a great spiritual joy. After I had become joined with the stars I was given the letters (of the alphabet) in spiritual marriage. I told this vision of mine to one who would take it to a man versed in visionary lore, bidding him conceal my name. When he related my vision to the man he said, "This is a measureless ocean and the one who has seen the vision shall have revealed to him knowledge of the highest things, of mysteries, of the properties of the stars, such as will be shared by no one in his time."[226]

In a symbolic usage of "marriage" here, the manyness of the letters (or the Names) disappears in the unifying Essence of the One. In order to advocate the concept of *waḥdat* in returning to the One, the letters or the Names are wedded together to remove any signs of *kathrah* ("multiplicity") by becoming unified in the being of the Perfect Man. Although every one of the letters or the Names, points to the Oneness of the Absolute, they become one (in the symbolism of spiritual marriage) with the Perfect Human Being to manifest the unity of the One in their collectedness as well. The very kernel of

---

224. *Futūḥāt*, II, cited in Chittick, *The Sufi Path of Knowledge*, 62.

225. See Austin, *Sufis of Andalusia*, 35.

226. *Futūḥāt*, IV, cited in Austin, *Sufis of Andalusia*, 35. This dream has been often quoted or referred to by contempoarary scholars. For example, see Suleyman Uludag, *Ibn 'Arabī*, trans., Dā'ūd wafā'ī (Tehran: Nashr-i Markaz, 1387), 27. See also Addas, *The Voyage of No Return*, 68.

the "knowledge of highest things" in the above interpretation of Ibn 'Arabī's dream, which is the knowledge brought to the prodigies among Perfect Human Beings, is the eminent realization of unity through which the Perfect Man, as the chief envoy of such realization, experiences the "highest mystery of the Path," which is *tawḥīd*. In other words, the return of the Perfect Man to the One, through his eminent realization or knowledge of unity, is tantamount to the return of the entire existence to the Absolute One.

In his description of the ties between *Alif* and everything else (or the rest of the letters), Ḥamūyah views the combination of the letters (from second to the last), or existence in its totality, as the *maẓhar* ("loci of manifestation") for *Alif* (i.e., the Absolute).[227] He also considers *Alif* as the Source that makes the manifestation of everything else [or every other letter] possible (*muẓhir*). Every letter (or any form of multiplicity) reveals the principles (*mabānī*) through which the Existence of *Alif* is manifested. *Alif* is also *bānī* ("the Founder/Foundation") of all letters.[228] Ḥamūyah seems to suggest the relationship of *'ayniyyah* ("sameness") between "the letters and *Alif*" as the uniformity between *anhār* ("streams of water") and *baḥr-i ḥayāt* ("the Sea of Life").[229] Although Ḥamūyah states that the streams of water (or letters) are the same as the Sea of Life (or *Alif*), this sameness does not suggest an exact type of uniformity or likeness in their essence. Ḥamūyah further explains that "the letters (*ḥurūf*) function as the arteries (*'urūq*) of *Alif* and the meaning of *Alif* flows through the letters like [their] spirit."[230]

In his *Kitāb al-Ma'rifah*, under the heading of *mas'alah* ("question") 281, Ibn 'Arabī offers a certain category of *tawḥīd* through which one might grasp a mystical method of envisioning *waḥdat* ("unity") within a limitless manifestation of *kathrat* ("multiplicity"). Ibn 'Arabi divides the concept of *tawḥīd* into three phases.[231] The first is *'ilm* ("knowledge"), the second is *ḥāl* ("spiritual state"), and the third phase is also *'ilm* ("knowledge"). The *'ilm al-awwal* ("first type of knowledge") corresponds to *tawḥīd al-dalīl* ("Oneness of God proved by reasoning"), which, as Ibn 'Arabī explains, is an understanding of *tawḥīd* by *'ulamā al-rusūm* ("exoteric

227. See Ḥamūyah, *al-Miṣbāḥ*, 61.
228. Ibid.
229. Ibid.
230. Ibid.
231. See Ibn 'Arabī, *Kitāb al-Ma'rifah*, 180.

scholars"), whom Ibn 'Arabī considered to be common people who practice *tawḥīd al-āmmah* ("Oneness of God as understood by the common people").[232]

In the second phase of *tawḥīd*, which seems to be a major transitional phase in understanding the Absolute's unity, *tawḥīd al-ḥāl* provides the mystic with an awareness of the Absolute's Oneness through entering into an effective *ḥāl* ("spiritual state"). In this phase, the the Truth Almighty becomes the *na't* ("attribute") of the mystic (*an yakūna Haqq ta'ālā na'tak*).[233] This phase is assigned to the Perfect Man who is aware of the surrounding presence of the Absolute.[234]

In order to manifest a unifying concept between the reality of the Absolute's attribute and the Perfect Man's attribute, Ibn 'Arabī utilizes the well-know Qur'ānic verse "*... thou (Muḥammad) threwest not when thou didst throw, but Allāh threw...*"[235] (8:17). By citing this verse, Ibn 'Arabī concludes that the Perfect Man's attribute is "not his or inside him, but is Him (*fatakūna Huwa*)."[236] He seems to suggest that the Absolute's attribute dwells within the very being of the Perfect Man and thus occupies it.

The third phase of *tawḥīd*, or *al-'ilm al-thānī* ("second type of knowledge") that arrives after *ḥāl* is *tawḥīd al-mushāhadah* ("the unity of witnessing").[237] In Ibn 'Arabī's view, in this phase of *tawḥīd*, the Perfect Man is able to witness all things (*al-ashyā'*) from the standpoint of inclusive unity (*min ḥaith al-waḥdāniyyah*). Thus, as Ibn 'Arabī states, "he [the Perfect Man] sees nothing but the One (*falā tarā ill-al-wāḥid*)."[238] This statement shows the unique capability of the Perfect Man in his move from *kathrat* ("multiplicity") towards *waḥdah* ('unity") in the phase of unity of witnessing. From here on, Ibn 'Arabī manifests a doctrinal creativity, according to which the Perfect Man is also able to witness a substantial *waḥdah* within an infinite array of *kathrah*. In order to depict the consistency of this phase (i.e., unity of witnessing), Ibn 'Arabī utilizes the term *maqāmat* ("spiritual stages") which points to its con-

232. Ibid.
233. Ibid.
234. See ibid.
235. For the verse (8:17), I have used its English translation by M. Pickthall.
236. See Ibn 'Arabī, *Kitāb al-Ma'rifah*, 180.
237. Ibid.
238. Ibid.

tinuity and endurance compared to the second phase, which was referred to by the term *ḥāl* ("spiritual state").[239]

As mentioned above, Ibn 'Arabī affirmed that in the phase of *tawḥīd al-mushāhadah* ("unity of witnessing"), the Perfect Man does not see any but *wāḥid* ("the One"). In a statement which immediately follows his previous elaboration, he mentions that "*wāḥid* ("the One"), through His manifestations, becomes *waḥdāt* ("many ones/unities") in [the multitude] of spiritual stages (*wa bi-tajallī-hi fi'l-maqāmāt-i takūn al-waḥdāt*)."[240] In Ibn 'Arabī's model, "the entirety of the world (or existence) is the [multitude of] many ones/unities (*fa'l-'ālam kulluh waḥdāt*)." These *waḥdāt*, as he states, turn into *murakkabāt* (series of compounds) by being added to each other (*iḍāfah*), and thus, become transformed into *ashkāl* ("shapes/forms").[241]

Ibn 'Arabī concludes that in order to realize *tawḥīd al-mushāhadah* ("unity of witnessing') in this world (*hādh al-'ālam*), these limitless combinations of "unities" need to become "one" *mashhad* ("locus of witnessing") for the Perfect Man. In other words, this profound mystical experience (i.e., the unity of witnessing) which provides the Perfect Man with the supreme knowledge of unity (or *'ilm al-thānī* in Ibn 'Arabī's term) occurs only in one locus of witnessing, which is the realm of multiplicity or *waḥdāt* ("multiude of ones/unities"). Therefore, this world contains within itself "one" locus of witnessing which consists of boundless "ones/unities." This one locus of witnessing is nothing but the world itself.

Ibn 'Arabī's approach to the problem of multiplicities in the above *mas'alah* ("question"), facilitates an essential move from *waḥdat* ("unity") towards *waḥdāt* ("unities"). His concise but effective argument reveals a very substantial reciprocation between the two concepts of *waḥdah* ("unity") and *kathrat* ("multiplicity"). Through this approach, both "unity and unities" complement each other in every respect without any contradiction. In Ibn 'Arabī's words, the unities (*waḥdāt* or the world/existence itself) function as the most perfect realm for the "most elevated mystical experience" (i.e., unity of witnessing intertwined with an elevated knowledge of unity).

---

239. See ibid.
240. Ibid.
241. Ibid.

The Perfect Man who carries essential capabilities to experience such an extensive awareness of unity, realizes the core inner-relationship between the inclusive unity (*waḥdaniyyah/wāḥid*) and Its manifestation (*bi-tajallīhi*)[242], which appears as *waḥdāt* ("unities"), and thus, provides him with the perfect *'ilm* ("knowledge') of *tawḥīd al-mushāhadah* ("unity of witnessing"). In his dialectical depiction of "unity and unities," Ibn 'Arabī also pinpoints the significance of understanding "multiplicity" as one of the most essential requisites for understanding "unity." Here, Ibn 'Arabī, instead of using the term *katharāt* ("multiplicities"), creatively utilizes the expression *waḥdāt* ("unities"), in order to highlight the absence of any contradiction between between the two concepts of unity and multiplicity.

The unities, which constitute the entirety of the world itself (*hādh al-'ālam,*[243] in Ibn 'Arabī's term), become the only realm for the most elevated mystical experience of the Perfect Man. In this regard, multiplicities (i.e. unities) become the most essential asset for reaching the most prominent awareness of unity. In the above approach, Ibn 'Arabī also reminds us of a dialectical comradeship between *tashbīh* and *tanzīh*. *Wāḥid* ("the One") through His manifestation (*bi-tajllīhī*) is seen as *waḥdāt* (unities).[244] Within the infinite array of these manifestations, the mystic is able to see multiplicities or *ashyā'* ("entities/things") as *wāḥid* ("the One"), for they point to the inclusive unity (*min haith al-waḥdāniyyah*, in Ibn 'Arabī's words). Thus, without having these unities (i.e., the mediums of *tashbīh*) there would be no understanding of the unity (i.e., *tanzīh*).

In the next *mas'alah* (question 282), Ibn 'Arabī explains the place of the Names (*asmā'*) in his understanding of multiplicity.[245] Here, instead of the term *wāḥid* ("the One at the level of inclusive unity"), he refers to *aḥadiyyah* ("exclusive unity"). He also employs the expression *āḥād* ("individuals") instead of *waḥdāt* ("unities"). *Aḥadiyyah* ("exclusive unity") is manifested (*ẓāhirah*) through individuals and concealed within their compounded totality (*al-majmū' fi'l-murakkabāt*).[246] This "manifest and concealed" unity, as Ibn 'Arabī states, is called the *asmā'* ("Names") in the lan-

242. See ibid.
243. Ibid.
244. See ibid.
245. See ibid., 181.
246. Ibid.

guage of *shar'*("revelation"). He then asserts that through inclusive unity (*wāḥid*) numbers come into existence. In this process, based on *al-tartīb al-ṭabī'ī* ("natural ordering"), numbers spread from the second to infinity (*mā-lā yatanāhī*).[247] As Ibn 'Arabī concludes, if *wāḥid* vanishes, numbers will disappear too.[248]

Ibn 'Arabī's elaborations on the concept of *waḥdah*, detailed above, might explain Ḥamūyah's approach to the letter *Alif* and its correlation with the rest of the letters. As mentioned earlier, the Kubrawī master sees the locus of manifestation for the letter *Alif*, from the second (*bā'*) to the last letter (*yā'*). *'Alif* is also the foundation of all letters. Without *Alif*, any other "letter" joins non-existence, in the same way that none of the "numbers" (in Ibn 'Arabrī's approach) remains if *wāḥid* fades away.

The prominent ninth/fourteenth century Persian advocate of Ibn 'Arabī, Nur al-Dīn 'Abd al-Raḥmān Jāmī also refers to *Alif* in a manner similar to that of Ḥamūyah. He views *Alif* as the foundation and returning abode of all letters: "[Although] entities of the letters (*a'yān-i ḥurūf*) are different in [their] forms (*ṣuwar*), all of them [i.e., letters] are gathered in the Essence of *Alif*. [Although] all [letters] are named with different names, but in reality they are the same as *Alif* (*hama 'ayn-i Alifand*)."[249]

Through explaining substantial ties between *Alif* and the rest of the letters, Ḥamūyah creatively delves into the concepts of *anwār* ("lights") and *asrār-i ilāhī* ("Divine secrets").[250] By doing this, he points out the role of Perfect Human Beings in reaching *dūst* ("the Friend").[251] He seems to compare each of the letters with one spark of light which performs as both *mishkāt* and *hijāb* ("niche and veil") for the Divine secrets. The Perfect Man needs to remove these veils which are scattered over the reality of spiritual meanings (*niqāb ba-rūyi ma'ānī*).[252] Ḥamūyah sees these veils (or letters except *Alif*) to be like *shikl-i ādam* ("the human body") that veils *jawhar-i insānī* ("the human essence or the essence of being human"). The human essence is also considered by Ḥamūyah to be a veil for the *ṣirr* ("secret") of *subḥānī* ("Divine"), *raḥmānī* ("Merciful") and *sulṭānī*

---

247. See ibid.
248. Ibid.
249. Jāmī, cited in Dahbāshī, *Sharḥ-i Rubā'iyyāt*, 133.
250. See Ḥamūyah, *al-Miṣbāḥ*, 61.
251. Ibid.
252. Ibid.

("Majestic").[253] In order to reach the Friend, the Perfect Man needs to pass through all these veils. Here, Ḥamūyah refers to secrets (*sirr*) related to both aspects of *jamāl* and *jalāl* ("Absolute's Beauty and Majesty," or secrets of *raḥmānī* and *sulṭānī*).

This combination of secrets might manifest in the fact that the Perfect Man is not able to reach a collected awareness of Reality beyond the multitude of veils, except by considering the Absolute in both realms of *jamāl* and *jalāl*. In other words, in order to reach a collected awareness of Reality, one needs to consider both aspects of *tashbīh* and *tanzīh*, which reminds us of Ibn 'Arabī's expression of *huwa lā-huwa* ("He/not He") or seeing the Absolute in both realms of "He" (similarity) and "not He" (peerlessness). It is interesting to note Ḥamūyah's usage of the term *sirr* ("secret") to describe the aspects of *jamāl* and *jalāl*, instead of the more commonly utilized term *ṣifāt* ("attributes").

We might claim that in Humaūyah's view, the ardent mystic of the Path does not attain the *secret of perfection* except by having both eyes (*dhū'l-'aynayn* in Ibn 'Arabī's term) for envisioning the Face of the "Friend" (or *dūst* in Ḥamūyah's term). Each of the never-ending manifestations of the Absolute offers a never repeating *wajh* ("Face") of the Reality that is not thoroughly witnessed unless by both eyes of *tashbīh* and *tanzīh* or *jamāl* and *jalāl*. This might be one of the most essential "secrets of perfection" in the view of both Ibn 'Arabī and Ḥamūyah. The *ẓāhir* ("manifest") or the "entire existence" is the ground for *tashbīh* ("Absolute's similarity") and the *bāṭin* ('Non-manifest") is the realm of *tanzīh* ("Absolute's peerlessness"). Witnessing these two realms together, or as Ibn 'Arabī suggests "*in*" each other," is the essential task for the Perfect Man in experiencing *waḥdat al-wujūd* ("unity of existence") through attaining an authentic knowledge of perfection. In his *Futūḥāt al-Makkiyyah*, Ibn 'Arabī explains this mystical progression as follows:

> He who sees the day does not see the night, and he who sees the night does not see the day. The actual situation is manifest and nonmanifest, since He is the Manifest and the Nonmanifest. So there is a Real and a creation. If you witness creation, you will not see the Real, and if you witness the Real, you will not see creation. You will not see both creation and the Real. On

253. Ibid.

the contrary, *you will witness this in that and that in this – a witnessing through knowledge – since one is a wrapper and the other enwrapped.*[254] [Emphasis added]

Najm al-Dīn Kubrā also refers to the stage where the dual manifestations of the "Absolute's Being and man's being" dissolve into the unity of the Absolute's Being. Through this progression, the Perfect Man finds his essential being through manifestations of the Absolute's Names of *jamāl* ("Beauty") and *jalāl* ("Majesty"): "At first, you perish (*tafnā*) with all the base (*madhmūmāt*) qualities of your being and necessarily (at first), the qualities of His Being, qualities of Awesome Majesty (*al-jalāl*) and Sublime Refulgence (*al-jamāl*) overcome you (*taghshāka*)."[255] Kubrā then elaborates upon the Perfect Man's experience of *fanā'* ("mystical annihilation") on the path towards unity: "Then your essence (*dhātuka*) is annihilated (passes away, *tafnā*) and His Being over comes you (*taghshā*), there being no being at that time except His Being."[256]

Utilizing the expressions such as *fardāniyyah* and *waḥdāniyyah* in his elucidation on the Perfect Man's progression towards unity with the Absolute, Kubrā then pinpoints the unique characteristic of the One Who Has No Second. He also refers to the meaning of the most comprehensive of the Absolute's Names (i.e., Allāh). In this Name, as mentioned earlier, both concepts of Beauty and Majesty or *tashbīh* and *tanzīh* find their unifying abode:

> Then you find the promise made good: "Whose is Dominion on that Day – Allah's, the One, the Irresistible." The meaning of Allah in the stage (*maqām*)...of epiphany (*tajallī*) of the Divine Essence (*al-dhāt*) is The One (*al-wāḥid*) for it is necessary in every respect that there not be a second, another existent—for the characteristic nature (*khāṣiyah*) of The One denies the possibility of a second existent. The meaning of the Irresistible is The One for He masters (*yagḥaru*) the rudder of individuality (*sukkān al-fardāniyyah*) by His Unity (*waḥdāniya-tihī*).[257]

In Kubrā's understanding, by denying any duality, the very es-

---

254. *Futūḥāt*, II, cited in Chittick, *The Sufi Path of Knowledge*, 225.

255. David Martin, "The Return to the One in the Philosophy of Najm al-Din Kubrā," in *Neoplatonism and Islamic Thought*, ed. Parvīz Morewedge (Albany: State University of New York Press, 1992), 237.

256. Ibid., with some modification.

257. Ibid., with some modification.

sential characteristic of the One leads the Perfect Man to the concept of the Absolute's unity. The most profound stage of this experience (i.e., experience of unity) occurs through the *tajallī* ("manifestation") of the Name Allāh. The most comprehensive Name of the Absolute finds its image in the person of Perfect Man. In other words, the most perfect of the Absolute's Names (in terms of Its comprehensiveness or *jāmi'iyyah*), which represents all the Names together, meets its most comprehensive image in the most perfect existent beings (i.e., the Perfect Man). The manifestation of the Name Allāh, becomes the essential ground for the Perfect Man's most essential mystical experience, the experience of unity.

Sa'd al-Dīn Ḥamuyah's symbolism of *Alif* and the rest of the alphabetical letters seem to resemble a similar correlation between the Name Allāh and the rest of the Names. Both Letter *Alif* and the Name Allāh are the essential foundations and reservoirs for the rest of the letters and the Names. These two, Letter and Name, also constitute the ultimate manifestations of Unity.

Ibn 'Arabī refers to the reciprocity between the twenty-eight letters of the alphabet (as the manifestations of creation), and *nafas al-Raḥmān* ("the Breath of the Merciful"). Through these letters or the Divine Words, which constitute and form the Names and are presented by His Breath, the Absolute governs all the affairs of creation. Ibn 'Arabī also makes an essential correlation between the All-Merciful's Breath, and the human breath. He states as follows:

> The Essence of the Divine Words, twenty-eight in number (i.e., the number of the letters in the Arabic Alphabet) and endowed with multiple aspects, emanate from the Breath of the Merciful, which is the Cloud where our Lord stood at the time where He created the world. The Cloud corresponds to the human breath and the manifestation of the world out of the void and into the various levels of being is like the human breath emanating from the heart, spreading out through the mouth and forming letters on the way. These letters are like the manifestation of the world from the Cloud, which is the Breath of God the Real and Merciful spreading into the specific levels [of existence] out of a potential and non-physical expanse, that is from the void filled by creation.[258]

258. *Futūḥāt*, II, cited in Pierre Lory, "The Symbolism of Letters and Language in Work of Ibn 'Arabī," *Journal of Muḥyiddīn Ibn 'Arabī Society* 22-23 (1998):34.

The concept of *'amā* ("Cloud") is associated with a well-known Prophetic *ḥadīth* in which he responds to a question regarding the Existence of the Lord before creation of the creatures.[259] The Prophet states that "He came to be in a Cloud, neither above which nor below which was any air."[260] Ibn 'Arabī suggests that the Cloud (Absolute at the level of *aḥadiyyah*), through Its correlation with the Breath of the Merciful,[261] reciprocates with the breath of the human being.[262] The Perfect Man, as the creation *par excellence*, and the *barzakh* ("mediator/medium") between the Absolute and creation,[263] deciphers, interprets and experiences the entirety of existence through renewing the Absolute's words.

Ibn 'Arabī also explains the fundamental ties between the concepts of the letters and the Names more clearly. Through this clarification, Ibn 'Arabī explains the role that human breath plays in creating letters by his reciprocation with the Divine Names.

> Each name has two forms. One of them is ours and is formed by our breath from the letters that we assemble. It is through (these Names) that we invoke Him, and they are the names of the Divine Names, like cloaks that they put on. Through the form of these names, we describe the Divine Names. The forms of that latter are close to the Most Merciful in so far as He speaks and is qualified by speech. Behind these forms there are meanings (*ma'ānī*) which are like the spirits of the forms. The forms of these Divine Names by which God refers to Himself in His discourse (i.e., the Qur'ān) have their existence in the Breath of the Most Merciful.[264]

Ibn 'Arabī also makes a parallel comparison between the manifestation of entities within the Absolute's Breath and the appearance of letters within man's breath by referring to a well-known Qur'ānic verse (16:40) regarding the creation of entities.

> God says, "Our only speech to a thing, when We desire it"— here "Our speech" refers to the fact that He is a speaker (*mutakallim*) — "is to say to it 'Be!'" (16:40). "Be!" is exactly

259. See Chittick, *The Sufi Path of Knowledge*, 125.
260. See ibid.
261. See ibid., 126.
262. See ibid., 127.
263. See ibid., 126.
264. *Futūḥāt*, II, cited in Lory, "The Symbolism of Letters," 35.

> what He speaks. Through it that to which He says "Be" become manifest...Thereby the entities become manifest within the Breath of the All-merciful, just as letters become manifest within the human breath.[265]

In Ibn 'Arabī's view, the Breath of the All-Merciful manifests the essence of creation (i.e., the letters and words of existence) within the breath of the most perfect *nash'a* – (i.e., the Perfect Man):

> From the Breath of the All-Merciful become manifest the letters of engendered existence and the words of the cosmos in accordance with the different levels of the places of articulation within the breath of the human breather, for the human being is the most perfect of all configurations (*nash'a*) in the cosmos. These places of articulation are twenty-eight letters. Each letter has a name which is determined by its own place of vocalization (*maqṭa'*).[266]

In Ibn 'Arabī's understanding, the Perfect Human Being is the most essential truth manifested in the most perfect Word of God, the Qur'ān. In other words, the Perfect Man who carries the knowledge of the Absolute's Names and also appears as their most perfect and comprehensive manifestation, is the fundamental reality of the Absolute's Word *par excellence.*

> The Total (Universal) Man, according to the essential reality, is the incomparable Quran descended from the Presence of Itself into the Presence of the One who gives existence...In the nearest heaven, it became "differentiation" (*furqān*) and came down in a divided form, in accordance with the Divine Realities, for their authority is exerted in many ways and that is why Man also became divided into separate forms...The Quran which descended is Truth as God has so designated it, thus all immediate truth "comprises an ultimate truth," and the ultimate truth of the Quran is Man.[267]

In Ibn 'Arabī's view, as mentioned above, through the Breath of the All-Merciful, the letters, and the words of the cosmos (the

---

265. *Futūḥāt*, II, cited in Chittick, *The Sufi Path of Knowledge*, 128.

266. Ibid., 128-129.

267. *Kitāb al-Isfār 'an Natā'ij al-Asfār*, cited in Lory, "The Symbolism of Letters," 37.

entire creation) become manifest within the Perfect Man's breath. Through these letters, the Perfect Man contemplates the Divine Names.[268] Through these Names, which become unified in the most comprehensive Name (Allāh), the Absolute's *ḥaḍarāt* ("presences"), as the essential ground for the Perfect Man's mystical experience, turn into one unifying *ḥaḍra* ("Presence"). The Perfect Man who has the most comprehensive realization of this Presence subsists within the *ḥaḍrat al-jāmi'*[269] ("Presence of the Absolute's comprehensiveness") and experiences His *waḥdah* ("Unity") everlastingly.

Sa'd al-Dīn Ḥamūyah's aforementioned approach to the letter *Alif* and Its comprehensiveness as the Foundation of all letters, also leads us to the realization of *Alif* as the Absolute at the level of *aḥadiyyah* (in Ibn 'Arabī's words). In Ḥamūyah's approach, the rest of the letters, from *bā'* to *yā'*, symbolize the concept of *kathrah* ("multiplicity"). These symbols of multiplicity, like the entire creation, return towards the One Whose essential *khāṣiyah*[270] ("characteristic," using Kubrā's expression) rejects any duality in existence. In the constant renewal of this never-ending experience, the Perfect Man is the most proficient wayfarer who witnesses the entire existence being returned to the Presence of the Absolute's Unity (*waḥdāniya-tihī*[271]) through His Names at each moment.

268. See Chittick, *The Sufi Path of Knowledge*, 129.
269. See ibid., 54.
270. See Martin, "The Return to the One," 237.
271. See ibid.